COSTS, ORGANIZATION AND MANAGEMENT OF HOSPITALS

The Book is published by arrangement with

HIGHER SCHOOL OF LABOUR SAFETY
MANAGEMENT (WSZOP) IN KATOWICE

JAGIELLONIAN UNIVERSITY IN CRACOV

UNIVERSITÉ PARIS 13

COSTS, ORGANIZATION AND MANAGEMENT OF HOSPITALS

edited by
Jan Stępniewski
and Marek Bugdol

Jagiellonian University Press

REVIEWERS
prof. dr hab. Stanisław Pajączkowski
dr hab. Wiktor Adamus
dr hab. inż. Wojciech Mniszek

COVER DESIGN *Anna Sadowska*
EDITOR *Mirosław Ruszkiewicz*
PROOFREADING *Marta Janiszewska-Hanusiak*
TYPESETTING AND TECHNICAL EDITOR *Ewa Ślusarczyk*

Monografia dofinansowana ze środków Wyższej Szkoły Zarządzania Ochroną Pracy (WSZOP) w Katowicach w ramach nowo utworzonej specjalności Zarządzanie Organizacjami Służby Zdrowia realizowanej przy współpracy z Uniwersytetem Paryż 13.

Monografia dofinansowana jest ze środków pochodzących z projektu „Reorganizacja rachunku kosztów na potrzeby zarządzania szpitalami" o numerze 0473/B/H03/2008/35 z dnia 22.09.2008. Instytucją zamawiającą jest Ministerstwo Nauki i Szkolnictwa Wyższego.

ISBN 978-83-233-3008-0

Jagiellonian University Press
Editorial Offices:
Michałowskiego St. 9/2, 31-126 Cracov
Phone: + 48 12 631 18 80, + 48 12 631 18 82, Fax: + 48 12 631 18 83
Distribution: Phone: +48 12 631 01 97, Fax: + 48 12 631 01 98
Cell Phone: + 48 506 006 674, e-mail: sprzedaz@wuj.pl
Bank: PEKAO SA, IBAN PL80 1240 4722 1111 0000 4856 3325

We would like to dedicate this book
to the memory of President of Poland Lech Kaczyński
and President of Poland in exile Ryszard Kaczorowski and the others
who sacrificed their lives in the plane crash near Smoleńsk
on 10 April 2010 on their way to Katyń to celebrate the 70th anniversary
of the mass murder of the Polish officer corps.

Editors

AUTHORS OF PARTICULAR PARTS

1.1.   **Didier Castiel** – Centre d'Économie de l'Université Paris 13 (CEPN--CNRS)

      Pierre-Henri Bréchat – Centre for Public Health Policy Analysis (CAPPS), EHESP – French School of Public Health, and Sciences-Po, Rennes & Paris, France

1.2.   **Agnieszka Kister** – UMCS Lublin

1.3.   **Iwona Mazur** – Dzienny Ośrodek Psychiatrii i Zaburzeń Mowy dla Dzieci i Młodzieży, Zespół Badawczy „Avicenna" – Uniwersytet Jagielloński

1.4.   **Magdalena Jaworzyńska** – UMCS Lublin

1.5.   **Elżbieta Izabela Szczepankiewicz** – Uniwersytet Ekonomiczny w Poznaniu

1.6.   **Marian Kachniarz** – Uniwersytet Ekonomiczny we Wrocławiu

2.1.1.   **Jacek Klich** – Uniwersytet Jagielloński

2.1.2.   **Camal Gallouj** – Centre d'Économie de l'Université Paris 13 (CEPN--CNRS)

      Souheila Kaabachi – EBS Paris

2.1.3.   **Jan Stępniewski** – Centre d'Économie de l'Université Paris 13 (CEPN--CNRS), Zespół Badawczy „Avicenna" – Uniwersytet Jagielloński, WSZOP w Katowicach

2.1.4. **Jerzy Błaszczuk** – Akademia Medyczna we Wrocławiu, Zespół Badawczy „Avicenna" – Uniwersytet Jagielloński

2.1.5. **Jerzy Błaszczuk**

2.1.6. **Dominique Brissaud** – Centre Hospitalier des 4 Villes – St Cloud, Université Paris 13, **Paul Lombard** – IO Conseil

2.2.1. **Piotr Karniej** – Akademia Medyczna we Wrocławiu, Zespół Badawczy „Avicenna" – Uniwersytet Jagielloński, **Lotfi Azzabi** – Université Paris 13, Institut Européen des Affaires de Paris

2.2.2. **Artur Piotrowicz** – Uniwersytet im. Mikołaja Kopernika w Toruniu, Szpital w Golubiu-Dobrzyniu

3.1.1. **Beata Buchelt** – Uniwersytet Ekonomiczny w Krakowie

3.1.2. **Marcin Kęsy** – Wyższa Szkoła Menedżerska w Legnicy, Zespół Badawczy „Avicenna" – Uniwersytet Jagielloński

3.1.3. **Danuta Kunecka** – Pomorska Akademia Medyczna w Szczecinie

3.2.1. **Agata Krukowska-Miler** – Politechnika Częstochowska

3.2.2. **Marek Bugdol** – Zespół Badawczy „Avicenna" – Uniwersytet Jagielloński

3.2.3. **Piotr Jedynak** – Uniwersytet Jagielloński, **Patrycja Gruca-Wójtowicz** – Szpital Wojewódzki im. św. Łukasza SPZOZ w Tarnowie, Firma doradczo-szkoleniowa Qualto s.c.

3.2.4. **Radosław Wolniak** – Wyższa Szkoła Zarządzania Ochroną Pracy w Katowicach

3.2.5. **Marta Cholewa-Wiktor** – Politechnika Lubelska

CONTENTS

PREFACE 11

INTRODUCTION 13

PART I. Costs and finances in hospitals 15

    1.1.   New changes in public hospital funding: The French DRGs (GHS) and their consequences on Low-income patients and social disabilities 17

    1.2.   Cost accounting and its role in the management of a hospital ... 32

    1.3.   The aspect of resources in activity based costing for hospital management purposes 40

    1.4.   The use of cost accounting systems in health care units in the Lublin area 47

    1.5.   The role of internal audit in hospitals 52

    1.6.   Construction of the soft budget restrictions and health unit debt .. 60

    Bibliography 67

PART II. Innovation, organization and management of hospitals 73

    2.1. Organizational innovations of hospitals 75

        2.1.1. Innovations in hospitals 75

        2.1.2. Innovation and organisation in the hospital: a French perspective 84

2.1.3. Organizational innovations in production of hospital
       service 95

2.1.4. Organisational standards of the endoscopic surgery ward ... 105

2.1.5. Organisation of one day surgery clinic 110

2.1.6. Information systems and risk management in health
       institutions. A practice-based approach 114

2. 2. Management of hospitals 126

2.2.1. The application of the process-oriented management concept
       in improving the productivity of hospital operation 126

2.2.2. Functioning of hospitals after commercialization 133

Bibliography 141

PART III. Human resource, patients' rights and quality service
of hospitals 149

3.1. Human resource of hospitals 151

3.1.1. Perspective of personnel function development in Polish
       hospitals 151

3.1.2. Interpersonal and intergroup communication process
       in the hospitals 159

3.1.3. Ethical aspects of competitions on managing position
       of hospitals 169

3.2. Patients' rights while quality of medical services 179

3.2.1. Quality of medical services from a point of view of
       patients'rights 179

3.2.2. Patients' satisfaction in the medical services quality
       management – research problems 188

3.2.3. Perspective of patient in managing quality of medical services .. 195

3.2.4. Quality improvement in hospital using the QFD method 204

3.2.5. Ethical programme of hospitals 218

Bibliography 230

CONCLUSIONS   237

SUMMARY   239

PREFACE

The book has its genesis in establishing the international studies *Medical and Social Care Organizations Management* (MOSS) specialty by Wyższa Szkoła Zarządzania Ochroną Pracy (WSZOP) w Katowicach (Higher School of Labour Safety Management in Katowice), in biliteral cooperation with Paris University 13. International in its character, it was to honor the inauguration ceremony of the studies on the 19th September, 2009 and to initialize a discussion at International Conference on *Organizational Innovations in Hospitals* (18–19/09/2010), held by Wyższa Szkoła Zarządzania Ochroną Pracy (WSZOP) w Katowicach in collaboration with two distinguished universities – respectable Jagiellonian University in Cracov and one of the well-known French universities – Université Paris 13.

The main aim of the book is to be used as a manual for overseas students of MOSS, students of medicine and nursing, economics and management and also for the managers of health, doctors , nurses and paramedic employees in hospitals.

The editors' purpose is to start the discussion in the environment of medical practitioners on organizational innovations in hospitals and promoting scientific research among academics on the organization and management of hospitals. We asked experienced health care managers and doctors, scientistis from France and Poland, who represented different interests, to contribute to the book.

It presents a rare example in Poland of a successful collaboration of a private school with eminent public universities which has resulted in: international studies in accordance with the idea od Bologne Convention, financed by EU, a common international top-level manual for students and the international scientific conference, all those happening at one time and one place.

We express our congratulations and acknowledgements to the main organizer – Wyższa Szkoła Zarządzania Ochroną Pracy (WSZOP) w Katowicach, while wishing the readers strong impressions.

The Editors

INTRODUCTION

Innovativeness is a term which has not been used in medical organizations until recently. It is connected with implementing new solutions, reform, improvement, inventiveness. It may concern all aspects and fields of activities, also in health care sector.

Nowadays contemporary hospitals cannot limit their interests to providing medical services, not taking into account their quality, health care or medical personnel organization. It is proved that the management of medical organizations is interdisciplinary domain where such disciplines as economics, costs, quality are entwined with technique and technology, law, knowledge management and IT. Each manager of a medical organization has to think about all these aspects simultaneously because all of them are equally important for hospital's existence.

They are presented as benchmark solutions implemented in France and a reader can learn about the analysis of costs of medical services, organizational changes personnel management, quality of medical services which exist in Polish hospitals or are recommended to be introduced.

The complex situation presents the need for introducing organizational, management, personnel innovations in health care sector, also it requires changes in financing and cost accounting systems. It is necessary to show a strong determination not only to break old stereotypes and habits but also to put health care units in the group of business entities whose activity provide profit for their owners. It is surprising that in Poland private health care units are regarded as reliable trading partners, good loanees and required associates in finances while public units are not in the group. Organizational innovations seem to be the instruments which may make public hospitals required and reliable partners in economic aspects, just like it is in other European countries.

The present book is published as a result of collaboration of Wyższa Szkoła Zarządzania Ochroną Pracy (WSZOP) in Katowice (Higher School of Labour Safety Management) with Institute of Economics and Management (*Research on Organization and Management of Hospitals* – „*Avicenna*") of Jagiellonian University in Cracov and Medical Department of Paris 13 University.

Management of a health care unit concerns finding solutions to many practical problems being analyzed practically and theoretically at the same time, which shows that practitioners should not be opposed to theoreticians. It is essential to treat hospital management practically because health care is not a 'chosen' discipline and is not extracted from economy and law and so it is not 'marked' either, which makes a health care manager use both practice and theory to be effective. The reports of the practitioners, dealing with problems every day are significant, especially those that may be used by others in similar situations.

The attempts of theoretical solutions implementations should not be ignored. They appeared as experience of other businesses and if their aim is really to improve the condition of hospitals functioning and they are innovative, despite being underestimated or not recognized, the practitioners believe they should be implemented out of concern for patients wellness and economic interest of hospitals.

The authors of the articles present both issues and attitudes. Many a scientist, dealing with the problems of health care management in theory is supported by practitioners who are engaged in health care unit management in Poland and France, making decisions significant to the units and their patients in such conditions.

Part I

COSTS AND FINANCES IN HOSPITALS

1.1. NEW CHANGES IN PUBLIC HOSPITAL FUNDING: THE FRENCH DRGs (GHS) AND THEIR CONSEQUENCES ON LOW-INCOME PATIENTS AND SOCIAL DISABILITIES

1.1.1. INTRODUCTION

The "health benefit basket" in France is to be reformed. The Social Security Act of 18 December 2003 (Loi de Financement de la Sécurité Sociale, LFSS) changed the inpatient acute care funding rules.[1]

Since 1 January 2008, services provided for inpatient or outpatient acute care are financed through a payment-per-case system. This is based on a diagnosis-related group type. A nationally fixed tariff (Groupe Homogène de Séjour, GHS, Homogeneous group of stays) is applied to each GHM (Groupe Homogène de Malades, diagnosis related group).

Health insurance expenditure is required to be efficient, effective and useful within the constraints of the financial implementation of GHS.[2] GHS represented 787 GHMs (or DRGs) in the 2007 database (Version 12) and 24 major diagnostic categories (MDC). Medicine, surgery and obstetrics covered 78% of these 787 GHMs. Until now, GHS described only the average length of stay and associated cost by GHM. Since 2004, a rationing budgeting system (Tarification à l'Activité, known as T2A in France) has been set up progressively to allocate financial resources to hospitals according to their activities, just like the Medicare program does in financing hospitals with DRG in USA. At the present stage of development, it covers 35% of hospital budgets in 2006 for the 1,006 public and 1,871 private hospitals (SAE [statistique annuelle des établissements], DREES [Direction de Recherche, des Etudes, de l'Evaluation et des Statistiques], French health ministry), to reach 100% in 2008 for

[1] M.M. Bellanger, V. Cherilova, V. Paris (2005), *The "Health Benefit Basket" in France*, European Journal Health Economics [suppl. 1] 6, p. 24–29.

[2] C. Segouin, P.H. Bréchat, L. Lebrun, F. Sahraoui (2006), *Les révolutions du PMSI et de la T2A: Bilans et perspectives* [in:] P.H. Bréchat, E. Salines, C. Segouin (dir.), *Médecins de santé publique*, Éditions ENSP, Rennes, p. 212–223.

public hospitals. As in all countries having a prospective payment system, case-mix puts together patients with comparable levels of resource use. Patients are allocated to a group based on diagnosis, procedures, age and gender with no consideration of their social and/or physical disabilities.[3]

In England, the prospective payment system has been rolled out to cover all hospital and community services from April 2008.[4] The objective of this program is to improve funding transparency and hospital efficiency.

Compared to the United States, it is a new challenge. Since the introduction of the DRG system for USA Medicare patients in 1983, case payment mechanisms have gradually become the principal means of reimbursing hospitals in most developed countries, especially in Europe. The use of case payments nevertheless poses severe technical and policy challenges. Many unsolved issues remain in their implementation.[5] The social dimension associated with funding DRG is far from being considered in those countries. For example, in England, Carpenter et al.,[6] have shown that in a restrictive field like physical disability, 65% of the patients had a growing level of physical disability. That results in a four-day longer hospital stay than predicted by the healthcare resource group (HRG: UK-DRG). This extra cost is not provided for in the HRG tariffs. In the meantime, socioeconomic deprivation is a growing phenomenon.[7,8,9] Such deprivation is one element of a multidimensional social disability, linked to seven supposedly distinct but interrelated areas: health, resources, cultural integration, working conditions, relations with others, housing, assets. These areas constitute a working definition of social disability, of which socioeconomic deprivation resulting from low income is the ultimate stage.[10,11] A 1998 study in the French context showed that "low income" patients spent on average 2.52 more days in hospital than the population as a whole. Their stays cost 33% more than for "non-disadvantaged" patients.[12]

---

[3] *Ibidem.*

[4] I. Carpenter, J. Bobby, E. Kulinskaya, G. Seymour (2007), *People admitted to hospital with physical disability have increased length of stay: implications for diagnosis related group re-imbursement in England*, Age. Ageing. 36, p. 73–78.

[5] R. Busse, J. Schreyogg, P.C. Smith (2006), *Hospital case payment systems in Europe*, Health Care Manag. Sci. 9, p. 211–213.

[6] I. Carpenter, J. Bobby, E. Kulinskaya, G. Seymour (2007), *People admitted to hospital with physical disability have increased length of stay: implications for diagnosis related group re-imbursement in England*, Age. Ageing. 36, p. 73–78.

[7] R. Carr-Hill, P. Chalmers-Dixon (2005), The *public health observatory handbook of health inequalities measurement*, South East England Public Health Observatory (SEPHO), Oxford.

[8] J.P. Mackenbach (2006), *Health Inequalities: Europe in Profile*, An independent, expert report commissioned by the UK. Presidency of the EU.

[9] J.P. Ruger (2006), *Ethics and governance of global health inequalities*, J. Epidemiol. Community Health 60, p. 998–1002.

[10] J.L. Borkowski, L. Kasparian (1991), *Construire des indicateurs d'inégalités – Enquête « Étude des conditions de vie » 1986–1987*, Document de travail F9106. INSEE, Paris.

[11] A. Villeneuve (1991), La *mesure des inégalités sous son aspect multidimensionnel – Enquête « Étude des conditions de vie » 1986–1987*, Document de travail F9105. INSEE, Paris.

[12] C. Mathy, M. Bensadon (2002), *Le surcoût de l'hospitalisation des patients précaires*, JEM. 20, p. 263–278.

In 2008, the challenge in France and other such countries is to take into account this social dimension in the reformed system budget. The GHS system can neither financially cover the patients' personal social dimensions nor determine a specific budget necessary in response to these particular needs, which are not mainly medically based. There is currently no aid from the GHS tariffs[13,14,15] to take financial account of the personal social dimension of a patient[16] or to allow a discretionary or specific budget to meet these particular needs.

Our aim is to design a tool to measure social disability (not exclusively its perception) of patients in a public hospital to learn: 1) the disability distribution and particular needs linked to the social disability, as well as the patients' medical needs; 2) whether or not these needs mobilize additional funding resources; 3) the extra resources that can be covered by the public hospital so that it fulfils its public service mission. The GHS associated with social disability indicators[17,18,19,20] would provide better knowledge on patients admitted to a public hospital and on the average length of stay and number of additional hospital days. Our objective is to propose a method of estimating patients' social disability in order to have its measurement and to include the costs not funded by public authorities and the additional budget to be allocated.

The French case studied here should be an example for all European countries which meet this particular problem of dealing with longer hospital stays resulting from personal social dimensions of a patient.

1.1.2. METHODS. AN INVESTIGATIVE STRATEGY BASED ON FOUR COMPLEMENTARY EVALUATIONS

1) Social disability: The evaluation of social disability was conducted with an anonymous questionnaire [Table 1] based on the Borkowski et al.[21] and Villeneuve[22] works. Compiled by statisticians of INSEE (Institut National de la Statistique et des

[13] C. Segouin, P.H. Bréchat, L. Lebrun, F. Sahraoui (2006), *Les révolutions du PMSI et de la T2A: Bilans et perspectives*, [in:] P.H. Bréchat, E. Salines, C. Segouin (dir.), *Médecins de santé publique*, Éditions ENSP, Rennes, p. 212–223..

[14] C. Mathy, M. Bensadon (2002), *Le surcoût de l'hospitalisation des patients précaires*, JEM. 20, p. 263–278.

[15] C. Segouin, P.H. Bréchat, L. Lebrun, F. Sahraoui (2006), *The new French hospital financing system: challenges for 2006*, Presse Med. 35, p. 565–567.

[16] P.H. Bréchat, A. Bérard, C. Magnin-Feysot, C. Segouin, D. Bertrand (2006), *Consumers and health policies: reports and perspectives*, Sante Publique 18, p. 245–262.

[17] J.L. Borkowski, L. Kasparian (1991), *Construire des indicateurs d'inégalités – Enquête « Étude des conditions de vie » 1986–1987*, Document de travail F9106. INSEE, Paris.

[18] A. Villeneuve (1991), *La mesure des inégalités sous son aspect multidimensionnel – Enquête « Étude des conditions de vie » 1986–1987*, Document de travail F9105. INSEE, Paris.

[19] *Ibidem.*

[20] *Ibidem.*

[21] J.L. Borkowski, L. Kasparian (1991), *Construire des indicateurs d'inégalités – Enquête « Étude des conditions de vie » 1986–1987*, Document de travail F9106. INSEE, Paris.

[22] A. Villeneuve (1991), La *mesure des inégalités sous son aspect multidimensionnel – Enquête « Étude des conditions de vie » 1986–1987*, Document de travail F9105. INSEE, Paris.

Études Economiques, the French National Institute of Economic Studies and Statistics), it constituted a comprehensive evaluation of social disability. Our questionnaire included six of the seven areas of social disability considered as follows: the "working conditions" figure largely in the field of "health".[23] Each of the six areas grouped two to four specific indicators, i.e. a total of 14 indicators [Table 1]. Some of these indicators are the sum of several variables, giving a total of 30 variables. The indicators were not redundant. The questionnaire on social disability included 213 items and the responses were used to obtain a social disability score based on variables, indicators and areas. Villeneuve[24] showed a population naturally endowed by 4.3 disabilities on average. Under four disabilities, we can define a non-social disability situation. Following Villeneuve,[25] we postulate that the presence of 1 to 4 accumulated disabilities does not indicate social disability (class 1 = no social disability). Villeneuve[26] determined the class 1 range (1 to 4 indicators). So we are left with 10 indicators to dispatch into disability classes. In a first approach, we decided to compute three other homogeneous classes: from 5 to 7 disabilities, a slight social disability (class 2); from 8 to 10 disabilities, an important social disability (class 3); over 10 disabilities, a severe social disability (class 4). In a second approach, we could merge two classes together in case we get too small a number of patients in one class to make a sensitivity analysis. The final disability score is not obtained by the sum of the scores in each area but by the presence of a number of indicators identified as the worse. Since social disability is often associated with a language barrier, the questionnaire was translated into English and Mandarin[27,28] to cater to a wider range of respondents.

2) Quality of life: The quality of life level associated with a social disability level was estimated with a general quality of life questionnaire (Euroqol). According to the resource allocation model,[29] quality of life is potentially a good indicator of resources required; particularly when the hypothesis of correlation between social disability and quality of life is confirmed. The quality of life questionnaire was completed by a visual analogic scale to study the correlation between severe social disability and diminishing quality of life. As the social disability questionnaire included 213 items, the Euroqol questionnaire was chosen (EQ5-D, French version, 5) because it consists of five quick to answer questions. −The responses to the quality of life questionnaire were given a score by Prieto et al.[30] who showed that the same weighting can be given to each answer without affecting significantly the results. The "measured life qual-

---

[23] J.L. Borkowski, L. Kasparian (1991), *Construire des indicateurs d'inégalités – Enquête « Étude des conditions de vie » 1986–1987*, Document de travail F9106. INSEE, Paris.

[24] A. Villeneuve (1991), *La mesure des inégalités sous son aspect multidimensionnel – Enquête « Étude des conditions de vie » 1986–1987*, Document de travail F9105. INSEE, Paris.

[25] *Ibidem.*

[26] *Ibidem.*

[27] D. Castiel, P.H. Bréchat, M.C. Mathieu-Grenouilleau, R. Rymer (2009) *Social disability and public hospitals: towards a model of resource allocation*, Santé Publique 2, p. 195–212.

[28] *Ibidem.*

[29] D. Castiel (1995), *Equité et santé*, Éditions ENSP, Rennes.

[30] L. Prieto, J.A. Sacristan (2004), *What is the value of social values? The uselessness of assessing health-related quality of life through preference measures*, BMC. Med. Res. Methodol. 4, 10.

ity" corresponds to what is measured with the Euroqol questionnaire. Direct reading of the results provided by the patients on the visual analogic scale was termed "perceived quality of life".

3) Hospitalization time: The average length of stay (ALS) in hospital was assessed for each patient and compared with the national cost scale according to the level of social disability for each patient. The data were obtained from the anonymized data of the GHS [Table 1].

4) Extra hospital days: The number of extra days due to social disability was estimated for the whole hospital from the quality of life and differences between the ALS observed and the national cost scale. The quality of life resulting from each class of social disability was compared to estimate the additional resources (RS) required: RS = Q1 / Qi (with Q1, the average quality of life observed in class 1 [no social disability] and Qi, the average quality of life observed in the other classes i, i $\neq$ 1). The extra resources required (ERS) can be calculated as the average weighted by the frequency observed for each social disability. We thus obtain:

$$\text{ERS} = \sum_{i=1}^{j} \frac{ni}{n} \, RSi \text{ for the i classes of social disability}$$

(i=1 to j, with j the last class computed and n represents sample size and n_i, sample size for class i).

Estimation of differential hospital cost according to the length of stay: The length of stay observed for each class of disability per GHS for each patient makes it possible to extrapolate the number of extra days needed for the care of social disability to the whole hospital. It is interesting to compare this result with that obtained from the quality of life method. By analogy with the previous method, we have: RS = ALS1 / ALSi (with ALS1: the differential average length of stay observed in class 1 compared with the ENC [Echelle Nationale de Coût, national cost scale]; ALSi: the differential average observed in class i compared with the ENC). ENC has been taken as a comparator because it is the gold standard for length of stay (theoretical reference). The cost associated with each GHM was evaluated by the national data based on 40 participating hospitals. Thus, the national scale is a reference in terms of length of stay but not in terms of cost. Using the ENC will guarantee that any deviation is not due to a difference in the hospitalized GHM of any social class. A theoretical distribution of stays according to disability class can be obtained by applying the distribution of disabled patients to the total number of stays. A number of extra days corresponds to each disability class, except for patients in the reference class 1. For each disability class, the number of extra days observed is then multiplied by the number of theoretical stays to obtain the number of additional days resulting from social disability. The average differential observed can be compared with the ENC for each patient and for each class of disability.

Table 1. Data from the French DRG (GHS) and chosen indicators of social disability

DATA FROM THE FRENCH DRG (GHS)	
1 – Average length of stay (ALS)	
2 – Diagnosis related group (DRG)	
3 – Treatment	
Chosen indicators of social disability	
1 – "Health"	
	Morbidity indicator (MORBI): from the sum of diseases and declared symptoms
	Incapacity indicator (INCAP): from the sum of mobility and autonomy problems and difficulties in daily tasks
	Risk indicator (RISKI): from the sum of three variables: smoking, alcohol, combination of both
	Working conditions indicator (RISKE): made up of four variables: night shifts (NUI), arduous work (PEN), combination of both (CUM), poor housing (ACUM)
2 – "Resources"	
	Standard of living indicator: income level (REVENU)
	Deprivation indicator (PRECAT): made up of four variables: financial difficulties (DEF), degree of financial help (TAF), unemployment without benefits (CHOM) accumulation of risks of socioeconomic deprivation (PRESTENDETT)
3 – "Cultural integration"	
	Schooling indicator (SCOL)
	Cultural activity indicator (CULTU): made up of three variables: reading newspapers, books, and an indicator of cultural integration disability
4 – "Relations with others"	
	Family relations indicator (FAMILLE)
	Neighbourly relations indicator (VOISINS)
5 – "Housing"	
	Indoor conveniences indicator (CI): made up of four variables: sanitation (DF), durable goods (EQ), number of inhabitants (IP), additional equipment (EC)
	The location of the accommodation (LOCA): made up of three variables: the proximity of amenities (DIS), criticism of the environment (CRIT) and ownership or tenancy (L)
6 – "Assets"	
	Property indicator (IMMO)
	Movable property indicator (MOBI)

1.1.3. MATERIAL

The public Lariboisière Fernand-Widal Hospital (AP-HP) in Paris was chosen. It is quite specific for our purpose because it is situated in an area where a large part of the population is underprivileged. So the probability of meeting this population is high. This hospital is a public teaching hospital with departments in medicine, surgery and obstetrics which cover more than half of the stays.

The questionnaire on social disability was conducted between 8 and 23 November 2005 for admissions between 7 and 22 November. French, English or Mandarin speakers, uncooperative (with or without a given reason) or unhealthy patients, people discharged at the time of the interview or who did not return the questionnaire or whose forms were incomplete, were retained. Patients in geriatrics, follow-up care, rehabilitation and psychiatry were excluded due to the slow turnover and those in ophthalmology and cardiology as well due to the quick turnover (less than 24 hours).

The size of the sample was calculated by hospital activity data to distinguish the difference in resource consumption between deprived and nondeprived patients. The results were obtained using Epi Info 6.0 software. The number of patients to be included is 480, assuming *a priori* that deprived patients represent 20% of the hospital population. The recruitment period adopted depended on the hospital activity between 2002 and 2004. The present study was conducted during one of the months identified as having an activity corresponding to the annual average.

The social disability questionnaire was administered to each patient upon admission (the first day or the day after in the case of an intervention or after intensive care). It was generally filled out by the patient, although occasionally by the interviewer helping a patient too sick or by providing him with some explanation in case of no comprehension.

1.1.4. STATISTICAL ANALYSIS

The variables constituting indicators were validated on the basis of a factor analysis of correspondences led by the statisticians of INSEE.[31,32]

They did it for each indicator consisting of a number of variables. Each variable is independent of others. Correlation between two variables is low even null. That can be verified in our sample by computing correlation matrix between each indicator. As we got 14 indicators, in order to clarify and simplify the results presentation, we give only correlation matrix results for the six areas.

---

[31] J.L. Borkowski, L. Kasparian (1991), *Construire des indicateurs d'inégalités – Enquête « Étude des conditions de vie » 1986–1987*, Document de travail F9106. INSEE, Paris.

[32] A. Villeneuve (1991), *La mesure des inégalités sous son aspect multidimensionnel – Enquête « Étude des conditions de vie » 1986–1987*, Document de travail F9105. INSEE, Paris.

The average differences between length of stay and/or costs for each class of social disability were analyzed using a paired student's t-test at the 5% level. Age differences in social disability classes were analyzed using the same test.

1.1.5. RESULTS

The percentage of usable questionnaires was 46.1% (504/1,094), despite the length and personal nature of the questions. Eight were completed in Mandarin and one in English. Only 85 (7.8%) of the 1,094 patients recruited refused to participate. Eighty patients were too ill to respond. Thirty-six patients were dismissed the day after hospitalization. Seven patients deceased. Forty-nine patients did not understand any of the languages of the questionnaire, and 333 questionnaires were poorly filled out (less than 70% completed and/or poorly completed).

Although we needed 480 patients, the sample is based on 504 patients. Having chosen to compute all hospitalizations of one day, we got 24 patients more than necessary the last day of the recruitment. The questionnaire was generally well completed out by 504 patients: 75 to 100% completion for 14 indicators. The average age of the participants was 47.8 ± 18.6 years,, with a median of 46.0 years. The age was unknown for one patient (0.2%). 55.9% were female and 0.4% of unknown gender. The average household included 2.45 ± 1.78 people. Compared with INSEE data of 2004 [18], our sample was almost completely professionally representative: except we got no farmers in our sample.

1.1.6. DETERMINATION OF THE LEVEL OF SOCIAL DISABILITY

By summarizing the 14 indicators of social disability, we could deduce disability classes showing the number of patients with a given disability and a number with worsened disabilities [Table 2]. The number of patients in class 4 was 18, so we decided to merge class 4 with class 3 to obtain a new class 3. A third of the patients presented no serious social disability, 42% presented a moderate and 24.8% a severe one (class 3). The levels of deterioration for the most affected indicator in each disability class show that all patients present the same order of disability and that the most socially disabled patients have a higher number of disabilities and a more deteriorated indicator [Table 3]. Correlation coefficients matrix between each area is given [Table 4]. Correlation between two areas is very low, excepted between resources and cultural integration (correlation coefficient is 0.36), but it is acceptable.

As for the quality of life, computed for only 477 patients, 70 patients (14.7%) considered their health state better now than over the past 12 months, while 239 patients considered it identical (50.1%) and 168 worse (35.2%). The quality of life was not different between classes 1 and 2 of social disability. The average score is 0.61 for the measured quality of life versus 0.63 for the perceived quality of life for patients in class 1, and respectively 0.55 and 0.60 for those in class 2 (p=0.07 and 0.18). The scores differ significantly between classes 2 and 3, depending on which tool is used (p=0.01 for measured quality of life and p=0.0004 for perceived quality of life) and respective scores of 0.44 and 0.51 for patients in class 3.

Table 2. Distribution of patients according to the number of known and worsened disabilities

Number of disabilities	Known disabilities (%)	Worsened disabilities (%)	Grouping according to disability	Final grouping according to disability
0	0	5 (1.0)		
1	1 (0.20)	17 (3.4)	Class 1	Class 1
2	2 (0.40)	28 (5.6)	n=168	n=168
3	1 (0.20)	48 (9.5)	(33.3%)	(33.3%)
4	2 (0.40)	70 (13.8)		
5	4 (0.80)	71 (14.1)	Class 2	Class 2
6	4 (0.80)	65 (12.9)	n=211	n=211
7	6 (0.70)	75 (14.9)	(41.9%)	(41.9%)
8	21 (4.3)	55 (10.9)	Class 3	
9	23 (4.6)	34 (6.7)	n=107	
10	26 (5.2)	18 (3.6)	(21.2%)	Class 3
11	44 (8.8)	12 (2.4)		n=125
12	81 (16.1)	5 (1,0)	Class 4	(24.8%)
13	70 (13.9)	1 (0.2)	n=18	
14	219 (43.6)	0	(3.6%)	
Total	504 (100)	504 (100)	504 (100)	504 (100)

Table 3. Levels of deterioration of the most affected indicators according to the class of disability % (rank)

Disability	Heading	Class 1	Class 2	Class 3
1 – "HEALTH"				
1	MORBIDITY INDICATOR (MORBI)	35.1 (4)	54.7 (7)	65.6 (8)
2	Incapacity indicator (INCAP)			
3	Risk indicator (RISKI)			
4	Working conditions indicator (RISKE)			
2 – "Resources"				
5	Standard of living indicator (REVENU)	41.3 (3)	82.5 (3)	99.1 (2)

6	Socioeconomic deprivation indicator (PRECAT)			65.5 (9)
3 – "Cultural integration"				
7	Schooling indicator (SCOL)		55.6 (6)	81.8 (6)
8	Cultural activity indicator (CULTU)			71.0 (7)
4 – "Relations with others"				
9	Family relations indicator (FAMILLE)			53.8 (10)
10	Neighbourly relations indicator (VOISINS)			
5 – "Housing"				
11	Indoor conveniences indicator (CI)	50.4 (2)	88 (2)	94.8 (3)
12	Location of accommodation (LOCA)		61.2 (5)	86.3 (5)
6 – "Assets"				
13	Property indicator (IMMO)		69 (4)	90.9 (4)
14	Movable property indicator (MOBI)	72.4 (1)	93.1 (1)	99.2 (1)

Table 4. Coefficients correlation matrix between areas of social disability

	Cultural integration	Housing	Assets	Relations with others	Resources	Health
Cultural integration	1	0.05	0.09	0.20	0.36	0.24
Housing		1	0.19	0.12	0.22	−0.003
Assets			1	0.18	0.23	0.13
Relations with others				1	0.27	0.11
Resources					1	0.14
Health						1

1.1.7. EVALUATION OF EXTRA RESOURCES REQUIRED TO TREAT THE SOCIALLY DISABLED PATIENTS

Estimation according to quality of life. The estimation of additional resources (ERS), all disability classes included, by the chosen estimation method of quality of life, is: measured quality of life: ERS = 1.14; perceived quality of life: ERS = 1.08 [detailed in Table 5].

Table 5. Estimation of the additional resources required (RS coefficient) according to "Measured quality of life" method and "Perceived quality of life" method

	Measured quality of life (1)	RS (2)*	Weight (ni/n) (3)	ERS = (2)x(3) (4)	Perceived quality of life (5)	RS (6)*	ERS = (3) x(6) (7)
Class 1	0.61	1	0.33	0.33	0.63	1	0.33
Class 2	0.55	1.11	0.42	0.47	0.60	1.05	0.44
Class 3	0.44	1.37	0.25	0.34	0.51	1.23	0.31
Total				1.14			1.08

*RS = Q1 / Qi (see methods)

Features of the GHS database. The database concerned 504 stays, 85 hospitalizations less under 24 hours, GHS unknown or alteration of nomenclature, i.e. 419 stays. Analysis of stays by MDC shows the activity to be representative of the normal medicine, surgery and obstetrics hospital activities during 2005 compared with activities in 2002–2004. The distribution of GHS was statistically the same year after year and our sample followed this distribution. The main disorders concerned the musculo-skeletal system and conjunctive tissue (104 MDC8); pathological pregnancies, births and postpartum complaints (74 MDC14); disorders of the nervous system (67 MDC1) and circulatory system (54 MDC5). GHS analysis showed that the sample ranged over 160 different GHSs. Although the disorders were representative of the diversity of medical, surgical and/or obstetrical hospital activities, each GHS count came with low numbers, from one to seven, except for straightforward vaginal deliveries (37 14Z02A), straightforward caesareans (11 14C02A), complications of antepartum complaints with or without surgery (9 14Z03B) and other disorders of genital organs for women under 70 years without severe associated comorbidity (7 13M04V). Only two GHSs had severe associated comorbidity.

None of the GHS induced an under- or overestimation of length of stay. The Average length of stay was 6.40 days and the average length of stay adjusted for each GHS number is 6.41 days.

Differential duration of stay and costs. Taking all disability classes together, the patients stayed on average 1.53 days less than indicated by ENC data. Patients in class 1, however, stayed 2.45 days less than in the ENC sample, whereas patients in class 3 stayed only 1.16 days less. Finally, those patients (class 3) stayed 1.29 days longer than those in class 1 (2.45 – 1.16; p=0.08), whereas those in class 2 stayed 1.41 days longer than those in class 1 (p=0.03). Age and gender could not explain these differences.

Extrapolation to patients at hospital. In 2005, 23,331 stays of over 24 hours were recorded, representing 187,821 hospital days. An estimation of the additional cost resulting from social disability can be expressed in numbers of hospital days: a total of 21,342 additional days, which is an 11.4% increase in 2005 theoretically attributable to social disability [Table 6]. Over 11% of the activity in the hospital involves social disability, representing an extra 3,500 stays at an average cost of 3,200 euros each and a budget of 11.2 million euros solely for the care of social disability.

Table 6. Hospital over-expenditure due to social disability in 2005

	% of the patients admitted (1)	Number of theoretical stays (2)	Additional length of stay * (3)	Number of extra days (2) x (3)
Class 1	33 %	7,699	–	–
Class 2	42 %	9,799	1.41	13,817
Class 3	25 %	5,833	1.29	7,525
Total	100 %	23,331	1.53	21,342

* Compared with patients in class 1

1.1.8. DISCUSSION

The used method has enabled us to meet the objective of quantifying the extra hospital costs associated with social difficulties. A model combining the GHS and social disability indicators that makes it possible to determine the specific budget allocations for socially disabled patients can now be generalized. Our results provide new possibilities for the comparison of hospital performances. Our sample was representative of the diversity of activities within the hospital.

The study has two limitations:

The number of patients participating was low, with a complex tool and a rapid turnover of patients. In fact, the tool was too complex because 333 patients did not complete it in a usable way. A shorter version of the questionnaire on social disability could be presented. Although the number of each GHS is low, the impact on the results should not be significant because average length of stay is not influenced by the number of patients. Length of stay seems to be homogeneous in medicine, surgery and obstetrics.

A study for each GHS was not possible due to the low numbers in each one. Such a study could be developed in other hospitals those having sufficiently large samples per GHS and populations with and without a social disability for comparison. That would also refine the indicators for a more accurate budget allocation for patients with social disabilities in a context of economic constraints.[33]

Assessment of social disability is both possible and desirable in the current context of health cost containment, particularly since low income patients are thought to

---

[33] C. Segouin, P.H. Bréchat, L. Lebrun, F. Sahraoui (2006), *Les révolutions du PMSI et de la T2A: Bilans et perspectives* [in:] P.H. Bréchat, E. Salines, C. Segouin (dir.), *Médecins de santé publique*, Éditions ENSP, Rennes, p. 212–223.

be the major healthcare consumers.[34,35,36] The health state of the socially disabled is only one aspect of the problem although it is a dominant factor linked with economic deprivation in the literature.[37,38,39,40]

Socioeconomic inequalities are studied in conjunction with a given pathology, such as cancer,[41] diabetes,[42] obesity[43] or heart attacks.[44] Usually studies simply describe the poor state of health associated with a low social class.[45,46] Our results confirm our hypotheses and put forward others which should alter the way low income people are considered. In our study, the area of health concerns four indicators: morbidity, incapacity, risk exposure and working conditions. Only the morbidity indica-

[34] C. Mathy, M. Bensadon (2002), *Le surcoût de l'hospitalisation des patients précaires*, JEM. 20, p. 263–278.

[35] J.J. Moulin, V. Dauphinot, C. Dupré, C. Sass, E. Labbe, L. Gerbaud, R. Guéguen (2005), *Inégalités de santé et comportements: comparaison d'une population de 704 128 personnes en situation de précarité à une population de 516 607 personnes non précaires, France, 1995–2002*, BEH. 43, p. 213–216.

[36] C. Sass, J.J. Moulin, R. Guéguen, L. Abric, V. Dauphinot, C. Dupré (2006), *Le score Epices: Un score et mesure des relations avec des données de santé, dans une population de 197 389 personnes*, BEH. 14, p. 93–100.

[37] R. Carr-Hill, P. Chalmers-Dixon (2005), The *public health observatory handbook of health inequalities measurement*, South East England Public Health Observatory (SEPHO), Oxford.

[38] J.P. Ruger (2006), *Ethics and governance of global health inequalities*, J. Epidemiol. Community Health 60, p. 998–1002.

[39] J.J. Moulin, V. Dauphinot, C. Dupré, C. Sass, E. Labbe, L. Gerbaud, R. Guéguen (2005), *Inégalités de santé et comportements: comparaison d'une population de 704 128 personnes en situation de précarité à une population de 516 607 personnes non précaires, France, 1995–2002*, BEH. 43, p. 213–216.

[40] C. Sass, J.J. Moulin, R. Guéguen, L. Abric, V. Dauphinot, C. Dupré (2006), *Le score Epices: Un score et mesure des relations avec des données de santé, dans une population de 197 389 personnes*, BEH. 14, p. 93–100.

[41] J. Adams, M. White, D. Forman (2004), *Are there socioeconomic gradients in stage and grade of breast cancer at diagnosis? Cross sectional analysis of UK cancer registry data*, BMJ. 329, p. 142–143.

[42] D.A. Lawlor, M. Harro, N. Wedderkopp, L.B. Andersen, L.B. Sardinha, C.J. Riddoch, A.S. Page, S.A. Anderssen, K. Froberg, D. Stansbie, G. Davey Smith (2005), *Association of socioeconomic position with insulin resistance among children from Denmark, Estonia, and Portugal: cross sectional study*, BMJ. 331, p. 183–188.

[43] J. Wardle, N.H. Brodersen, T.J. Cole, M.J. Jarvis, D.R. Boniface (2006), *Development of adiposity in adolescence: five year longitudinal study of an ethnically and socioeconomically diverse sample of young people in Britain*, BMJ. 332, p. 1130–1135.

[44] F.A. McAlister, N.F. Murphy, C.R. Simpson, S. Stewart, K. MacIntyre, M. Kirkpatrick, J. Chalmers, A. Redpath, S. Capewell, J.J. McMurray (2004), *Influence of socioeconomic deprivation on the primary care burden and treatment of patients with a diagnosis of heart failure in general practice in Scotland: population based study*, BMJ. 328, p. 1110–1113.

[45] T. Doran, F. Drever, M. Whitehead (2004), *Is there a north-south division in social class inequalities in health in Great Britain? Cross sectional study using data from 2001 census*, BMJ. 328, p. 1043–1045.

[46] P.B. Reagan, P.J. Salsberry, R.J. Olsen (2007), *Does the measure of economic disadvantage matter? Exploring the effect of individual and relative deprivation on intrauterine growth restriction*, Soc. Sci. Med. 64, p. 2016–2029.

tor figures among the most deteriorated indicators in each disability class and it is found at the bottom of the list of the most deteriorated indicators. For patients in class 3, the morbidity indicator is eighth in the list of disability factors [Table 3]. In other words, while the health of low income patients is worse, the health issue is secondary compared to other factors constituting social disability. This broader perception is contrary to many health studies[47,48,49,50] which avoid the other aspects emphasizing social disability.

Similarly, lack of income is not a major determinant of social disability. The three most specific factors of social disability are poor cultural integration, socioeconomic deprivation, disrupted or nonexistent family relations, which add to the other factors but is not itself the most affected.

Quality of life appears to reflect social disability, as it deteriorated with an increasing level of disability. A further study is needed to determine whether it is a scaled-down expression of social disability.

The multifactoral nature of social disability, the objective appreciation of this disability by the doctor and its codification (ICD 10) are complex. The socially disabled patient is treated for his health condition but rarely for his social disability. Such a patient is typically discharged from the hospital at least one day later on average, due to the time needed to find an appropriate service. The department of gynaecology and obstetrics is involved for women having just given birth (lack of decent housing for example). The increasing ALS between disability classes 1 and 3, combined with the associated cost, is not linked to a more serious case-mix, as shown by analysis of their GHSs.[51]

The additional resource allocation results in a slightly longer average stay. Both the ALS and the quality of life methods of assessing the additional hospital days required to deal with the social disability lead to similar results: a 10 to 11% increase in resources (8% with the perceived quality of life method, 14% with the measured quality of life, 11% with the ALS method). The trend is not towards an increase in the length of stay, same as for the socially disabled, contrary to the findings of Mathy et al.[52] The public hospital continues to take care of the social needs in a difficult medi-

---

[47] J.J. Moulin, V. Dauphinot, C. Dupré, C. Sass, E. Labbe, L. Gerbaud, R. Guéguen (2005), *Inégalités de santé et comportements: comparaison d'une population de 704 128 personnes en situation de précarité à une population de 516 607 personnes non précaires, France, 1995–2002*, BEH. 43, p. 213–216.

[48] C. Sass, J.J. Moulin, R. Guéguen, L. Abric, V. Dauphinot, C. Dupré (2006), *Le score Epices: Un score et mesure des relations avec des données de santé, dans une population de 197 389 personnes*, BEH. 14, p. 93–100.

[49] C. Allonier, P. Dourgnon, T. Rochereau (2006), *Santé, soins et protection sociale en 2004*, Série résultats, No.1621. IRDES, Paris.

[50] Observatoire national de la pauvreté et de l'exclusion sociale. *Rapport 2005–2006* (2006), La documentation française, Paris.

[51] C. Mathy, M. Bensadon (2002), *Le surcoût de l'hospitalisation des patients précaires*, JEM. 20, p. 263–278.

[52] *Ibidem.*

cal and economic context.[53,54] The GHS system could better contribute by taking into account these results, as has been suggested.[55,56,57] The use of the GHS in our study enabled us to complete the information required for the different analyses by supplying complementary information. There is need for improved awareness and better training for those who gather and encode data, though this appears hypothetical[58] or else a scaled-down investigative tool. Additional resources appear necessary to improve the state of health of the socially disabled and to meet the additional hospital expenditures.[59,60,61,62,63]

Global care of patients with severe social disabilities appears to be a better solution than allocating additional resources to small administrative areas. Because, as Connolly et al.[64] note, people living in deprived circumstances can move from place to place, and therefore additional resources may not be appropriate to cover changing social needs and inequalities over time. Hospital funding dealing with social disabilities should be more efficient.

[53] C. Segouin, P.H. Bréchat, L. Lebrun, F. Sahraoui (2006), *Les révolutions du PMSI et de la T2A: Bilans et perspectives* [in:] P.H. Bréchat, E. Salines, C. Segouin (dir.), *Médecins de santé publique*, p. 212–223. Éditions ENSP, Rennes.

[54] C. Segouin, P.H. Bréchat, R. Rymer (2006), *The new French hospital financing system: challenges for 2006*, Presse Med. 35, p. 565–567.

[55] L. Borella, P. Peuvrel, M. Sauvage, D. Maraninchi, T. Philip (2000), *A study based on national DRG data to evaluate work load and practice relating to cancer patients in not-for-profit hospitals*, Rev. Epidemiol. Sante Publique 48, p. 53–70.

[56] P. Fender, A. Weill (2004), *Epidemiology, public health and medical databases*, Rev. Epidemiol. Sante Publique 52, p. 113–117.

[57] A.M. Schott, T. Hajri, B. Gelas-Dore, C.M. Couris, S. Couray-Targe, V. Trillet-Lenoir, B. Dumeril, J.P. Grandjean, G. Lledo, J.L. Poncet, C. Colin, N. Cautela, F.N. Gilly (2005), *Analysis of the medical activity related to cancer in a network of multidisciplinary hospitals using claims databases, the reseau Concorde Oncology Network*, Bull. Cancer 92, p. 169–178.

[58] C. Segouin, P.H. Bréchat, L. Lebrun, F. Sahraoui (2006), *Les révolutions du PMSI et de la T2A: Bilans et perspectives* [in:] P.H. Bréchat, E. Salines, C. Segouin (dir.), *Médecins de santé publique*, Éditions ENSP, Rennes, p. 212–223.

[59] M.M. Bellanger, A. Jourdain (2004), *Tackling regional health inequalities in France by resource allocation: a case for complementary instrumental and process-based approaches?* Appl. Health Econ. Health Policy 3, p. 243–250.

[60] D. Castiel, A. Jourdain (1997), *Equity and health planning: critical analysis of the SROS and implications for a model of resource allocation*, Cah Sociol Demogr Med. 37, p. 205–235.

[61] A. Jourdain (2000), *Equity of a health system*, Eur. J. Public Health 10, p. 138–142.

[62] P. Lombrail (2000), *Accès aux soins* [in:] A. Leclerc, D. Fassin, H. Grandjean, M. Kaminski, T. Lang (dir.), Les inégalités sociales de santé, La Découverte/INSERM, Paris, p. 403–418.

[63] A.R. Tarlov, R.F. St. Peter (2000), *Introduction* [in:] A.R. Tarlov, St. Peter RF, *The society and population health reader*, Vol. II: *A state and community perspective*, The Press, New York, p. IX–XXV.

[64] S. Connolly, D. O'Reilly, M. Rosato (2007), *Increasing inequalities in health: Is it an artefact caused by the selective movement of people?*, Soc. Sci. Med. 64, 2008–2015.

1.2. COST ACCOUNTING AND ITS ROLE IN THE MANAGEMENT OF A HOSPITAL

1.2.1. INTRODUCTION

The reform of health protection system which goes back to the end of the 19th century, sets as a purpose to improve the quality of services provided and to reduce operating costs of the entities in the medical market. Years of experience have made the hospitals look for different ways to cut down on costs. The size of costs depends on many factors, among which there are: gradual ageing of the society, the higher health awareness of people and taking advantage of costly, yet modern medical technologies.

Hospitals, as any other businesses subject to accounting, are obliged to make cost accounting reports. It has a traditional function, i.e. reporting and analytical, controlling or to, a lesser degree, managing one. Its result is to set the costs of services provided and the estimate the effectiveness of management of the unit.[65] Its main idea is to provide the information about the costs of different sections and various kinds of business activities (basic, remaining, financial and out of ordinary). The costs are classified as direct and indirect, where the criterion is the relation to a cost carrier and also the fact whether the cost entry is assigned to a document directly or indirectly.

The article presents a diagnosis of the results of the costs accounting records kept in the Regional Hospital of Kardynal Stefan Wyszyński in Lublin and it indicates the usefulness of the chosen, out of the record cost accounting in the health care units.

1.2.2. COST ACCOUNTING IN THE UNITS PROVIDING MEDICAL SERVICES

Hospitals need an appropriate and multi-section cost information for the purpose of management. Cost accounting in those units is kept according to balance and tax regulations. In addition the accounting rules are described in the Act on health care units[66] enforcing the rules of accounting of enquities, public health care units and Regulation of the Ministry of Health and Social Care of the 22nd of December, 1998,[67] which differentiates: cost centers connected with providing health service, called the centers of basic operation; cost centers connected with activities supporting the basic operation, called the cost centers of supporting operation and cost center connected with hospital management as an entity – the center of managerial costs. Public health

---

[65] E. Nowak (1999), *Rachunek kosztów*, Ekspert, Wrocław, p. 16.

[66] Act of the 30th August, 1991 on health care units (Dz. U. 1991, No. 91, item 408 with subsequent amendments).

[67] Regulation of the Ministry of Health and Social Care of the 22nd of December, 1998 on specific rules for cost accounting in public healthcare units (Dz. U. No. 164, item 1194), par. 1, point 1.

care units have also task centers: centers of basic health care (general health centers, centers for children, dental and dermatological), specialist centers, hospital wards and emergency rescue teams. Separating such centers, treated as the costs centers, becomes a challenge for cost accounting to satisfy management.

The centers responsible for the costs are to improve both the effectiveness of the hospital operation and the control of the costs. It is necessary to give the opportunity for measuring the level of implementing costs tasks in every aspect (plan, implementation, execution) and to define the aims, tasks and measuring instruments for the assessment of the level of the implementation. Each responsibility center should also have motivational system and make decisions independently.[68] Decentralization of responsibility in such centers gives a company, here a hospital, calculable benefits. They may be: broadening the knowledge of how to improve services for clients, quickening decision-making in particular situations (e.g. threat to life or health), rising motivation due to personal responsibility, specifying and synchronizing managerial aims.[69]

In the costs centers of basic operation, being hospital wards, the cost carrier is 'a day of care per a person' and a patient with his/her medicaments and assigned medical procedures. In other costs centers of this operation the medical procedures are the cost carriers, while in the cost centers of supporting operation – the services provided by them become the costs carriers.[70] The Regulation shows in detail that the costs should be regarded as a variation system, it also specifies which costs should be counted as direct costs. Indirect costs, as the costs of supporting centers, are to be calculated according to properly applied criteria, determined by the unit's manager, along with the accepted cost carriers.

When deciding on the basis for calculating indirect costs, the relation between the calculated costs and the amount is taken into account, e.g. in case of material-consuming service it is the amount of the used materials or the laborage if the service is costly or only direct costs, when the amount is comparable. But it is possible to use other approach. The value of the directly used resources on operating a medical procedure is established with average amount of use and current prices of the materials and payment rates plus margins, which constitutes normative single direct costs of the particular procedures.[71] The amount of single medical service costs depends on the sorts of diagnostic and therapeutic cases and the methods of dealing with them. A properly calculated cost accounting aims at creating the basis for optimal ways of operating, which is the starting point of costs reduction, service valuation and rating. It is usually not precise in its traditional form due to inaccurate valuating of service costs as an inadequate approach is applied to calculate indirect costs.

---

[68] S. Nowosielski (1998), *Centra kosztów i zysku w przedsiębiorstwie*, "Ekonomika i Organizacja Przedsiębiorstwa", No. 7.

[69] A. Karmańska (ed.) (2006), *Rachunkowość zarządcza i rachunek kosztów w systemie informacyjnym przedsiębiorstwa*, Difin, Warszawa, p. 162.

[70] Regulation…, par. 1, point 3.

[71] *Ibidem*, article 5, point 4.

1.2.3. Precision in defining the costs of a hospital – using operating costs accounting

Problem accounting which concerns for example: operating costs accounting serve the controlling and decision-making process in the company. The function of all out of the record, problem costs accounting is to help with the solving problems with the control or decision. The information on costs supports the management: planning, controlling, organizing, motivating and communication. The use of such accounting sets the basis for valuating resources, processes and cost units (a patient, service). It is also the source of rationalizing of costs. Informative utility of the accounting boils down to: defining the amount of costs to make price decisions, calculating profitability in the section of products/service, clients, operation and departments/centers of responsibility and finding the reasons for costs.[72]

Applying a process approach, which characterizes accounting, leads to focusing on processes and operations and their results, not on chosen aspects of the units' activities. Its idea is to assume that operating at using the resources intentionally contributes to arising costs. Thanks to detailed accounting procedures, when using the approach, precise information on costs, the reasons for costs may be provided, which favors the effectiveness of costs management.

Planning costs is connected with taking into account certain activities that are bound to process of providing the service directly or indirectly. The planning allows to define the costs of all processes, essential and non-essential. This method of costs accounting has become a foundation for the activity based management method (ABM). The idea of ABM is continual analysis and planning activities in the range, e.g. their size. The reasons for costs are also analyzed so the costs may be planned on optimal level. Besides the operating cost accounting there are two other accounting systems that may be applied in health care entities: quality cost accounting and target cost accounting.

1.2.4. Cost information in management – quality cost accounting and target cost accounting

Cost accounting as the methods of management accounting contribute to the improvement of the quality of products, processes and services. Costs data are used to make decisions on the basis of costs patterns. Cost accounting is an instrument of control of hospital resources distribution thanks to which it is possible to eliminate the sources of wastage and to optimize the use of the resources. Quality cost accounting is an example of such situation. The idea of it in as follows: an analysis of quality costs according to products/services and the place of origin,

---

[72] I. Sobańska (ed.) (2003), *Rachunek kosztów i rachunkowość zarządcza*, C.H. Beck, Warszawa, p. 426.

1) coordination of activities (defining the tasks, controlling their implementation and execution),

2) preventing, controlling and reducing mistakes,

3) executing responsibility for the costs of mistakes.[73]

Quality costs contribute to showing where loss is generated. There are three types of them in hospital. The first type of quality costs is connected with the activities leading to avoiding mistakes and failures: personnel trainings, planning and the work of teams which promote, analyze and control the quality, expenditure on projecting, introducing and maintaining the quality system (defining the norms for processes and final services, preparing procedures for reliability of services provided, preparing training programs on quality). The second type is the cost of quality controlling. They are notably connected with the work of the teams which supervise the introducing of quality. They are the costs of checking if the expected result has been gained. Detailed data of the cost group means the verification of the processes in response to particular requirements, quality system control, assessment of service and product providers. The third type of these costs is related to the costs of abnormalities (called failure costs) revealed inside and outside of hospital. The inner failure costs concern wrong instructions and procedures and the costs of preparing the new procedures, useless reports, repeated control, delay in payments. The outer failure costs regard complaints on inappropriate service, appeals and claims, they are connected with court verdicts and compensations.

It is reasonable to introduce quality cost accounting to hospitals, but it is labor-consuming and requires all staff and management involvement. The information generated from the accounting allow for thorough the analysis of costs, especially those which are associated with inappropriate quality of the services provided. Also a patient, assessing the quality contributes to the results of quality monitoring, which helps to valuate the cost of quality and the result of the quality effect.

It may be a full scale improvement of activities including either all aspects of the unit's operating scope or a part of it. The implementation of a continual developing process requires a system of encouragements, motivational instruments, popularizing the method by an instituting team. Target costing is the accounting which focuses on the analysis of costs appearing at the initial stage of creating a service. It allows for service costs managing at the moment of a project. The idea of it is to minimalize all costs components of a product or service, engaging many different departments of the company or hospital.[74] It comprises a set of instruments and tools used for cost planning, supervising and managing.[75] Its purpose is to ensure that a service will be profitable, as expected, in the market. It takes into account the costs of the service life cycle and the cost accounting system allows to control and reduce them. Target costing demands permanent market research and analyzing clients' needs to offer

---

[73] T. Kiziukiewicz (ed.) (2003), *Zarządcze aspekty rachunkowości*, Polskie Wydawnictwo Ekonomiczne, Warszawa, p. 252–253.

[74] *Ibidem*, p. 244.

[75] M. Sakurai (1989), *Target Costing and How to Use It*, "Journal of Cost Management", Summer, p. 42.

a proper service. It results in describing the price for a client (only as a sale price possible to achieve), reducing a target margin from it and setting a target cost.

Market value of a product as an essential outer factor for setting target costs depends on such factors as: the level of meeting clients' needs by the service, its quality and practicality, the level of differential price of services in the market. Target cost is compared with, often varying, cost valuated by employees of different departments. To define the differences a lower profit margin may be accepted, the project or assumption about the service may be verified or it may be relinquished in favor of outsourcing. Hospitals face the problem of adapting the costs of services provided to the prices which are offered in the market. Thus the methodology of target cost accounting seems to be the future of these entities.

1.2.5. Cost accounting of the Regional Hospital of Kardynal Stefan Wyszyński in Lublin

The hospital uses a traditional, reporting cost accounting. The register is kept as a variation system with analytical elaboration. There are 102 items of the costs constituting the direct costs. The basic activity costs concern hospital wards and specialist centers. The costs are collected and registered within the fifth group, as the source of the costs. In accordance with the MF Regulation indirect costs appear while implementing non-medical activities and they are generated by such responsibility centers as: Administration (administrative-technical, administrative and financial-accounting units), Maintenance Unit, Boiler House, Pharmacy, Laboratory, Histopathology Room, Radiology Department (Computer-Assisted Tomography-CAT, Vascular Unit, X-Ray Room, Echography Room), Nuclear Medicine, Sterilization, Casualty Department, Chemotherapy Center, Endoscopy Room and Central Operational Section.

In 2008 the procedures for pricing the medical services were prepared in the hospital. Proper codes were applied to the procedures in accordance with the International Medical Procedures Classification (Polish edition ICD-9CM). Yet not all procedures are updated as far as the standard costs values are concerned. Preparing a list of the medical procedures implemented should be followed by keeping the register of executing them. Such attempt was made in chosen centers at the end of 2009 and the beginning of 2010.

Table 7. Allocation keys for indirect cost accounting

	Centers of costs origin	Allocation key
1.	Administration and Maintenance Unit	Pay costs
2.	Boiler House	Percentage share of the heating area of servicees
3.	Pharmacy	Value of medicaments taken
4.	Laboratory	Value of examinations, being executed
5.	Histopathology Room	Value of examinations
6.	Radiology Department Z	Value of examinations, being executed
7.	Nuclear Medicine	Value of executed examinations

8.	Sterilization	Value of executed sterilization services (boxes and packages)
9.	Casualty Department	Number of patient admitted to the wards
10.	Chemotherapy Center	Value of executed examinations
11.	Endoscopy Room	Value of executed examinations
12.	Central Operational Section	Amount of operating hours in aid of the wards

Source: The author's analysis based on the hospital's data.

The normative costs are the content of the procedure. They are established by calculating and average use of resources and current prices. The pricing of the procedures in based on the level of direct materials and pay costs (work time). In relation to a big fluctuation of the levels of pay and price costs, unit costs of direct procedures have changed. The increase in pays resulted in changing prices of services and large cost variances appeared.

Defining the cost of medical procedure is possible thanks to previously description of the way the procedure should be implemented and necessary resources to introduce it. In the hospital there are clearly established rules for indirect costs calculating presented in Table 7.

Exact valuating of a procedure costs requires a precise marking of the initial materials and defining new rules for storage management. In the analyzed hospital there are no detailed procedures for using different materials or lasting time of a procedure.

Analyses of costs in variation system, especially subjective, are often carried out. The implementation of the budgeting process based on historic costs influences the costs reduction although there are some constraints ton the process. The constraints may be legal qualification, system of medical service contracts, limiting medical services and inability to influence the price for particular service implementation. There is no computer network within the hospital, which would connect all departments into a coherent entity. It makes it impossible to provide information to all managerial ranks, integrate the data within one system and eliminate multiplied inputting the same data.

1.2.6. METHODS OF THE HOSPITAL'S COSTS REDUCTION

Regional Hospital of Kardynal Stefan Wyszyński in Lublin in an independent public health care unit. In view of an enormous debt of about 90 ml PLN, in 2008 the hospital started implementing a reconstructive plan with reducing costs by redundancy as its main assumption. Also restructuring the wards, i.e. creating new ones and making the operating ones smaller. The achieved savings concerned typical costs of the unit such as payments, energy and water consumption. Basic activity costs decreased from 135,054,792.76 PLN in 2008 to 125,864,349.47 PLN in 2009, so there was a significant costs reduction of 9,190,443.29 PLN. The budgeting system introduced in the hospital was to control the costs and plan them. It contributed to reducing operating costs of the hospital: maintenance, service and treatment costs. The effects of the restructuring activities in the 4th quarter of 2008 and the 1st quarter of 2009 are presented in Table 8 as the reduced costs.

Table 8. Activity costs in the 4th quarter of 2008 and the 1st quarter of 2009

account	Cost variation	Average monthly costs in the 4th quarter of 2008	Average monthly costs in the 1st quarter of 2009	% rate
401	Material consumption	2,389,020.22 PLN	2,186,042.90 PLN	91.50%
402	Energy consumption	364,236.21 PLN	459,854.15 PLN	126.25%
403	Transport service	13,211.89 PLN	14,434.60 PLN	109.25%
404	Renovating service	55,005.15 PLN	59,508.27 PLN	108.19%
405	Outsourcing	684,185.79 PLN	591,079.04 PLN	86.39%
406	Wages in total	6,892,487.04 PLN	5,486,643.88 PLN	79.60%
407	Social insurance	1,181,390.02 PLN	957,519.01 PLN	81.05%
408	Other costs	37,297.59 PLN	36,415.66 PLN	97.64%
409	Employees benefits	2,389,020.22 PLN	2,186,042.90 PLN	91.50%
410	Taxes and payments	364,236.21 PLN	459,854.15 PLN	126.25%
411	Bank service	13,211.89 PLN	14,434.60 PLN	109.25%
	Sum up	11,864,812.10 PLN	10,054,259.13 PLN	84.74%
400	Amortization	402,507.82 PLN	508,326.40 PLN	126.29%
	In total	12,267,319.92 PLN	10,562,585.53 PLN	86.10%

Source: The hospital data.

The data in the table show that basic activity costs of the 1st quarter of 2009 decreased in comparison with the 4th quarter of 2008. The reduction of material consumption was observed because of an intensive control of purchasing and regular monthly stock-taking of the wards' medicines kits. In case of outsourcing the costs lowered because of laundry service. Also there were regular controls of servicing the medical equipment. The fall in wages of 15 % was observed thanks to the liquidation of managerial jobs and reduction of employment for definite and indefinite period contracts. The data are shown in Table 9.

Table 9. Changes in employment as the result of restructuring in 2008–2010

Personnel group	30.04.2008		28.02.2010		Difference in employment IV 2008 – II 2010	
	Person	Jobs	Person	Jobs	Person	Jobs
Doctors	249	228.96	226	206.89	−23	−22.07
Nurses and birth assisstants	571	563.00	523	515.63	−48	−47.37
Senior personnel	49	47.00	53	52.25	4	5.25
Middle personnel	157	155.25	153	152.00	−4	−3.25
Paramedics, hospital attendants and emergency medic	245	244.50	193	193.00	−52	−51.50
Junior personnel	30	30.00	10	9.50	−20	−20.50
Administration	86	84.25	74	71.25	−12	−13.00
Service	105	104.50	89	89.00	−16	−15.50
Employees in total	1492	1457.46	1321	1289.52	−171	−167.94

Leaves without pay	19	19.00	6	6.00	−13	−13.00
Maternity leaves	32	32.00	18	17.75	−14	−14.25
Rehabilitation benefits	4	4.00	8	8.00	4	4.00
Absent – totally	55	55.00	32	31.75	−23	−23.25
Employed – total	1547	1512.46	1353	1321.27	−194	−191.19

Source: The hospital data.

The table shows that there was reduction in employment in particular workers groups (apart from the senior personnel).

To reduce costs such activities were implemented: checking the necessity to use expensive medicaments, and limiting the consumption of antibiotics (the percentage share of antibiotics in total medicine consumption was falling down systematically since 2002 from 14.81% to 9% in 2009). The amount of laboratory tests, time of hospitalization were reduced and the system of transferring information improved slightly.

In 2010 further costs rationalizing started by creating a so called 'purchasing group' – to minimalize purchases down to € 14,000. Buying up to this amount in a not regulated form of spending money, beyond control and it may be done in any way giving freedom of activity. The rationalization of energy consumption costs took place in the form of the change of a tariff group, introducing the rules for planning and controlling the power consumption in cheaper time zones, modernizing the transformer station to lower the costs of so called 'energy waste tg φ.' The estimated savings were about 10%. Instead of gas, oil was used, as an alternative and the control of energy fuels use increased. It brought 25% of savings. The hospital management was considering buying the cleaning services. Currently, average monthly cost of cleaning was about 773,000 PLN in 2008. Annually, the hospital spent 9,276,000 PLN on cleaning. The market price of cleaning offered by outsource companies was much lower. It should be treated as an investment with a rate of return for several years. With all the predicted costs, the outsource service cost returns in the seventh month of the second year of the contract and it will bring savings after this time which may reach even 667.000 PLN of profit in the second year.

Also computerization of the hospital may result in savings. The unit does not have an integrated management system. The computer system planned should help in current analyses of effectiveness factors of the processes and bring such benefits: ordering the workflow in the hospital, gaining easier access to the medical and economic information. It will be possible to keep a detailed computer record of medical service in the system of medical documentation: a filing system of patients' turnout, a turnover of medicines and materials used in treatment, a record of examinations, treatments, consultations and medical procedures and other data important in medical documentation. An integrated system will allow to record economic processes and it will help to value the normative costs of services, to calculate the costs of treatment and to establish prices. The introduction of a part of so called Back Office system has been finished. It will supervise the infrastructure, secure the sensitive data, monitor the work efficiency and also will record the hardware and software, the electronic mail or the website service. To reduce costs, the system of laboratory duties has been eliminated, diagnostics has been enriched with coagulology, activities have been consolidated, e.g. Angiosurgery Ward broaden its offer with intravascular surgery employing X-ray Unit personnel, a contract system of providing services in specialist centers has been introduced, also for doctors and X-ray technicians, anaesthesiology and operating room nurses. New diagnostic and treatment techniques have been applied, which shortened the time of patient's hospitalization.

1.2.7. CONCLUSION

Traditional cost accounting is kept according to the regulations on finance reporting. The data about costs are analyzed in detail monthly in regard to the plan – execution sections. They are used not only to control the operating of the unit as an entity but also to assess the activity of particular responsibility centers. The information serves to price the costs of medical services in accordance with the law regulations.

Implementing the strategy of costs reduction, it is possible to reduce the excessive costs of the hospital's activity thanks to the effective way of using the resources, decreasing the costs of the implemented processes and shortening the time of patients' hospitalization. In the surveyed health care unit the changes contributed to the reduction in work costs, also it started using outsource services. The savings are seen in the rationalization of the use of the resources (work force, materials, equipment).

1.3. THE ASPECT OF RESOURCES IN ACTIVITY BASED COSTING FOR HOSPITAL MANAGEMENT PURPOSES

The increasing importance of cost information in the process of managing a hospital is reflected by a growing interest of managers in modern methods of cost accounting. The ultimate goal is to increase the quality and reliability of the cost information as well as prompt availability of thereof. Quality of the information gets top priority in the decision making process and one can observe a rising interest in introducing the so-called activity based costing (ABC) method in hospitals. The process approach to hospital organisation gradually gains a widespread acceptance and understanding among managers. Control of the process of performing medical services and achieved results should be analysed against the cost accounting. Cost accounting ought to be treated, among other things, as a controlling tool and a means of streamlining consumption of resources by the hospital's internal units.

Resources which are at the hospital's disposal get more and more importance and this is due to the fact that hospitals, just like any other enterprises, have to function and make do with restricted resources.

The resources aspect often tends to be undervalued in the process of constructing the activity based costing and in many other cases results in failed attempts in the implementation phase. In the ABC system, costs are treated as a financial measure of consumption of particular resources. Health care services create a demand for realising certain activities and these are a direct cause of consuming certain resources, which, as a result, leads to generating costs. From this perspective, the costs carrier is actually not the product/service but the activity necessary for its realisation.

Picture 1. Model of activity based costing

COST PERSPECTIVE

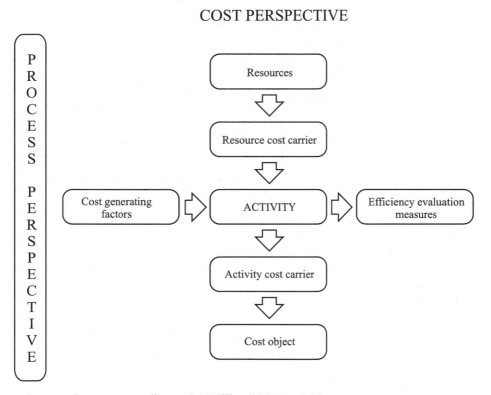

Source: Concept according to J.A Miller (2000), p. 216.

According to the assumptions of the activity based costing, functioning of the hospital should be perceived as a set of activities. The fundamental cause of realising activities are the hospital's patient/s customers. It is the fulfilment of their needs which requires undertaking certain activities aimed at realisation of the medical service. Costs are a result of the performed activities but not their cause.

Cost accounting, among other things, is supposed to help to answer the question about which activities cause consumption of particular resources of the hospital or how many and which resources we need to realise given activities and, in consequence, medical services. Traditional cost accounting makes it actually impossible to find the answer to such a question.

Picture 2. Position of resources in activity based costing

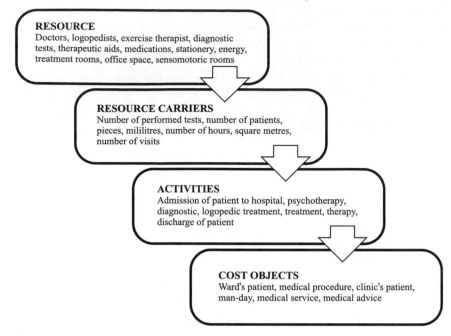

Source: Author's own concept based on data from the analysed health care centre.

"The Theory of activity based costing, regarded as a modern and innovative concept, relying on very clear and understandable or even obvious assumptions, has substantially facilitated a better perception of the business reality by executives".[76]

The model of activity based costing is built on two basic perspectives: cost perspective and process perspective.

The key element in both perspectives is the performed activity but realising activities would not be possible if the hospital did not possess appropriate resources.

Picture 3. Relationships between resources and activities

ACTIVITIES	RESOURCES
Admission of patient	• Receptionist • Psychiatrist • Nurse • Doctor surgery
Psychological examination	• Psychologist • Psychological tests • Therapeutic aids • Psychologist's office

---

[76] R. Piechota (2005), *Projektowanie rachunku kosztów działań*, Difin, Warszawa, p. 24.

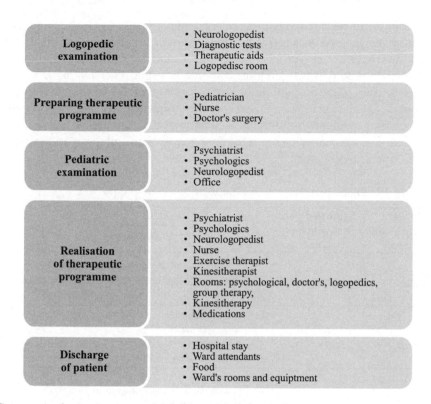

Source: Author's own concept based on data from the analysed health care centre.

The diagram above illustrates the resources and activities identified for the analysed health care centre, displaying in particular the importance of resources in the cost accounting designed for the given unit. The next diagram shows the relationships occurring between the identified activities and the resources which are at the centre's disposal.

Resources are all the economic elements used or consumed during realisation of activities and consequently in the process of performing medical care services.

Hospital can and should be perceived not only as a set of activities but also as a set of resources which have been gathered in order to conduct medical services. The costs incurred by the hospital result from both the fact of acquiring and possessing them and the fact of using them in the process of realising medical services. Limited financial resources force the managers to pay more and more attention to economical use of the possessed resources.

The source of information about the resources should be the subject cost calculation that is the cost centre (CC), but the costs should be organised so as to represent particular resources. Resource based costing method accounts the costs with reference to particular hospital resources which are in turn set in the management hierarchy i.e. organizational structure. Moreover, the distinguished resource categories are assigned certain costs by type (hence the need for accounting costs in the type system) e.g. the fixed assets are assigned depreciation, materials – consumption of materials, employees – remuneration. Here is an example of such cost accounting for human resources.

In order to consider properly costs of consumed and used resources and to allow for appropriate resource management in the hospital, classification of costs should go beyond the standard four type classification according to the cost type.

The very first step in designing the resource based cost accounting is to identify the key resources of the hospital. If the cost information follows this approach, it will help provide the managers with a better way to efficiently manage the level and extent of resource consumption. Besides, it constitutes the basis for the unused resource calculation. The resource element is the first one to exert influence on the precision of all the further calculations.[77]

Table 10. Human resources cost accounting according to type

Types/ categories of resources	Synthetic costs According to types	Analytical costs According to types
Human resources	Remuneration	1. Remuneration under employment contract 2. Remuneration under specific work contract 3. Remuneration under specific task contract
Human resources	External services	1. Doctor contracts 2. Nurse contracts 3. Psychologist contract 4. Logopedist contract
Human resources	Social insurance and other benefits for employees	1. Contributions to Company Social Benefits 2. Protective and labour clothing 3. Benefits in kind for employees 4. Social insurance premiums towards: retirement, annuities, accident, early retirement 5. Social insurance premium towards Labour Fund 6. Training courses
Human resources	Other costs	1. Business trips and allowances 2. Contributions to State Fund for Rehabilitation of the Disabled

Source: Author's own concept.

Table 11. Key resources in Mental Health Care Centre CC

Resources in the centre	Cost (PLN)	Carrier	Carrier amount	Carrier unit value
1. Human resources				
2. Psychologists	32,472	working hours	1,584h	20.5 PLN
3. Doctors	67,200		1,680h	40.0 PLN
4. Nurses	816		48h	17.0 PLN
1. Floor space of ward rooms	18,000	m²	60m²	25 PLN / 3.2 per 1h

[77] T. Zieliński (2007), *Odkrywanie prawdy o zyskach*, Akademia Menedżera Sp. z o.o., Poznań, p. 78.

1.	Computers	6968	no. of hours of computer work	3312h	2.1 PLN
1.	Rests, therapeutic aids	9504	no. of working hours of psych.	1584h	6.0 PLN

Source: Author's own analysis based on data from the analysed health care centre.

The concept of the resource based costing will be discussed based on the example of a cost centre (CC) which is, for instance, the Mental Health Care Centre. The centre realises the two key processes of patient diagnosis as well as treatment and therapy. Part of the diagnosing process (reaching diagnosis) are, among other things, diagnostic sessions conducted by psychologists. According to an interview with a psychologist, it seems that usually one patient needs three diagnostic sessions. During such a visit the patient is interviewed and, if necessary, their family members are asked questions too. As a rule, the following actions are undertaken: diagnostic tests are made, observations are made, patient's drawings are analysed, the medical casebook is updated, patient's health state is assessed, a diagnosis is made and a therapeutic programme is designed. The last activity is signing the so-called therapeutic contract with the patient.

On the basis of a description of the course of the diagnostic session, resources necessary for its realisation were assigned. First of all, we identified the resources which were at the mental health centre's disposal, assigned costs to them, determined the resource cost carriers and their amounts which in turn allowed us to calculate the unit value of the cost carrier.

The next stage was to assign the resources to the activity 'psychological diagnostic examination' (diagnostic session) realised by a psychologist.

In order to realise the psychological diagnostic examination session, the following resources are necessary: psychologist, room, computer and tests and therapeutic aids. The duration time of the session is 1 h. Based on the data included in the table above, it was quite easy to assign all the necessary resources and calculate the cost of such activity: 1h of psychologist's work – 20.5 PLN, computer – 2.1 PLN, aids and tests – 6.0 PLN, cost of the ward room per 1h is – 3.2 PLN which **in total is 32.8 PLN. If there was a need to hold three sessions, the total cost of the psychological diagnostic procedure will be 98.4 PLN.**

Another area where the resource based costing will bring tangible benefits is assessment of the resource consumption and calculating the so-called unused costs, not consumed in realisation of particular activities. It is a very important issue as the costs of unused resources in traditional methods of cost accounting are added costs of the services realised in the particular place of cost creation (CC), which makes the service unit cost increase and, as a result, distorts the view of its profitability. According to the paper's author,[78] costs of unused resources should be related directly to the financial result, which will allow to maintain the accuracy of the unit cost and profitability of the services/session.

---

[78] This view is also shared by Rother authors: G. Swiderska, K. Rybarczyk.

The above issue will be discussed based on the example of the activity of "admission of patient to ward" by analysing and comparing its potential capability of admitting patients to its actual performance. The analysed ward can admit to ward 75 patients daily and provide them with full medical and nursing care, which means performing 1500 man-days monthly. The costs connected with admission of a patient to hospital and their stay at the ward amount to 100,000 PLN monthly. A period of six months was analysed and the actual man-day performance was as shown in the table.

Table 12. Potential and actual man-days realised in the ward.

	X	XI	XII	I	II	III
Cost of patient's stay (PLN)	100,000	100,000	100,000	100,000	100,000	100,000
Potential capability	1,500	1,500	1,500	1,500	1,500	1,500
Actual use of man-days	1,350	1,200	1,300	1,000	1,200	1,100
Unit cost of a man-day						
According to capability	66	66	66	66	66	66
According to actual use	*74*	*83*	*77*	*100*	*83*	*90*
Costs of unused man-days (PLN)	**9,900**	**19,800**	**13,200**	**33,000**	**19,800**	**26,400**

Source: Author's own analysis based on data from the analysed health care centre.

Analysis of the above table shows that the costs of the unused man-days increase the unit cost of the man-day and the patient's stay. It goes without saying that it is possible to calculate the loss the ward generates because of not using its real potential.

The information gathered from the managers indicates that over the last three years the actual use of the ward's capability has remained approximately at the same level. Therefore, taking into account the above findings, it would be advisable to make a decision to adjust the resources volume to the real needs and allocate the human resources to the performed ambulatory activity.

Similar analyses can be applied to other resources of the health care centre in order to assess the level of their effective use. It is possible to assess the effectiveness of use of the medical apparatus and equipment and use of working time by particular profession groups. The cost information organised in this manner will enable the managers to aim more successfully at effective management of the level and degree of resource usage.

The resource based costing gives a possibility of creating cause and effect models of activity based costing (ABC). The important thing is that, knowing the costs and the resources possessed by the ward, it is no longer difficult to find the right formula to assign the costs to activities.

In conclusion, the benefits resulting from introducing the resource based costing are indisputable as thanks to this solution it is possible to reduce the overall costs of the performed activity by controlling the costs and potential of particular resources which are at the medical centre's disposal. It forms the basis for building the activity based costing. The fact, that each cost must be assigned to a particular resource contributes to reducing the number of the so-called 'cost sacks'.[79] It allows to adjust 0.5 of the resource level to the activity volume including the value of the contract concluded with the National Health Fund. It actually constitutes invaluable support for any investment decisions. These are just a few of the numerous advantages of the resource based costing method.

1.4. THE USE OF COST ACCOUNTING SYSTEMS IN HEALTH CARE UNITS IN THE LUBLIN AREA

1.4.1. INTRODUCTION

Every business activity undertaken by health care units necessitates the use of financial resources, human work, and services, which in turn results in incurring costs. The importance of costs as an element affecting the management decision-making process comes from the fact that incurring costs by health care units is inevitable; however, costs may and should be reduced.

A crucial source of information regarding expenditures of health care units is the applied cost accounting system. It reflects the character of the entire activity of a given unit, including all processes that take place there, and generates information on costs for various levels of management.[80] The tasks of cost accounting systems used in hospitals are as follows:[81]

– obtaining information on the individual and total cost of the already provided medical services,

– determining factors that influence the level and structure of costs,

– enabling reaching sound decisions that may include setting prices of services provided in health care units, allocating financial resources within health care units, developing plans for their activity etc.,

– determining the results of the activity of separate organizational units, costs that they are to cover, and their participation in the overall expenditures of a given health care unit,

– monitoring costs incurred,

– monitoring results of the activity of specific organizational units or results of different types of activity,

– controlling and analyzing effects and costs of the activity of health care units in time and space,

[79] T. Zieliński (2007), *Odkrywanie prawdy o zyskach*, Akademia Menedżera Sp. z o.o., Poznań, p. 91.

[80] J. Gierusz, M. Cygańska (2009), *Budżetowanie kosztów działań w szpitalu*, Ośrodek Doradztwa i Doskonalenia Kadr Sp. z o.o., Gdańsk, p. 89.

[81] M. Hass-Symotiuk (ed.) (2008), *Rachunkowość i sprawozdawczość finansowa zakładów opieki zdrowotnej*, Ośrodek Doradztwa i Doskonalenia Kadr Sp. z o.o., Gdańsk, p. 430–431.

– analyzing and evaluating the management of resources used by health care units to improve their efficiency,

– providing all staff members of health care units with economics training.

The cost accounting system used in publicly funded health care units is based on Ministry of Health and Welfare order from 22nd December 1998 regulating the application of this system in public health care units. The order, which has been in effect since 1st January 1999, has changed the concept of cost calculation which now aims at precise calculation of costs of particular medical care services provided to patients in hospitals.

The cost accounting system that has been used in health care units since 1999 is a typical, traditional full cost accounting system. It requires proper registration of costs and fixing the individual cost of services provided.

The aim of the study presented in this article was to evaluate the solutions applied to cost accounting systems in chosen health care units, and to show the ways of improving them. For the purpose of the study, we have used domestic and foreign literature, legislative acts, and surveys.

1.4.2. THE APPLICATION OF COST ACCOUNTING SYSTEMS IN CHOSEN HEALTH CARE UNITS

In our survey, a questionnaire was sent by mail to 40 independent public health care units in the Lublin area. The units were chosen from the register of health care units in the aforementioned area.[82] We chose independent public health care units with the HP. 1 department code (hospital system).[83] For the purpose of the empirical study, which was conducted between October and November 2009, a research device – a questionnaire – was worked out. It was addressed to finance directors and chief accountants of health care units.

In the course of our study, a total of 14 units responded, which accounts for 35% of all the addressed. Considering survey effectiveness, it is a satisfactory result.

The traditional system of full cost accounting by nature and by source is used in only 64.3% of those health care units where the study was carried out.

Cost accounting by nature includes all individual costs that illustrate the amount of resources used in hospitals to provide patients with health care and therapeutic treatment. Cost accounting by nature only indicates changes in the level of various costs in relation to changes in services provided; it does not show the reason why such costs are covered.

---

[82] Register of health care units can be retrieved from the following webpage: www.rejestrzoz.gov.pl.

[83] HP 1–5 are department codes of specified organizational units within health care units, provided for in the annex to the Minister of Health order from 16th July 2004 on the system of department identification codes for health care units and on details concerning the assignment thereof.

Cost accounting by source, on the other hand, indicates the source of costs and the person responsible for their amount. It also shows expenditures of chosen functional units in hospitals, making it possible to control and analyze the management of financial resources in individual organizational units.[84]

What is of crucial importance is the classification of costs in the system of cost accounting by element which allows individual costs of specified calculation items to be determined. A calculation item is a category in cost accounting systems to which all incurred costs are attributed. In hospitals, calculation items may include: single medical care services, one-day hospital stays, patients, medical cases, and medical procedures. Thanks to such data, all factors affecting the level and structure of costs can be taken into consideration in the funding process.[85]

All health care units that participated in our study use the system of cost accounting by nature; 57.1% of all respondents use the system of cost accounting by source, and only 28.6% classify costs with the use of the cost accounting system by element.

Two out of fourteen respondents apply additional criteria to the cost accounting system, which enables them to use the variable cost accounting model.

None of the examined health care units has implemented modern models of cost accounting into their financial management. Activity-based costing (ABC), which is more and more often introduced into health care units in Western Europe and the USA, reflects the actual structure of costs incurred in the patient care process to a larger extent than traditional models.[86] As a consequence of developing modern medical technologies and the increase in the importance of quality and variety of provided services, a considerable growth in indirect costs has been noted. Research has shown that in case of medical procedures, the participation of indirect costs in the overall manufacturing cost amounts to around 70%.[87] The increasing participation of indirect costs as well as their being independent from the size of a given activity could make managers of health care units interested in developing some of the ABC model solutions, particularly for the use of hospitals.

In 64.3% of the studied cases, cost accounting includes distinction of cost sources. The accounting system applied by 57.1% of respondents encompasses a list of organizational units responsible for costs covered. In all studied health care units, the system of cost accounting by nature is always accompanied by cost accounting by source and/or by element.

In order to determine total costs, it is necessary not only to apply a properly designed cost accounting system, but also to distinguish cost sources on the basis of a health care unit's activity, type of contractual services it provides, and its manage-

---

[84] M. Kludacz (2005), *Funkcje budżetowania kosztów i ich realizacja w polskich szpitalach* [in:] M. Hass-Symotiuk (ed.), *Sterowanie kosztami w zakładach opieki zdrowotnej*, Wydawnictwo Uniwersytetu Szczecińskiego, Szczecin, p. 139.

[85] M. Hass-Symotiuk, U. Wawer (1997), *Wykorzystanie informacji o kosztach w zarządzaniu placówkami opieki zdrowotnej*, "Zeszyty Teoretyczne Rady Naukowej Stowarzyszenia Księgowych w Polsce", Warszawa, p. 61.

[86] J. Gierusz, M. Cygańska, *op. cit.*, p. 113.

[87] J. Stępniewski (ed.) (2008), *Strategia, finanse i koszty szpitala*, Wolters Kluwer, Warszawa, p. 178.

rial needs. The extent of detail in distinguishing cost sources is conditioned by the size of a given health care unit, the type of its management and supervision, as well as types of contracts it has signed with the NFZ (the Polish National Health Fund).[88]

In 71.4% of the examined health care units, the calculation item in basic cost sources is one-day hospital stay, and in 21.4% – medical procedure. Yet, when it comes to additional cost sources, the main source of incurred costs is the number of provided services – 71.4% of respondents; and the number of points indicating the use of material and human resources – 28.6% entities.

The basis of the adequate accounting of all costs in the area of their appearance is the assignment of used resources value in individual cost centers and the accounting for cost considering some cost centers' operations for the benefit of other centers. The basic problem for the appropriate indirect cost accounting is the adequate choice of keys to share the indirect costs. Therefore, the management should take the real, not the forged costs into consideration. In order to be certain that the cost information is correct, both direct costs and indirect costs' statistical key figures should be rearranged.

The managers of all units declare the use of information from cost accounting for financial reports preparation, internal services costs taxing and the budget estimation. It is interesting to say that the information from cost accounting is not enough support for management processes.

The main cost carrier in health care units is patients and tests run for their sake, medical procedures and administered drugs. The transition to the system of contracts of medical services according to homogeneous groups of patients requires the knowledge about individual patient treatment costs and their structure.

In the examined health care units, only 57.1% of entities calculates individual costs of patient treatment. Among these, 62.5% of respondents estimate costs considering the average hospitalization costs, and 37.5% of entities estimate costs taking all the ICD-9 positions assigned to patient's personal identity number into consideration.

The individual patient treatment costs estimation requires the combination of medical and economic data. The sign chart of a patient will be a helpful tool for gathering information concerning the treatment of disease in individual patient.

The task of the sign chart should be not only to list all medical procedures during patient's stay in the hospital but also to include economic data. The cost of patient hospitalization includes all treatment costs, e.g.:[89]

– costs of in-ward treatment (the product of the number of days of treatment and the daily cost of medical care),

– costs of medical procedures provided by other medical cost centers,

– costs of pharmacotherapy (the total of drug use and accounted costs of the pharmacy),

---

[88] M. Trojnacka (2008), *Ocena przydatności tradycyjnych systemów rachunku kosztów do celów zarządczych w zakładzie opieki zdrowotnej* [in:] E. Nowak (ed.), *Rachunkowość zarządcza w warunkach globalizacji*, Prace Naukowe Uniwersytetu Ekonomicznego we Wrocławiu Nr 15, Wrocław, p. 438.

[89] M. Hass-Symotiuk (2008), *Metodyka ustalania kosztów jednostkowych leczenia pacjenta* [in:] E. Nowak (ed.), *Rachunkowość zarządcza…*, p. 97–101.

– costs of patients' stay (the product of one-day in-patient nutrition and the number of days in the hospital; the product of individual accommodation costs and the number of days spent in the hospital).

The correctly estimated costs of patient treatment may be the basis for:[90]

– healthcare contract negotiations with the payer,

– estimation of medical service prices for sale,

– making out bills (for National Health Service or patients) for the treatment according to real costs – patients will be aware of their treatment cost,

– preparations of standards of patient treatment, groups and disease entities.

There are many variables determining a specific disease entity. Therefore, in order to achieve the most accurate data to compare the costs of patient treatment with National Health Service's price, one should calculate all disease cases in the given group treated at the specified time.

Applied medical procedures and administered drugs constitute the differentiating factor of the in-ward patient treatment. It is associated with various factors such as body reaction to the applied treatment or the disease stadium. Therefore, it is necessary to calculate the cost of medical procedure.

In the study of chosen health care units, only 35.7% of them tax medical procedure. Among them 80.0% tax the procedures according to ICD-9 classification and 20.0% according to the hospital service catalogue.

Medical procedure cost estimation is one of the stages of cost accounting. Its main task is to support the business activity by providing adequate information. Estimation should collect data which will be basis for the evaluation of economic efficiency of the particular entity.

Respondents, who tax the medical procedure were asked about the benefits such a practice gives. All examined units have basis to negotiate the contract with the payer. Half of the respondents may compare their price with the fixed cost of the procedure. 33.3% of subjects may assess the efficacy of used resources.

Medical procedure estimation is more important in these units, where the continuous negative financial result is the main cause of problems. Without taxed procedures it is impossible to estimate the individual profitability, and therefore, to show the most cost-absorbing areas and determine the influence of particular procedures on the financial result.

On the basis of survey results we may conclude that not all health care units calculate the individual patient's costs or tax the procedures. It may prove that health care units' priority is the treatment, not money.

1.4.3. SUMMARY

To sum up the considerations on the topic of cost accounting systems, we may come to the conclusion that not all examined health care units use cost accounting systems according to the Ministry of Health and Social Care regulations from 22nd December

---

[90] *Ibidem*, p. 103.

1998 and follow its directives. The causes of not using the cost accounting systems in accordance with regulations in health care units were defined in literature and confirmed by surveys. Most common are:[91]

– the lack of an adequate, integrated computer system enabling to combine the medical and economic data,

– the lack of data-gathering and organizing tools,

– difficulties in the interpretation of directives, which trigger individual conceptions of and modifications to the use of the rules,

– the lack of standards of medical procedures leading to a considerable diversity in methods applied in a health care unit,

– too big an engagement of hospital administration employees in the preparation of reporting documents for the National Health Service as a result of an overcomplicated system of health care units accounting for their contracts,

– the lack of adequately trained administration and medical personnel able to tax the medical services, and the employment restrictions as a result of unit's reorganization,

– the lack of coherence between the Accountancy Act's regulations and legal instruments of the Ministry of Health,

– the lack of hospital management systems, which would systematize the range and ways of the use of information from the accounts.

The existing solutions within cost accounting systems need to be adjusted to the needs created by modern management techniques applied to health care units. It may appear in the process of introducing new concepts of cost accounting systems, such as e.g. operations cost accounting systems, thanks to which managers will have an effective service costs management tool. Thanks to accurate estimation of costs of medical care services, it will be possible to determine their real profitability.

1.5. THE ROLE OF INTERNAL AUDIT IN HOSPITALS

1.5.1. INTRODUCTION

For the past several years Polish public finance sector has adopted internal audit to control public finance. The obligations and rules connected with internal audit were introduced to the public finance sector units in January 2002 by virtue of the Public Finance Act. A subsequent yet a significant amendment of this Act, which has been effective since 2010, extends the list of the sector units obliged to implement internal audit. The Act specifies also healthcare sector units, because, among others, the

---

[91] J. Kogut (2009), *Ocena prawidłowości dokonywania wyceny usług medycznych w SP ZOZ: Rachunkowość a controlling*, Prace Naukowe Uniwersytetu Ekonomicznego we Wrocławiu Nr 56, Wrocław, p. 200.

healthcare reform should lead to the establishment of a modern health care system, which would efficiently treat patients, be favorable to the sector employees as well as effectively manage public funds.

It is the primary objective of the currently binding internal audit regulations and standards to support a manager in efficient unit management. Internal audit is a management instrument used by unit managers to gain rational assurance that objectives and tasks of a given unit are attained, procedures resulting from acts of law or adopted by a unit manager are implemented and observed, while internal audit mechanisms and procedures adequately and correctly support unit's operation. Presently internal audit not only analyzes internal control efficiency but also public finance management control. Furthermore, it is a vital tool for risk management estimation and execution of corporate governance and public governance tasks.

This work aims to present the fundamental acts of law and standards related to internal audit, which are in force in 2010 in the healthcare sector units, in hospitals in particular. Qualification requirements for the function of a unit's internal auditor and the basic rules and scope of operation of an internal audit division are elaborated on. Additionally, the conditions and rules for internal audit outsourcing were listed.

1.5.2. FORMAL BASES OF INTERNAL AUDIT IN HEALTHCARE SECTOR

The Public Finance Act,[92] executive orders issued pursuant thereto by the Minister of Finance as well as the guidelines of the Minister of Finance published in the communications and the International Standards for the Professional Practice of Internal Audit, which were adopted as internal audit standards in the public finance sector units, govern the internal audit in use and operation.

In 2010 in accordance with the amended Public Finance Act internal audit is obligatory for the following healthcare sector units: The Ministry of Health, The National Health Fund, Independent public healthcare facilities and Other state or independent corporate persons from the sector established pursuant to separate acts of law to execute public tasks, provided that they collect substantial public funds or make substantial public outlays.

On the basis of a delegation of the Public Finance Act the Minister of Finance issued numerous **executive regulations and instructions**. In 2010 internal audits in hospitals are based, *inter alia,* on the following regulations:

    1. The ordinance concerning internal audit execution and documentation,[93]

    2. Communication No. 1 concerning the internal audit standards,[94]

    3. Communication No. 13 concerning the management control standards,[95]

---

[92] Ustawa z 27 sierpnia 2009 r. o finansach publicznych (Dz. U. Nr 157, poz. 1240).

[93] Rozporządzenie Ministra Finansów z 1 lutego 2010 r. w sprawie przeprowadzania i dokumentowania audytu wewnętrznego (Dz. U. Nr 21, poz. 108).

[94] Komunikat Nr 1 MF z 19 lutego 2009 r. w sprawie standardów audytu wewnętrznego w jednostkach sektora finansów publicznych (Dz. Urz. MF Nr 2, poz. 12).

[95] Komunikat nr 23 MF z 16 grudnia 2009 r. w sprawie standardów kontroli zarządczej dla sektora finansów publicznych (Dz. Urz. MF Nr 15, poz. 84).

4. Communication No. 16 concerning the announcement of the "Internal Audi-tor's Code of Ethics" and the "Internal Audit Charter".[96]

5. Communication No. 25 concerning the form of information about the internal audit task execution.[97]

Furthermore, at its website the Ministry of Finance publishes and recommends **other documents to be used by managers and internal auditor**s in the public finance sector units. Additionally, for the execution of the internal audit tasks concerning **information system audits** in the public finance sector units, that is in hospitals, internal auditors are recommended by the Minister of Finance to apply standards and guidelines published by the international **Information Systems Audit and Control Association (ISACA)**, i.e.:

– SISA[98] – standards and guidelines for information systems audit and

– COBIT[99] – guidelines for Information Technology management.

The currently effective public finance act, which pertains to internal audit in the public sector, governs among others the following matters:

1) Internal audit definition,

2) Internal audit rules,

3) Definition and rules of management control, which is evaluated by an internal auditor,

4) The obligation to inform the councilors from a local government about, among others, the results of a financial economy audit and report from the execution of an audit plan for the previous year,

5) Deadline for development of a report from the execution of an audit plan for the previous year until January the following year,

6) A possibility of internal audit outsourcing to a party unemployed by a unit, for instance, to an auditor. The act specifies the units the provision applies to provided that they meet the requirements referred to therein,

7) A list of professional qualifications for internal auditors in public finance sector units.

In accordance with Article 275 of the Public Finance Act **an internal audit is carried out by an internal auditor employed by a unit or a service provider un-employed by a unit**. An internal auditor must be employed by:

– The Ministry of Health,

– The National Health Fund,

– Independent public healthcare centers,

Independent public healthcare centers are an exception to this rule, as they can outsource internal audit on the condition that neither revenue nor costs exceed PLN 100,000. thousand or the unit employs fewer than 200 people. The same applies to

---

[96] Komunikat Nr 16 MF z 18 lipca 2006 r. w sprawie ogłoszenia „Kodeksu etyki audytora wewnętrznego w JSFP" i „Karty audytu wewnętrznego w JSFP" (Dz. Urz. MF Nr 9, poz. 70).

[97] Komunikat Nr 25 MF z 18 grudnia 2009 r. w sprawie wzoru informacji o realizacji zadań z zakresu audytu wewnętrznego (Dz. Urz. MF z 2009, nr 15, poz. 85).

[98] Standards for Information Systems Auditing, ISACA 2002, www.isaca.org.pl.

[99] Control Objectives for Information and Related Technology. Management Guidelines (COBIT). IT Governance Institute, April 2001, www.itgi.org and www.isaca.org.pl.

departments headed by the Minister of Health, which can outsource internal audit upon his/her consent.

Additionally, healthcare sector units, which were established by local governments, can also outsource internal audit, if the local government's budgetary resolution stipulates income and revenue as well as expenses and costs are below PLN 100,000. thousand At a local government the tasks related to internal audit are assigned to its head in accordance with Article 276 of the Act, that is respectively to: the commune administrator, mayor, chairman of the a local government's management board.

The head of an internal audit division is obliged to conduct an internal audit, save for local government units, to present all the internal audit-related information and documents at the request of the Minister of Finance. Therefore, since 2010 the heads of independent public healthcare centers, which were not established by local government units, if revenue or costs recorded in the financial plan exceed PLN 40,000. thousand, are obliged to notify the Minister of Finance in writing about the commencement of an internal audit. This pertains also to other healthcare sector units, such as, for instance:

1. State budgetary units, if revenue or expenses recorded in the budgetary unit's financial plan exceed PLN 40,000. thousand.

2. Other public finance sector units, internal audits are conducted at the head's discretion.

It must be stressed that in 2010 an **audit committee** will be established at the Ministry of Health. The objectives of the audit committee were defined in the amended Public Finance Act in Article 289 and they in particular apply to the obligation to signal significant risks and weaknesses in management control and to put forward facilitation methods, set out priorities for annual and strategic internal audit plans. The committee should also review the internal audit results and monitor their implementation, review internal audit plan execution reports and evaluate management control. The committee will also monitor the performance of internal audits in units, review internal and external evaluation of the work of internal audit divisions and give consent to termination or modification of employment contracts of the heads of internal audit divisions. The objectives of the audit committee, which are enumerated above, apply both to the units headed by the Minister and to other healthcare sector units.

1.5.3. INTERNAL AUDITOR'S QUALIFICATIONS

A person with EU citizenship or a citizenship of any other country, the citizens of which, pursuant to international agreement or the European Community law regulations, are entitled to be employed in the Republic of Poland can perform internal audits in the units of the public finance sector. Such a person must be capable of performing legal activities, executing all public rights as well as must not be punished for any intentional crimes or any intentional fiscal crimes. Furthermore, he/she must be a university graduate and possess **pertinent qualifications** to perform an internal audit as specified in Article 286 of the Public Finance Act. Internal audits can be conducted by a person, who:

1. Holds an international certificate: Certified Internal Auditor (CIA), Certified Government Auditing Professional (CGAP), Certified Information Systems Auditor (CISA), Association of Chartered Certified Accountants (ACCA), Certified Fraud Examiner (CFE), Certification in Control Self Assessment (CCSA), Certified Financial Services Auditor (CFSA), Chartered Financial Analyst (CFA) or

2. In the years 2003–2006 passed the internal audit examination before the Examination Committee appointed by the Minister of Finance, or

3. Holds auditor's qualifications, or

4. Has a two-year internal audit practice and graduated from post-graduate studies in internal audit issued by an organizational unit, which, upon the diploma issue, was authorized to award Ph.D. titles in economics or law.

Moreover, internal audit practice means at least half-time employment documented by a head of a unit from the public finance sector, which is connected with:

1) conducting audits under the supervision of an internal auditor,

2) certifying and issuing EU financial assistance discontinuation declarations, which are referred to in the Fiscal Inspection Act, by fiscal inspectors,[100]

3) supervising or performing inspections, which are referred to in the Supreme Chamber of Control (Najwyższa Izba Kontroli) Act.[101]

As mentioned before internal audits in the units from the healthcare sector are conducted by internal auditors employed by the unit or by an outsourced service provider. **An outsourced internal auditor** can mean: a natural person, a natural person conducting business, for instance an auditor or other persons on conditions that they meet the above mentioned requirements specified in Article 286 of the Public Finance Act. A private partnership, a general partnership, professional partnership, limited partnership, limited joint stock partnership or a corporate person can act as an outsourced internal auditor provided that their employees conducting internal audit in a unit meet the requirements specified in Article 286 of the Public Finance Act.

1.5.4. THE ROLE AND TYPES OF INTERNAL AUDIT IN HOSPITALS

In accordance with Article 272 of the Public Finance Act internal audit means independent and objective activities, which support the Minister or a manager heading a given division or a unit in attaining their goals and executing their tasks by regular evaluation of management control as well as counseling. What is evaluated in particular is if management control in the government administration or a given unit is adequate, effective and efficient. Consequently, the idea behind internal audit is to identify and comprehend potential risks faced by a hospital and to examine and evaluate the effectiveness of the internal control system, which was implemented to control risks and financial safety. The underlying objective of an internal audit in a hospital is to support its management in attainment of its goals and execution of its tasks by regular management control evaluation of public spending.

---

[100] Ustawa z 28 września 1991 r. o kontroli skarbowej (Dz. U. z 2004 r. Nr 8, poz. 65, ze zm.).

[101] Ustawa z 23 grudnia 1994 r. o Najwyższej Izbie Kontroli (Dz. U. z 2007 r. Nr 231, poz. 1701 oraz z 2008 r. Nr 209, poz. 1315, Nr 225, poz. 1502 i Nr 227, poz. 1505).

In accordance with the Internal Audit Standards the fundamental goal of an audit is to add value and facilitate a unit's operation. Internal audits should provide hospital management with an unbiased and independent evaluation of management and internal control mechanisms, inclusive of financial control procedures, are in place and operate adequately, effectively and efficiently. An internal audit encompasses examination and evaluation of risk management and task execution quality.

Internal audits include assurance activities (evaluation) and counseling. Assurance activities constitute a fundamental task of an internal audit. An independent and unbiased management evaluation, inclusive of evaluation of risk management and control and unit's operation areas and systems, should assure a hospital management that its systems operate properly. Audit by counseling should also lead to the facilitation of hospital operation. An internal auditor can submit requests to the hospital management or the management of audited units, which should result in the facilitation of the operation of a hospital or its organizational units.

An internal audit should cover all areas of hospital operations. Internal audit is a management instrument used by unit managers to gain rational assurance that objectives and tasks of a given hospital are being attained, procedures resulting from acts of law or adopted by hospital management are being implemented and observed, while internal audit mechanisms and procedures adequately and correctly support hospital's operation. Internal audit should include in particular:

– A review of internal control mechanisms and reliability and credibility of operational, management and financial information,

– An identification and analysis of risks related to hospital operation, including evaluation of the effectiveness of risk management and internal control,

– An opinion if the control mechanisms put in place in the audited systems by hospital management are adequate and efficient,

– An opinion about procedures and practices of financial information development, classification and presentation,

– An opinion if acts of law, internal hospital regulations as well as programs, strategies and standards introduced by pertinent bodies are observed,

– An opinion about hospital property security, an evaluation of the effectiveness and economy of hospital resources use and public funds management,

– Submission of reports with conclusions and presentation of recommendations concerning enhancement of effectiveness of hospital's operation in a given area,

– A review of programs and projects to establish if a hospital generates planned results and meets its objectives,

– An evaluation if a hospital's operation is adjusted to the previously presented recommendations of an internal audit or a control.

The basic internal audit types include: operational audit, including compliance audit, which is sometimes referred to as separate audit type, performance audit, financial audit and information technology audit. The operational audit examines if hospital operations are in accordance with its operational and strategic objectives and evaluates a hospital's systems in operation. The results of an operational audit are later used to enhance a hospital's future operation. On the other hand, the financial audit is chiefly associated with the evaluation of the accounting system and the reliability of financial statements. The financial audit aims to identify all negligence and irregularities in the financial and accounting areas of hospital's operation.

1.5.5. RULES OF INTERNAL AUDIT

In accordance with the provisions of the Public Finance Act a multi-personal internal audit unit is managed by its head. In the case of an internal auditor employed in a one-person internal audit unit, the provisions of the Act are applied together with the ordinance concerning the internal audit performance and documentation as well as the instructions of the head of the internal audit unit.

In the event internal audit is outsourced, the Public Finance Act stipulates that an agreement concluded between a unit and such a service provider should provide for the internal audit is conducted in accordance with the regulations of the Act and its executive orders. Furthermore, the agreement with a service provider should specify how to handle documents, in particular it should indicate how to proceed with electronic documents, prepared for internal audit so as to make them accessible, protected against unauthorized dissemination, mutilation or destruction.

The internal audit standards,[102] which should be observed by auditors in public finance sector units, that is in hospitals, are divided into:

1. Attribute Standards (Series 1000), which pertain to the organization of an internal audit unit and the procedures for internal auditors,

2. Performance Standards (Series 2000), which characterize activities taken during internal audit, among others, planning, examination, reporting, as well as quality criteria for their evaluation,

They are supplemented by the Implementation Standards, which feature detailed instructions and procedures. They are defined separately for: Assurance activities (marked as A following Standard number, for instance 1130.A1) and counseling (marked as C following Standard number, for instance 2010.C1).

An internal audit can be considered properly performed if the following activities indicated in the standards were taken, that is, for instance:

1) the hospital management was responsible for the internal control system,
2) the audit was targeted to hospital operation facilitation,
3) risks were prioritized,
4) audit was of high quality,
5) the auditor's opinions were independent, impartial and unbiased,
6) the auditor was professional, knowledgeable and diligent,
7) internal audit results were used effectively,
8) information circulation and communication were problem-free.

Internal audits, which cover the evaluation of risk management, internal control systems and hospital management, are to a large extent based on the trust placed on an auditor. An internal auditor is trusted if he/she is ethical. The currently binding

---

[102] Komunikat Nr 1 MF z 19 lutego 2009 r. w sprawie standardów audytu wewnętrznego w jednostkach sektora finansów publicznych (Dz. Urz. MF Nr 2, poz. 12).

Code of Internal Auditor's Ethics in the public finance sector units was published in 2006. The Code supplements the internal audit standards and provides instructions for internal auditors in the public finance sector units. In the light of the Code of Ethics an internal auditor is obliged to audit and counsel in an honest, reliable and decent manner. It presents rules of internal audit practice and standard procedures expected for an internal auditor. The rules of internal audit practice in the public finance sector units include: honesty, objectivity, confidentiality, professionalism, internal auditor's procedures and relations between internal auditors and conflicts of interests. Each of the rules was specified in rules of conduct for internal auditors.

In accordance with acts of law and internal audit standards a person in charge of internal audit should set out rules and procedures to be observed during an audit. The form and content of the rules and procedures depends on the scale and structure of an internal audit as well as its complexity. The **internal audit charter** as well as the description of the internal audit procedures, which frequently in practice are referred to as **Internal Audit Book of Procedures**, constitute fundamental internal documents governing internal audit performance. The internal audit charter specifies the chief objectives and rules of an internal audit. Furthermore, it should define the basic rights, obligations and responsibilities of an internal auditor and specify his/her status in a unit as well as the relation with other control institutions such as the Supreme Chamber of Control, inspectors from the Inland Revenue Agencies and the Social Security Company etc. The Internal Audit Book of Procedures specifies the general provisions of the charter and describes the detailed audit methods, inclusive of the planning procedures, audit task execution, documentation development and reporting.

An internal auditor documents all activities and events, which are significant for internal audit. An internal auditor keeps the current internal audit files in order to document the internal audit and its results as well as the permanent internal audit files to collect information about risk areas, which can possibly constitute a subject of an internal audit. The obligation to document all the activities and events significant to perform an internal audit is stipulated in the ordinance concerning the internal audits and their documentation.

The hospital management, the head of the audited unit, in which an audit is performed as well as all authorized persons can gain access to current audit files. The internal audit documents are marked and stored in accordance with the general rules concerning the files left behind in a unit.

1.5.6. FINAL CONCLUSIONS

Public sector internal audit is and will continue to be constantly improved as *inter alia* it is introduced by virtue of the amended Public Finance Act effective as of January 1, 2010 as well as the new version of the International Standards for the Professional Practice of Internal Audit put in practice in 2009. Internal audit becomes obligatory in more and more public finance sector units, including the healthcare sector units, which means it is necessary and efficient for public sector operation.

Thus, in light of the currently binding regulations and adopted standards an internal audit should support a manager of a unit in effective unit management, evaluation of the efficiency of internal control, public finance management, risk management and execution of corporate and public governance tasks.

1.6. CONSTRUCTION OF THE SOFT BUDGET RESTRICTIONS AND HEALTH UNIT DEBT

1.6.1. INTRODUCTION

Despite the system transformation which took place in Poland in 1989, the health care sector remained unchanged until the end of the 1990s. It was the relic of the previous era both financially and in the way it was managed. Floating like stiff ice floes on 'the rough waters' of transformations, the sector was believed not to be subjected to any changes and it was clearer and clearer for the state authorities that they were not able to keep it stable any longer. Those two tendencies met head-on in the ground-breaking year of 1999 when systemic reforms of management and financing of Polish health care were introduced. On one hand, the health care stopped being financed by the state budget, assuming that it would adapt to the means offered by the insurance system in Poland. On the other hand, most of the health care units started being supervised by the local self-governments.

Despite the reform many public hospital still have serious problems with covering the costs of their activity. They are indebted significantly and the risk of insolvency and bankruptcy has appeared in many cases. Such situation results from two factors above all.

Firstly, it is a specific 'memory of the organization.' The health care units got used to making decisions which, after further analyses, appeared to be unfeasible and as a result were reversed. It concerned the sanitary conditions of the hospitals, the register of medical services (RUM), self-governing or the standards of accountancy. The situation seemed similar in cases of several clearing of debts, which were always regarded as final ones. It led to a common belief that a hospital cannot balance and that the source of clearing of debts must always be found.[103] That sort of habit to resist any changes was not appreciated by the reformers and it played an essential role in the lack of motivation for adapting its activity to new conditions.

Secondly, the measures to prevent the units from getting debt-ridden turned out to be too weak. The formula of autonomy units and the founding agents' limited influence on their activity caused the paralysis. At the same time the state consistently

---

[103] In the documents from the social boards' meetings there are discussions on absurd arguments of some of the Board members, sometimes quite amusing, e.g. shortage of money for medicaments or salaries. They prove that the managing staff presented the mentality of the previous system, really difficult to be changed.

refused to interfere. However, the moment its necessity was noticed, all the conditions of the situation were not thoroughly seen (Act of 15th April, 2005 *on the social help and the restructurization of public health care units*, Dz. U. No. 78, item 684). It resulted in a selective, not full-scale process of financial restructuring of hospitals.

It is the second aspect of the problem the article discusses.

Its main purpose is to present the rules of the soft budget restrictions in the legal structure of autonomy public health care unit.

The basic thesis is that the indebtedness of the health care units is the effect of using the soft budget restrictions in the structure of public hospitals in large measure.

The problem is really serious because the insolvency of self-governing organizational units providing medical services carries with it profound economic, social and political consequences. It may result in abandoning or reducing the range of medical services. The insolvency of self-governing organizational units may also lead to the loss of payment capacity of the self-governing local unit and finally, to disorganizing of the whole system of satisfying the local community's multiple needs.

1.6.2. THE SOFT BUDGET RESTRICTIONS – BASIC TERMS

The theme of the soft budget restrictions is widely discussed by A. Babczuk[104] in his works.

The term of the soft budget restrictions was mentioned by J. Kornai (1979) for the first time with reference to specific relations between the companies and the state authorities in the economies planned centrally. The author regards 'the budget constraint' as behavioral characteristics of decision-makers. If the budget constraint is hard the managers adapt (*ex ante*) the expenses of the company managed by them to the financial resources they expect from the product sale and all the other benefits coming from the company's assets.[105] A hard budget restriction sets the limits on business entities behavior (*ex ante*). *'The softening of the budget constraint takes place when an explicit correlation between expenses and profits loosens because expenses surplus in comparison to profits will be regulated by another institution, the state as usual.'*[106] Then the budget constraint stops being the factor hampering the decision-makers behavior.

---

[104] A. Babczuk (2008), *Miękkie ograniczenia budżetowe jako przesłanka niewypłacalności jednostek samorządu terytorialnego*, cz. I: *Zagadnienia teoretyczne*, "Finanse Komunalne" No. 3, p. 5–8; A. Babczuk, *Miękkie ograniczenia budżetowe jednostek samorządu terytorialnego* [in:] G. Borys (ed.) (2008), *Finanse i rachunkowość – teoria i praktyka*, Prace Naukowe Uniwersytetu Ekonomicznego we Wrocławiu No. 16, Wrocław, p. 11–15.

[105] J. Kornai (1979), *Resource-Constrained Versus Demand-Constrained Systems*, „Econometrica" Vol. 47, No. 4, p. 801–819; J. Kornai (1986), *The Soft Budget Constraint*, "Kyklos" Vol. 39, No. 1, p. 3–30; J. Kornai, E. Maskin, G. Roland (2003), *Understanding the Soft Budget Constraint*, "Journal of Economic Literature" Vol. 41, p. 1095–1136.

[106] J. Kornai (1986), *The Soft Budget Constraint*, "Kyklos" Vol. 39, No. 1, p. 22.

M. Dewatripoint and E. Maskin define such soft budget constraints as the supporting subjects' inclination for financial feeding of other organizations due to striving so as to avoid the loss of the input they had in the past. The attitude of the supporting subjects is predicted by the supported subjects.[107]

A. Babczuk thinks that the soft budget constraints have the traits of a social institution. He understands them as entrenched, common expectations of the participants of a social interaction that one party of the social or commercial contract will be eager to cover, directly or indirectly, the deficiencies of the other party. The budget constraints are soft only when the expectations to receive support are seen as likely to be realized. The soft budget constraints would not be strong and meaningful unless they created the expectations and attitudes of the surrounding subjects, especially the stakeholders of the supported party of the social or commercial contract.[108]

With reference to self-government health care units the problem of soft budget constraints (restrictions) may appear in many aspects. It may be seen in the relation between the health care unit and a local self-governing office which is its founding agent. In that case the hospital managers decisions are made with a conviction that the founding agent will support it on the brink of bankruptcy. An attempt to pass the unit's indebtedness on the agent may endanger the finances of the local self-governing office itself. Thus both the decision-makers and the managers of self-government health care unit may expect to be supported by the state authorities.[109]

1.6.3. THE IDEA OF AN AUTONOMY UNIT

Formal possibilities of establishing autonomy health care units have existed since the beginning of the 90s. Yet the idea was not too popular. In 1996 there were only 8% of public autonomy hospitals when the then Ministry of Health and Social Care started a pilot scheme called 'An Autonomy Hospital'.[110] In the accepted form of the system, the autonomy units were supposed to complement the whole system. It was only dedicated to the currently balanced hospitals. The other hospitals were supposed to act in the form of a public sector unit or company. Therefore the idea of autonomy was to be the confirmation of the statue of the unit marking out in the system.

The process of setting up the formal-legal base for such units activity was finalized with the Act of the 20th June, 1997 *on the changes in the Act on the health care units and some other Acts* (Dz. U. 1997, No. 104, item 661). It introduced e.g. the term 'autonomy public health care unit' ('spzoz' in Polish).

The structure of the units showed many inaccuracies because of which it was subjected to jurisdiction of the courts of various instances (including The Supreme Administrative Court and The Constitutional Tribunal). It is enough to mention that

---

[107] M. Dewatripont, E. Maskin (1995), *Credit and Efficiency in Centralized and Decentralized Economies*, "The Review of Economic Studies" Vol. 62, No. 4, p. 541–555.

[108] A. Babczuk, *Miękkie ograniczenia budżetowe jako przesłanka...*, p. 5–8.

[109] A. Babczuk, *Miękkie ograniczenia budżetowe jednostek...*, p. 11–15.

[110] J. Klich (2007), *Przedsiębiorczość w reformowaniu systemu ochrony zdrowia w Polsce. Niedoceniane interakcje*, Wydawnictwo Uniwersytetu Jagiellońskiego, Kraków, p. 84.

in 1991–2007 the Act was amended 46 times. In spite of that there are still no statutory definitions and it is not interpreted in a consolidated and commonly accepted way.[111] It evokes the problems with interpreting, decreases its efficiency and at the same time, increasing the risk for the changes undertaken.

The amount of the autonomy units jumped at the end of 1998. The reform introduced at the time assumed that only such statue would entitle to contract the services. That is why the process was rather obligatory to the hospitals which wanted to maintain their activity.

1.6.4. THE RULES OF FINANCIAL ECONOMY OF AN AUTONOMY HOSPITAL

Basic regulations for financial economy of an autonomy hospital are the terms: art. 35b, 35c and art. 50 i 60 point 1 of The Act on Health Care Units. They state that the unit itself covers the costs of business activity and commitments and that its business activity is based on the regulations defined by the Act on Public Finances. The unit should go by the efficiency in its assets use. However, art. 61 of the Act on Health Care Units neither predicts the consequences of the lack of annual balance confirmation nor defines, who is to verify it (the Board or the Council of the founding agent or a Community Council). The Director of the hospital does not need a vote of approval although it is a standard not only in economy units but also in the public financial sector.

The rules of financial economy defined in such a way are at variance with the provisions in art. 60 point 2 and 4 which state that the negative financial balance cannot result in ceasing the activity and also that the founding agent covers the balance of the unit. They are fundamental for the lack of supervision over the effectiveness of the hospitals. First it is said that the unit itself covers its costs while further on, in the same Act, the manager is provided with a sort of guarantee that the financial balance does not influence the further business activity of the unit. It is mentioned in point 4 of art. 60, which, according to many managers, describes the role of the agents in the system precisely – as those who take over the units' debts. It is difficult to disagree with that, as it may be concluded from the analysis of the statutory provisions. There is no other way to interpret the financial situation and the role of the founding agent if it is deprived of the opportunity to control and execute the effectiveness, being at the same time responsible for the hospital"s activity consequences.

It should be noted that the process of 'passing' the health care units on local self-governments took place in the atmosphere of conviction that unprepared system would adapt to new developments on its own. The hospitals' large inertia, resulting from clearing of their debts, did not disturb the positive thinking. In 1994 and 1995 budgetary grants were awarded twice for paying off debts of 2 billion PLN in total. In 1997 The State Treasury took over 1.7 billion PLN. The last clearing of debts,

---

[111] M. Dercz, T. Rek (2007), *Ustawa o zakładach opieki zdrowotnej. Komentarz*, Wolters Kluwer, Warszawa, p. 11–12.

proceeded in 1998 was of over 8 billion PLN.[112] The amount of debts of health care units in 1991–1998, cleared by the State Treasury was in total 11.7 billion PLN.[113]

In 2005–2008 autonomy hospitals received support in the form of loans granted from the state Budget. A special Act of the 15th April, 2005 *on social help and restructuring of public health care units* was adopted.

868 autonomy health care units took advantage of such help. Most of them were set up by Local District Governments or Voivodships. They were granted 2.2 billion PLN of loans in total. After a successful financial restructuring of the unit the loans might have been amortized at 70%.[114]

At the end of 2009 the hospitals' commitments were at the level of 9.5 billion PLN.[115] Thus it may be assumed that the amount of indebtedness, at present, is almost at the same level as a decade before, i.e. 10 years after the reform started.

Further promises to support the autonomy units were enclosed in the project of the Act of the 6th November on *the health care units*. Unfortunately it was vetoed by the President. That is why the Government has adopted long-term scheme called 'Support for the local self-government units in stabilizing the system of health protection' (so called plan B).[116] It is based on the current regulations for the health care units.

It is worth noticing that the undefined responsibility of the management is the factor which increases the risk of insolvency of an autonomy health care unit. It results from an apparent autonomy. The situation is that the responsibility for the manager's decisions falls on the founding agent. It violates the rule of a direct correlation between the decision-making authority and the responsibility for, which sets the basis for effective management. It should be noted that the dysfunction concerns the financial economy, one of the most important spheres of functioning of each unit. In vain would one look for any detailed rules concerning a manager's responsibility for the negative financial balance in the Act of the 30th August, *on the health care units*. Neither are they in the Act of the 30th June, 2005 *on public finances* (Dz. U. No. 249, item 2104 with subsequent amendments) nor in its new version of the 27th August, 2009 *on public finances* (Dz. U. No. 157, item 1240). Such situation contributes essentially to a kind of tension between the owner's authority and the autonomy of the

---

[112] D. Młodzianowska (2006), *Wady systemowe w ochronie zdrowia jako zagrożenie sukcesu komercjalizacji i prywatyzacji opieki zdrowotnej w Polsce* [in:] D. Wasilewski, M. Węgrzyn, *Komercjalizacja i prywatyzacja ZOZ. Kluczowe warunki osiągnięcia sukcesu*, Prace Naukowe Akademii Ekonomicznej we Wrocławiu No. 1103, Wrocław.

[113] *Analiza wykonania budżetu państwa i założeń polityki pieniężnej w 1998 roku*, Supreme Chamber of Control, Warszawa, June 1999.

[114] *Informacja o wynikach kontroli restrukturyzacji samodzielnych publicznych zakładów opieki zdrowotnej ze szczególnym uwzględnieniem wykorzystania pomocy publicznej*, Supreme Chamber of Control, No. 141/2008/P/07/100/KPZ, Warszawa 2008, p. 14–18, 49–50; *Uzasadnienie projektu ustawy o zmianie ustawy o pomocy publicznej i restrukturyzacji publicznych zakładów opieki zdrowotnej*, print No. 852, Sejm, Warszawa 2008, p. 1–5.

[115] *Dynamika zobowiązań ogółem samodzielnych publicznych zakładów opieki zdrowotnej w latach 2003 – IV kw. 2009*, Ministry of Health.

[116] Act No. 58/2009 of the Cabinet, the 27th April, 2009 *w sprawie ustanowienia programu wieloletniego pod nazwą "Wsparcie jednostek samorządu terytorialnego w działaniach stabilizujących system ochrony zdrowia"* (www.ratujemyszpitale.pl).

unit. It has many negative results, an ineffective use of the institutional potential of the organization, among others.[117] Then it seems that the improvements may go in two alternative directions. Either the manager of the unit will be autonomous within the hospital structure or the ownership structures, well-known in the economy sector, will be adapted. Both solutions should be based on full responsibility of a manager for the decisions made. It concerns criminal and financial responsibility. It is hard to imagine any successful system of management without these components.

The most serious dysfunctions result from creating the hospital 'autonomy' ex-temporaneously. The effect is that the autonomy is defined in the Act on health care units imprecisely. Moreover the regulations are not synchronized with other Acts, which are the bases for founding agents activity (both in competence and finances). As the result an autonomy health care unit is a non-elaborated, new legal creation, which is neither autonomous nor a part of specific administration, as it does not be-long to any forms of administration sectors. It is not on the traditional list of different forms of public service organization (public enterprise, budgetary unit or community company). So it is not surprising that the form of an autonomy health care unit is de-scribed as a formal-legal hybrid in many scientific works and expert reports.[118]

1.6.5. NECESSARY CHANGES

A systemic solution that eliminates most constraints identified in the autonomy hos-pital structure, meaning the current management, the ownership supervising and bet-ter accessibility to financial instruments, is restructuring hospitals into public compa-nies. According to article 8, point 7 of the Act on the health care units, a health care unit may be set up by a native or foreign body corporate.

The Act on the health care units allows the restructuring only as expanding, reducing the activity or joining two separate units (article 36 i 43). It also says about a change in its financial economy or its liquidation (article 60, point 3). Neither the Act regulations nor other statutory regulations give right to transform an autonomy hospital into an economy unit acting on the commercial code. The only way is to liquidate a current form of busi-ness activity and establishing a new business entity which will set up a non-public health care unit. In such case there is no legal consecution between the old and new entity.

The Supreme Court Act resolved the doubts over the restructuring hospitals into commercial partnerships against the Act on health care units.[119] It recognized the right of Local Governments to establish economic units which are to fulfill public job in health care.

---

[117] C. Włodarczyk (2003), *Reformy zdrowotne. Uniwersalny kłopot*, Wydawnictwo Uniwer-sytetu Jagiellońskiego, Kraków, p. 188.

[118] S. Golinowska, Z. Czepulis-Rutkowska, M. Sitek, A. Sowa, C. Sowada, C. Włodarczyk (2002), *Opieka zdrowotna w Polsce po reformie*, Reports CASE, No. 53; M. Boni, A. Kruszewski, M. Gorajek (2003), *Analiza sytuacji i program systemowych zmian w sektorze opieki zdrowotnej w Polsce*, Expert's report for Vice-Prime Minister Jerzy Hausner, Warszawa.

[119] Supreme Court Act of 22nd February, 2006 (Sygn. akt. II PZP 10/05).

The situation was to be changed in the suggestions prepared by the Prime Minister Tusk's Cabinet. The alteration in the Act on health care units assumed the formula of 'transforming' an autonomy hospital into the formula of a partnership, with legal consecution. However, it was vetoed by the President. Plan 'B' prepared by the Government allows taking advantage of existing law regulations.

1.6.6. CONSEQUENCES OF FINANCIAL INSTABILITY OF AN AUTONOMY HOSPITAL FOR THE FOUNDING AGENTS

As a result the indebtedness of hospitals reached the values which exceeded the possibilities of the agents to solve the problem. Art. 169 item 1 and art. 170 item 1 of the Act on public finances introduce the regulations setting limits on the way the local self-government units get in debts (up to 60% of worked-out income with an annual rate not exceeding 15% of the expected income). In comparison with the autonomy hospitals, the partnership units have hard budget restrictions. The situation will not allow to use the Government's support. The Government plan mentioned above, assumes the liquidation of autonomy hospitals and taking over their liabilities by the founding agents. After that the agent will receive a grant of the same value as the public-legal liabilities. Although a huge part of the liabilities will be compensated by the Budget, it may result in exceeding the hard budget restrictions. The time of taking over the liabilities is not synchronized with the time of receiving the grant – both dates may differ so much that the unit may risk the consequences of the hard budget restrictions.

The fact is proved by the analysis of the financial situation in Lower Silesia Districts. It lets us distinguish three groups, almost equal in the numbers of the units. In 30% of them the accumulated debt exceeds 100% of annual income (according to the data from 2007, debts of the District and the hospital; the record holder reaches 164%); next 30% remain within 60–100%, and the next 30% of local Districts' accumulated debt is below the statutory threshold (<60%) with a significant majority staying below the threshold. To sum up, 2/3 of Local Districts in Lower Silesia cannot cover the negative financial balance of their hospitals. They are excluded from the Government plan.

1.6.7. CONCLUSIONS

The soft budget restrictions became a specific social institution. Its idea is to persist in entrenched, common expectations of the social relation participants that one party of the trade or social contract will be eager to cover the other's financial deficiency, directly or indirectly. The soft budget restrictions defined this way may become one of the main reasons for a mass insolvency of entities of different sort, also self-government organization units and local units.

The formal-legal formula of an autonomy hospital is a traditional example of a unit based on the soft budget restrictions. The above analysis shows that such form of setting limits did not prevent the units from growing debts, just the opposite – it encouraged to create a specific sector awareness that it was impossible for a hospital to balance its activity. It created dysfunctions, leading to squandering a lot of effort and energy devoted to increasing its efficiency. A large inertia appeared in its real, financial dimension, in the form of a huge systemic indebtedness. Waiting for eliminating of the dysfunction turned out to be a waste of time. The lack of systemic solutions results in undertaking individual initiatives, using the existing but complicated legal possibilities. At the end of 2007, in our country, there were over 50 hospitals under the formula of community partnership. Generally the innovations prove that there is a possibility to eliminate the dysfunctions effectively by transposition of the formula of providing the services into that which is based on the hard budget restrictions. As consequence, there appears a specific transfer of responsibility for negligence (generated in the soft budget restrictions conditions) to the forms of hard restrictions (the founding agents). The fact, along with the restructuring hospitals into commercial partnership seems to confirm higher efficiency of the hard budget restrictions in the public sector.

BIBLIOGRAPHY

1. Act No. 58/2009 of the Cabinet 27th April, 2009 on establishing a long-term scheme called 'Support for the local self-government units in stabilizing the system of health protection' on the 9th June from: www.ratujemyszpitale.pl.
2. Act of the 20th June, 1997 *on the changes in the Act on the health care units and some other Acts* (Dz. U. 1997, No 104, item 661).
3. Act of the 27th August, 2004 on health care services finansed from public means (Dz. U. No. 210, item 2135 with subsequent amendments).
4. Act of the 30th August, 1991 on the health care units (Dz. U. 1991, No. 91, item 408 with subsequent amendments).
5. Act of 15th April, 2005 *on the social help and the restructurization of public health care units*, Dz. U. No. 78, item 684.
6. Act of the 30th June, 2005 *on public finances* (Dz. U. No. 249, item 2104 with subsequent amendments).
7. Act of the 27th August, 2009 *on public finances* (Dz. U. No. 157, item 1240).
8. *Analiza wykonania budżetu państwa i założeń polityki pieniężnej w 1998 roku*, Supreme Chamber of Control, Warszawa, June 1999.
9. Adams J., White M., Forman D. (2004), *Are there socioeconomic gradients in stage and grade of breast cancer at diagnosis? Cross sectional analysis of UK cancer registry data*, BMJ. 329, p. 142–143.
10. Allonier C., Dourgnon P., Rochereau T. (2006), *Santé, soins et protection sociale en 2004*. Série résultats, No. 1621. IRDES, Paris.
11. A. Babczuk (2008), *Miękkie ograniczenia budżetowe jako przesłanka niewypłacalności jednostek samorządu terytorialnego*, cz. I: *Zagadnienia teoretyczne*, "Finanse Komunalne" No. 3.
12. A. Babczuk, *Miękkie ograniczenia budżetowe jednostek samorządu terytorialnego* [in:] G. Borys (ed.) (2008), *Finanse i rachunkowość – teoria i praktyka*, Prace Naukowe Uniwersytetu Ekonomicznego we Wrocławiu No. 16, Wrocław.

13. Bellanger M.M., Cherilova V., Paris V. (2005), *The "Health Benefit Basket" in France*. Eur J Health Economics [suppl. 1] 6.
14. Bellanger M.M., Jourdain A. (2004), *Tackling regional health inequalities in France by resource allocation: a case for complementary instrumental and process-based approaches?*, Appl. Health Econ. Health Policy 3.
15. Boni M., Kruszewski A., Gorajek M., (2003), *Analiza sytuacji i program systemowych zmian w sektorze opieki zdrowotnej w Polsce*, Expert's report for Vice--Prime Minister Jerzy Hausner, Warszawa.
16. Borella L., Peuvrel P., Sauvage M., Maraninchi D., Philip T. (2000), *A study based on national DRG data to evaluate work load and practice relating to cancer patients in not-for-profit hospitals*, Rev. Epidemiol. Sante Publique 48.
17. Borkowski J.L., Kasparian L. (1991), *Construire des indicateurs d'inégalités – – Enquête « Étude des conditions de vie » 1986–1987*, Document de travail F9106. INSEE, Paris.
18. Bréchat P.H., Bérard A., Magnin-Feysot C., Segouin C., Bertrand D. (2006), *Consumers and health policies: reports and perspectives*, Sante Publique 18.
19. Busse R., Schreyogg J., Smith P.C. (2006), *Hospital case payment systems in Europe*, Health Care Manag. Sci. 9.
20. Carpenter I., Bobby J., Kulinskaya E., Seymour G. (2007), *People admitted to hospital with physical disability have increased length of stay: implications for diagnosis related group re-imbursement in England*, Age. Ageing. 36.
21. Carr-Hill R., Chalmers-Dixon P. (2005), *The public health observatory handbook of health inequalities measurement*, South East England Public Health Observatory (SEPHO), Oxford.
22. Castiel D. (1995), *Equité et santé*, Éditions ENSP, Rennes.
23. Castiel D., Bréchat P.H., Grenouilleau M.C. (2007), *Disadvantaged patients in public hospitals: need for additional funding*, Presse Med. 36.
24. Castiel D., Bréchat P.H., Mathieu-Grenouilleau M.C., Rymer R. (2009), *Social disability and public hospitals: towards a model of resource allocation*, Santé Publique 21.
25. Castiel D., Jourdain A. (1997), *Equity and health planning: critical analysis of the SROS and implications for a model of resource allocation*, Cah. Sociol. Demogr. Med. 37.
26. Connolly S., O'Reilly D., Rosato M. (2007), *Increasing inequalities in health: Is it an artefact caused by the selective movement of people?*, Soc. Sci. Med. 64.
27. Control Objectives for Information and Related Technology. Management Guidelines (COBIT). IT Governance Institute, April 2001, www.itgi.org and www.isaca.org.pl.
28. Dercz M., Rek T. (2007), *Ustawa o zakładach opieki zdrowotnej. Komentarz*, Wolters Kluwer, Warszawa.
29. Doran T., Drever F., Whitehead M. (2004), *Is there a north-south division in social class inequalities in health in Great Britain? Cross sectional study using data from 2001 census*, BMJ. 328.
30. *Dynamika zobowiązań ogółem samodzielnych publicznych zakładów opieki zdrowotnej w latach 2003 – IV kw. 2009*, Ministry of Health.

31. Fender P., Weill A. (2004), *Epidemiology, public health and medical databases*, Rev. Epidemiol. Sante Publique 52.
32. Gierusz J., Cygańska M. (2009), *Budżetowanie kosztów działań w szpitalu*, Ośrodek Doradztwa i Doskonalenia Kadr Sp. z o.o., Gdańsk.
33. Golinowska S., Czepulis-Rutkowska Z., Sitek M., Sowa A., Sowada C., Włodarczyk C. (2002), *Opieka zdrowotna w Polsce po reformie*, Reports CASE, No. 53.
34. Hass-Symotiuk M. (2008), *Metodyka ustalania kosztów jednostkowych leczenia pacjenta* [in:] Nowak E. (ed.), *Rachunkowość zarządcza w warunkach globalizacji*. Prace Naukowe Uniwersytetu Ekonomicznego we Wrocławiu Nr 15, Wrocław.
35. Hass-Symotiuk M. (ed.) (2005), *Sterowanie kosztami w zakładach opieki zdrowotnej*, Wydawnictwo Uniwersytetu Szczecińskiego, Szczecin.
36. Hass-Symotiuk M. (ed.) (2008), *Rachunkowość i sprawozdawczość finansowa zakładów opieki zdrowotnej*, Ośrodek Doradztwa i Doskonalenia Kadr Sp. z o.o., Gdańsk.
37. Hass-Symotiuk M., Wawer U. (1997), *Wykorzystanie informacji o kosztach w zarządzaniu placówkami opieki zdrowotnej*. "Zeszyty Teoretyczne Rady Naukowej Stowarzyszenia Księgowych w Polsce", Warszawa.
38. *Informacja o wynikach kontroli restrukturyzacji samodzielnych publicznych zakładów opieki zdrowotnej ze szczególnym uwzględnieniem wykorzystania pomocy publicznej*, Supreme Chamber of Control, No. 141/2008/P/07/100/KPZ, Warszawa 2008.
39. INSEE. (2005), *Tableaux de l'économie française*, 2005/2006, INSEE, Paris.
40. Institute of Public Affairs, *Przyszłość samodzielnych publicznych zakładów opieki zdrowotnej*, "Analizy i Opinie", No. 6 (2/2003).
41. Jourdain A. (2000), *Equity of a health system*, Eur. J. Public Health 10.
42. Kachniarz M. (2006), *Restrukturyzacja placówki medycznej – doświadczenia praktyczne* [in:] Węgrzyn M., Wasilewski D. (ed.), *Komercjalizacja i prywatyzacja ZOZ. Kluczowe warunki osiągnięcia sukcesu*, Prace Naukowe Akademii Ekonomicznej we Wrocławiu Nr 1103, Wrocław.
43. Kachniarz M. (2008), *Ekonomizacja administracji publicznej na tle koncepcji prawnych i społecznych* [in:] Borys T. (ed.), *Gospodarka a środowisko*, Prace Naukowe Akademii Ekonomicznej we Wrocławiu Nr 22, Wrocław.
44. Karmańska A. (ed.) (2006), *Rachunkowość zarządcza i rachunek kosztów w systemie informacyjnym przedsiębiorstwa*, Difin, Warszawa.
45. Kiziukiewicz T. (ed.) (2003), *Zarządcze aspekty rachunkowości*, Polskie Wydawnictwo Ekonomiczne, Warszawa.
46. Klich J. (2007), *Przedsiębiorczość w reformowaniu systemu ochrony zdrowia w Polsce. Niedoceniane interakcje*, Wydawnictwo Uniwersytetu Jagiellońskiego, Kraków.
47. Kludacz M. (2005), *Funkcje budżetowania kosztów i ich realizacja w polskich szpitalach* [in:] Hass-Symotiuk M. (ed.), *Sterowanie kosztami w zakładach opieki zdrowotnej*, Wydawnictwo Uniwersytetu Szczecińskiego, Szczecin.

48. Kogut J. (2009), *Ocena prawidłowości dokonywania wyceny usług medycznych w SP ZOZ, Rachunkowość a controlling*, Prace Naukowe Uniwersytetu Ekonomicznego we Wrocławiu Nr 56, Wrocław.
49. Komunikat Nr 1 MF z 19 lutego 2009 r. w sprawie standardów audytu wewnętrznego w jednostkach sektora finansów publicznych (Dz. Urz. MF Nr 2, poz. 12).
50. Komunikat Nr 16 MF z 18 lipca 2006 r. w sprawie ogłoszenia „Kodeksu etyki audytora wewnętrznego w JSFP" i „Karty audytu wewnętrznego w JSFP" (Dz. Urz. MF Nr 9, poz. 70).
51. Komunikat Nr 23 MF z 16 grudnia 2009 r. w sprawie standardów kontroli zarządczej dla sektora finansów publicznych (Dz. Urz. MF Nr 15, poz. 84).
52. Komunikat Nr 25 MF z 18 grudnia 2009 r. w sprawie wzoru informacji o realizacji zadań z zakresu audytu wewnętrznego (Dz. Urz. MF Nr 15, poz. 85).
53. Kornai J. (1986), *The Soft Budget Constraint*, "Kyklos" Vol. 39, No. 1.
54. Lawlor D.A., Harro M., Wedderkopp N., Andersen L.B., Sardinha L.B., Riddoch C.J., Page A.S., Anderssen S.A., Froberg K., Stansbie D., Davey Smith G. (2005), *Association of socioeconomic position with insulin resistance among children from Denmark, Estonia, and Portugal: cross sectional study*, BMJ. 331.
55. Lombrail P. (2000), *Accès aux soins* [in:] Leclerc A., Fassin D., Grandjean H., Kaminski M., Lang T. (dir.), *Les inégalités sociales de santé*, La Découverte/ INSERM, Paris.
56. Mackenbach J.P. (2006), *Health Inequalities: Europe in Profile*, An independent, expert report commissioned by the UK. Presidency of the EU.
57. Mathy C., Bensadon M. (2002), *Le surcoût de l'hospitalisation des patients précaires*, JEM. 20.
58. McAlister F.A., Murphy N.F., Simpson C.R., Stewart S., MacIntyre K., Kirkpatrick M., Chalmers J., Redpath A., Capewell S., McMurray J.J. (2004), *Influence of socioeconomic deprivation on the primary care burden and treatment of patients with a diagnosis of heart failure in general practice in Scotland: population based study*. BMJ. 328.
59. Miller J. (2000), *Zarządzanie kosztami działań*, WiG Press, Warszawa.
60. Młodzianowska D. (2006), *Wady systemowe w ochronie zdrowia jako zagrożenie sukcesu komercjalizacji i prywatyzacji opieki zdrowotnej w Polsce* [in:] Wasilewski D., Węgrzyn M., *Komercjalizacja i prywatyzacja ZOZ. Kluczowe warunki osiągnięcia sukcesu*, Prace Naukowe Akademii Ekonomicznej we Wrocławiu No. 1103, Wrocław.
61. Moulin J.J., Dauphinot V., Dupré C., Sass C., Labbe E., Gerbaud L., Guéguen R. (2005), *Inégalités de santé et comportements: comparaison d'une population de 704 128 personnes en situation de précarité à une population de 516 607 personnes non précaires, France, 1995–2002*, BEH. 43.
62. Nowak E. (1999), *Rachunek kosztów*, Ekspert, Wrocław.
63. Nowak E. (ed.) (2008), *Rachunkowość zarządcza w warunkach globalizacji*, Prace Naukowe Uniwersytetu Ekonomicznego we Wrocławiu Nr 15, Wrocław.
64. Nowosielski S. (1998), *Centra kosztów i zysku w przedsiębiorstwie*, „Ekonomika i Organizacja Przedsiębiorstwa", No 7.
65. Observatoire national de la pauvreté et de l'exclusion sociale. *Rapport 2005– –2006* (2006), La documentation française, Paris.

66. Piechota R. (2005), *Projektowanie rachunku kosztów działań*, Difin, Warszawa.
67. Prieto L., Sacristan J.A. (2004), *What is the value of social values? The uselessness of assessing health-related quality of life through preference measures*, BMC. Med. Res. Methodol. 4, 10.
68. Reagan P.B., Salsberry P.J., Olsen R.J. (2007), *Does the measure of economic disadvantage matter? Exploring the effect of individual and relative deprivation on intrauterine growth restriction*, Soc. Sci. Med. 64.
69. Regulation of the Ministry of Health and Social Care of the 22nd December, 1998 on on specific rules for cost accounting in public healthcare units (Dz. U. No. 164, item 1194) par. 1, point 1, 3, 4.
70. Regulation of the Ministry of Health and Social Care of the 19th August, 1998 *on detailed rules for competitions for managerial positions in public health care units, jury members and the competitions regulations* (Dz. U. No. 115, item 749 with subsequent amendments).
71. Rozporządzenie Ministra Finansów z 1 lutego 2010 r. w sprawie przeprowadzania i dokumentowania audytu wewnętrznego (Dz. U. Nr 21, poz. 108).
72. Ruger J.P. (2006), *Ethics and governance of global health inequalities*, J. Epidemiol. Community Health 60.
73. Rybarczyk K., Karwowski M. (2000) [w:] *Rachunek kosztów usług medycznych i zarządzanie finansami w ochronie zdrowia*, Materiały na konferencję, Szczecin.
74. Sakurai M. (1989), *Target Costing and How to Use It*, "Journal of Cost Management", Summer.
75. Sass C., Moulin J.J., Guéguen R., Abric L., Dauphinot V., Dupré C. (2006), *Le score Epices: Un score et mesure des relations avec des données de santé, dans une population de 197 389 personnes*. BEH. 14.
76. Schott A.M., Hajri T., Gelas-Dore B., Couris C.M., Couray-Targe S., Trillet--Lenoir V., Dumeril B., Grandjean J.P., Lledo G., Poncet J.L., Colin C., Cautela N., Gilly F.N (2005), *Analysis of the medical activity related to cancer in a network of multidisciplinary hospitals using claims databases, the reseau Concorde Oncology Network*, Bull. Cancer 92.
77. Segouin C., Bréchat P.H., Lebrun L., Sahraoui F.. (2006), *Les révolutions du PMSI et de la T2A: Bilans et perspectives* [in:] Bréchat P.H., Salines E., Segouin C. (dir.), *Médecins de santé publique*, Editions ENSP, Rennes.
78. Segouin C., Bréchat P.H., Rymer R. (2006), *The new French hospital financing system: challenges for 2006*, Presse Med. 35.
79. Sobańska I. (ed.) (2003), *Rachunek kosztów i rachunkowość zarządcza*, C.H. Beck, Warszawa.
80. Standards for Information Systems Auditing, ISACA 2002, www.isaca.org.pl.
81. Stępniewski J. (2008), *Strategia, finanse i koszty szpitala*, Wolters Kluwer, Warszawa.
82. Supreme Court Act of the 22nd February, 2006 (Sygn. akt. II PZP 10/05).
83. Swiderska G. (2002), *Rachunkowość zarządcza i rachunek kosztów*, T. I, Difin, Warszawa.
84. Tarlov A.R., St. Peter R.F. (2000), *Introduction* [in:] Tarlov A.R., St Peter R.F., *The society and population health reader*, Vol. II: *A state and community perspective*, The Press, New York.

85. Trojnacka M. (2008), *Ocena przydatności tradycyjnych systemów rachunku kosztów do celów zarządczych w zakładzie opieki zdrowotnej* [in:] Nowak E. (ed.), *Rachunkowość zarządcza w warunkach globalizacji*, Prace Naukowe Uniwersytetu Ekonomicznego we Wrocławiu Nr 15, Wrocław.

86. Ustawa z 27 sierpnia 2009 r. o finansach publicznych (Dz. U. Nr 157, poz. 1240).

87. Ustawa z 28 września 1991 r. o kontroli skarbowej (Dz. U. z 2004 r. Nr 8, poz. 65, ze zm.).

88. Ustawa z 23 grudnia 1994 r. o Najwyższej Izbie Kontroli (Dz. U. z 2007 r. Nr 231, poz. 1701 oraz z 2008 r. Nr 209, poz. 1315, Nr 225, poz. 1502 i Nr 227, poz. 1505).

89. Villeneuve A. (1991), La *mesure des inégalités sous son aspect multidimensionnel – Enquête « Étude des conditions de vie »* 1986–1987, Document de travail F9105. INSEE, Paris.

90. Villeneuve A. (1995), *Les formes multiples de la pauvreté et le rôle des difficultés de jeunesse* [in:] *La société française: Données sociales*, INSEE, Paris.

91. Wardle J., Brodersen N.H., Cole T.J., Jarvis M.J., Boniface D.R. (2006), *Development of adiposity in adolescence: five year longitudinal study of an ethnically and socioeconomically diverse sample of young people in Britain*, BMJ. 332.

92. Włodarczyk C. (2003), *Reformy zdrowotne. Uniwersalny kłopot*, Wydawnictwo Uniwersytetu Jagiellońskiego, Kraków.

93. Zieliński T. (2007), *Odkrywanie prawdy o zyskach*, Akademia Menedżera Sp. z o.o., Poznań.

Part II

INNOVATION, ORGANIZATION
AND MANAGEMENT OF HOSPITALS

2.1. ORGANIZATIONAL INNOVATIONS OF HOSPITALS

2.1.1. INNOVATIONS IN HOSPITALS

2.1.1.1. INTRODUCTION

In today's world health care providers deal with multiple complex and pressing problems including the aging population, an ever-increasing proportion of patients with chronic diseases, cancer deaths, childhood and adult obesity, escalating costs, regulatory interventions, and increasing responsibilities for patient safety. Health care innovation offers important promises to address many of these problems.[120] Many studies show that an emphasis on innovation is critical to efforts to fuel growth, maintain market share, and improve patient satisfaction and clinical quality, efficiency, and delivery.[121]

Innovation has been studied in depth by researchers belonging to various disciplines, such as psychology, sociology, economics, anthropology and organization theory. Researchers, though with different objectives, analyzed and offered several insights into the complex and dynamic nature of innovation. In spite of the richness of the studies, there appears to be a general lack of conceptual clarity.[122] All these make research on innovation challenging and exciting.

An innovation in health care is defined here as "a set of behaviors, routines and ways of working, along with any associated administrative technologies and systems" which are:
– perceived as new by a proportion of key stakeholders,
– linked to the provision or support of health care,
– discontinuous with previous practice,

[120] M. Toner, M.R. Tompkins (2008), *Invention, Innovation, Entrepreneurship in Academic Medical Centers*, "Surgery", Vol. 143 (2), p. 168–171.

[121] M. O'Brien (2008), *Leading innovation in a risk-averse healthcare environment*, "Healthcare Financial Management", August, Vol. 62 (8), p. 112–114.

[122] T. Ravichandran (1999), *Redefining Organizational Innovation: Towards Theoretical Advancements*, "The Journal of High Technology Management Research", Vol. 10 (2), p. 243–274.

– directed at improving health outcomes, administrative efficiency, cost-effectiveness, or the user experience, and

– implemented by means of planned and co-ordinated action by individuals, teams or organizations.[123]

The above definition arises from Rogers' concept according to which an innovation is "an idea, practice, or object that is perceived as new by an individual or other unit of adoption"[124] Although one may find other definitions of innovation developed for particular medical specializations,[125] we will stay with the general one presented above.

The main goal of this paper is to identify the main streams of theoretical and empirical research on innovations in hospitals (with special emphasis on organizational innovations) and to find the main determinants for hospital innovation success as indicated in the literature.

2.1.1.2. METHODOLOGY

The research was a desk study based on the resources from the following databases:
1. BMJ Journals
2. EIFL-EBSCOhost Web
3. ProQuest Medical Library
4. ScienceDirect
5. Springer Link
6. Wiley InterScience/Blackwell

The key words used for searching were:
– innovations in hospitals,
– innovations in health care,
– innovations and hospitals,
– innovations and health care,
– organizational innovations in hospitals,
– organizational innovations and hospitals.

The time span for search was the period of 1990–2010 but in few cases it occurred to be necessary to reach books and papers prior to 1990.

Having completed all the records showed in six databases mentioned above, the first selection aimed at elimination of overlaps was done. As a result a list of 338 files was completed. Then all of these files were checked basing on the content of

---

[123] T. Greenhalgh, G. Robert, P. Bate, O. Kyriakidou, R. Peacock (2004), *How to Spread Good Ideas: A Systematic Review of the Literature of Diffusion, Dissemination and Sustainability of Innovations in Health Service Delivery and Organization*, NCCSDO, London, p. 40.

[124] E.M. Rogers (1983), *Diffusion of Innovations*, Free Press, New York, p. 11.

[125] For example, a surgical innovation can be defined as a new intervention that is not viewed by the institution, community or profession as meeting the accepted standards of safety, reliability and familiarity with effects, side effects and complications in: M.F. McKneally, A.S. Daar (2003), *Introducing new technologies: protecting subjects of surgical innovation and research*, "World Journal of Surgery", Vol. 27, p. 930–934.

their abstracts. Consequently, a list of 128 papers dealing directly or indirectly with innovations in hospitals and in health care systems was prepared. Then all the papers from this list were looked through in order to identify the most relevant ones. Finally, the list of 47 papers was prepared and all these were analyzed with adequate scrutiny.

2.1.1.3. MAIN STREAMS OF RESEARCH ON INNOVATION IN HOSPITALS

Innovations in hospitals are often analyzed within the framework of innovation diffusion research. Here, after Rogers,[126] one may identify the main components of the innovation diffusion process which are:
- innovation,
- communication channels,
- time,
- social system.

Wejnert groups variables defined in diffusion research to explicate their influence on an actor's decision to adopt an innovation into three main components:[127]
- characteristics of the innovation itself and here two sets of variables are defined: public versus private consequences and benefits versus costs of adoption,
- characteristics of innovators (actors) that influence the probability of adoption of an innovation. Here six sets of variables are identified: societal entity of innovators (either people, organizations, states, etc.), familiarity with the innovation, status characteristics, socioeconomic characteristics, position in social networks, and personal qualities,
- characteristics of the environmental context (it incorporates four sets of variables: geographical settings, societal culture, political conditions, and global uniformity).

The above shows that the theory of diffusion of innovations constitutes a complex set of issues. Building on the categories stated above one may add: elements of diffusion of innovation, the adoption process (where knowledge, persuasion, decision, implementation and confirmation are further identified and explored), characteristics of innovations, adopter categories (and here one distinguishes between innovators, early adopter, early majority, late majority, laggards), diffusion in organizations, consequences of adoption, and diffusion and management. Consequently, all these constitute a rich field for further inquiries.

Trying to put light on the main streams of research and theoretical reflection regarding innovations in hospitals, one should refer to the fact that the theory of the diffusion of innovations in the health care context is underdeveloped.[128] Empirical studies of the diffusion of innovations in hospitals have nearly thirty years of history[129] but there is still a shortage of relevant studies and majority of them are mostly case studies.

---

[126] E.M. Rogers, *op. cit.*

[127] B. Wejnert (2002), *Integrating Models of Diffusion of Innovations: A Conceptual Framework*, "Annual Review of Sociology", Vol. 28, p. 297–326.

[128] T. Greenhalgh, G. Robert, P. Bate, O. Kyriakidou, R. Peacock, *op. cit.*

[129] R.H. Lee, D.M. Waldman (1985), *The diffusion of innovations in hospitals. Some econometric considerations*, "Journal of Health Economics", Vol. 4 (4), p. 373–380.

Available empirical studies show that innovations slowly spread over all hospitals and so different hospitals are operating under different technologies at the same point in time.[130] Innovation processes in hospitals are usually analyzed as either technological or organizational.[131] As Blank and Van Hulst showed in their very recent study inventoried specific and well-known innovations in the Dutch hospital industry between 1998–2008 – technical change is non-neutral and output-biased and some technologies affect cost in beneficial ways.[132]

Although the issue of diffusion of innovation in hospitals is important, it does not form the dominant stream in the theoretical and empirical research in this field.

The literature on innovation in hospitals can be divided into four groups (streams of thought) of uneven size, with each group adopting a different approach to the question.[133]

The first group, in which hospitals are broadly likened to firms, favors an approach in which hospitals are conceived as *production functions*.[134] These studies have drawn in particular on the economics of bureaucracy, agency theory, convention theory and the new industrial economics.

The second group adopts an approach in which a hospital is seen as a "set of technological and bio-pharmacological capacities". This group of studies is extremely heterogeneous in terms of the disciplines involved and the theoretical approaches adopted. The characteristic they all share is that they emphasize what may be called *medical innovation*, a term which can be used as a generic appellation for various types of (tangible and intangible) technological and bio-pharmacological innovations in the healthcare field. Within the medical innovation, the following three sub-groups can be identified:

– biomedical or bio-pharmacological innovation (new medicines, new chemical or pharmaceutical substances etc.),

– tangible or "hard" medical innovation, that is the introduction of technological systems for providing healthcare and biological analysis, whether they involve capital goods (e.g., MRI, scanners etc.), miscellaneous small items of equipment (e.g., dressing kits, syringe drivers, catgut, reabsorbable prostheses) or diagnostic or therapeutic equipment, including medical imaging technologies,[135]

---

[130] J.L. Blank, B.L. Van Hulst (2009), *Productive innovations in hospitals: an empirical research on the relation between technology and productivity in the Dutch hospital industry*, "Health Economics", Vol. 18 (6), p. 665–679.

[131] M. Garcia-Goñi (2006), *Diferencias y similitudes antre los procesos de adopción de innovaciones tecnológicas y organizacionales en los hospitals*, "Gaceta Sanitaria", Vol. 20, Suppl. 2, p. 51–62.

[132] J.L. Blank, B.L. Van Hulst, *op.cit.*

[133] F. Djellal, F. Gallouj (2005), *Mapping innovation dynamics in hospitals*, "Research Policy", Vol. 34, p. 817–835.

[134] M. Ahern (1993), *The softness of medical production and implications for specifying hospital outputs*, "Journal of Economic Behavior and Organization", Vol. 20, p. 281–294.

[135] P.C. Nystrom, K. Ramamurthy, A.L. Wilson (2002), *Organizational context, climate and innovativeness: adoption of imaging technology*, "Journal of Engineering and Technology Management", Vol. 19, p. 221–247.

– intangible or "soft" medical innovation, which includes what might be called the 'invisible' technologies, that is care protocols, diagnostic or therapeutic strategies etc.

This literature is concerned mainly with the following topics:
– the nature of medical innovation as captured through case studies and the development of more or less sophisticated typologies,[136]
– the dynamic of medical innovation, which is approached through the diffusion of medical innovation, its life cycle and its diminishing returns, the nature of the technological trajectory pursued and the constraints on medical innovation[137] – the impacts of medical innovation, considered in relation to a multitude of potential targets: the quality of the product (i.e. health), productivity, work organization, the nature of the work in question, health expenditure, externalities etc.[138]

Part of this "soft" innovations may be classified as organization innovations and referred to such activities as for example postoperative pain management using continuous infusion of local anesthetics,[139] innovations in less invasive surgical procedures (an example of which can be reparation of abdominal aortic aneurysms (endovascular aneurysm repair – EVAR),[140] or – on the other side – shared care in hearing aid provision.[141] Some innovations may be aimed at managerial functions related to certain fields like system redesign,[142] acute care delivery[143] or various restructurisation projects.[144]

---

[136] P.P. Groenewegen, J.B. Hutten (1989), *Improving primary health care through technological innovation*, "Health Policy", Vol. 13 (3), p. 199–211.

[137] P.C. Nystrom, K. Ramamurthy, A. Wilson (2005), *op. cit.*; B. Jerome-D'Emilia, J.W. Begun, *Diffusion of breast conserving surgery in medical communities*, "Social Science and Medicine", Vol. 60, p. 143–151.

[138] J.P. Newhouse (1992), *Medical care costs: how much welfare loss?*, "Journal of Economic Perspectives", Vol. 6 (3), p. 3–23.

[139] A. Banks (2007), *Innovations in postoperative pain management: continuous infusion of local anesthetics*, "Association of periOperative Registered Nurses Journal" (AORN Journal), Vol. 85 (5), p. 904–914.

[140] N.M. Danjoux, D.K. Martin, P.N. Lehoux, J.L. Harnish, R. Zlotnik Shaul, M. Bernstein, D.R. Urbach (2007), *Adoption of an innovation to repair aortic aneurysms at a Canadian hospital: a qualitative case study and evaluation*, "BMC Health Services Research", Vol. 7 (182), 15 November; retrieved on March 8, 2010 from: http://www.biomedicentral.com/1472-6963/7/182.

[141] J.P.C. Grutters, M.A. Joore, F. van der Horst, R.J. Stokroos, L.J.C. Anteunis (2008), *Decision-Analytic Modeling to Assist Decision Making in Organizational Innovation: The Case of Shared Care in Hearing Aid Provision*, "Health Services Research", October, Vol. 43 (5), Part I, p. 1662–1673.

[142] M.I. Harrison, J. Kimani (2009), *Building capacity for a transformation initiative: system redesign at Denver Health*, "Health Care Management Review", Vol. 34 (1), p. 45–52.

[143] G.M. Campbell, T. Briley (2008), *Bundled redesign: transformational reorganization of acute care delivery*, "Critical Care Nursing Clinics of North America", Vol. 20 (4), p. 489––498.

[144] M.T. Kinneman, K.S. Hitchings, Y.E. Bryan, M.A. Fox, M.J. Young (1997), *A pragmatic approach to measuring and evaluating hospital restructuring efforts*, "The Journal of Nursing Administration", Vol. 27 (7–8), p. 33–41.

As Grutters et al. assess, organizational innovations are being researched mainly within the framework of health technology assessment which focuses increasingly more on organizational innovations than on specific technologies.[145] With regard to decision making in organizational innovation there are two major issues: (1) there is not enough data to answer questions with enough precision for use in decision making and (2) collecting data is expensive and there is not enough budget to provide helpful answers.[146] This in turn may partly explain why organizational innovations in hospitals are underrepresented in the literature.

The third group comprises an increasingly large number of studies that consider hospitals as a kind of "data-processing machines" and address the question of innovation in hospitals from the perspective of the introduction of *information systems*. In the literature, innovation in services is very often reduced to the introduction of new information and communication technologies (NICTs). One of the consequences were changes in the structure of administrative departments, introduction of logistical departments and then further transformation into medico-technical departments.[147]

Medical IT now has a wide set of applications ranging from medical and patient care records to sophisticated imaging and remote network access for multiple purposes (training, diagnosis etc.). The favored topics in this literature are generally the same as in the literature that adopts the 'hospital as a set of technical and bio-pharmacological capacities' approach. They include the nature of innovation (with particular distinction being made between hybrid medical technologies and the NICTs that make remote diagnosis and treatment possible) and the diffusion of IT and its impact on the quality of healthcare and on wellbeing, job quality, skills and productivity.[148] Research by Paré and Trudel[149] on adoption and implementation of a picture archiving and communications system (PACS) in two of Canadian hospitals showed that PACS deployment was not simply a rollout of new technology but a project which transformed the two organizations. This in turn shows that it is crucial to anticipate and address organizational and behavioral challenges from the very first phase of the innovation process in order to ensure that all participants will be committed to the project. In other words, to maximize the likelihood of PACS success, it appears crucial to take into consideration all the technical, economic, organizational, and human factors, and does so from the very first phase of the innovation process. The findings

---

[145] J.P.C. Grutters, M.A. Joore, F. van der Horst, R.J. Stokroos, L.J.C. Anteunis, *op. cit.*

[146] J. Hadley (2000), *Better Health Care Decisions: Fulfilling the Promise of Health Services Research*, "Health Services Research", Vol. 35 (1), part 2, p. 175–186.

[147] I. England, D. Stewart, S. Walker (2000), *Information technology adoption in health care: when organisations and technology collide*, "Australian Health Review", Vol. 23 (3), p. 176–185.

[148] M.A. Hebert (1998), *Impact of IT on health care professionals: changes in work and the productivity paradox*, "Health Service Management Review", Vol. 11 (2), p. 69–79; F. Lau, A. Penn, D. Wilson, T. Noeworthy, D. Vincet, S. Doze (1998), *The diffusion of an evidence-base disease guidance system for managing stroke*, "International Journal of Medical Informatics", Vol. 51, p. 107–116; D.E. Burke, N. Menachemi (2004), *Opening the black-box: measuring hospital information technology capability*, "Health Care Management Review", Vol. 29 (3), p. 210–217.

[149] G. Paré, M.C. Trudel (2006), *Knowledge barriers to PACS adoption and implementation in hospitals*, "International Journal of Medical Informatics", Vol. 76 (1), p. 22–33.

by Greenhalgh et al. reinforced all the above. Greenhalgh et al proved that the process of the introduction of a centrally stored, shared electronic patient record (the summary care record: SCR) in England was determined by eight various interacting influences of technical, economic, social, and personal nature and that an intensive co-operation of all hospital professionals was needed.[150]

There is still a lot of innovative potential originating from emerging information technology. For example Health2.0 and user generated health care informatics, which are largely conducted through mobile phones, are co-evolving patient-driven health systems, and potentially enhance PHC and family medicine workforce development. This in turn can be used as an innovation, for example, in organizing primary health care in developing countries like India.[151]

Taking into account the subject of the inquiries mentioned above one may maintain that some of the issues covered within the third stream of research on innovation in hospitals can be classified as organizational innovations.

In the fourth group, which is the most recent and probably the least voluminous, hospitals are seen as "providers of complex services and healthcare system hubs". In this approach, hospitals are regarded as combinative providers of diverse and dynamic services, able to go beyond their own institutional boundaries by becoming part of larger networks of healthcare provision, which are themselves diverse and dynamic (inter-hospital agreements on the shared use of equipment, community health networks set up to tackle a range of pathologies or even social problems). This approach makes it possible to extend the model of hospital innovation to incorporate new forms of innovation and new actors in the innovation process, in accordance with the Schumpeterian tradition of openness. This can be illustrated by the research on the work of four interprofessional care co-ordinators (IPCCs) whose role was to speed patient through-put within a London teaching hospital.[152]

Thus, innovation in hospitals is not a black box (hospital seen in terms of its production function). Nor is it any longer simply the sum of more or less highly developed and spectacular medical technologies designed and/or used by a medical aristocracy (the hospital as a set of technical and bio-pharmacological capacities). And nor can it be reduced to a sophisticated and tentacular information system (hospitals as information systems). If innovation in hospitals is to be apprehended in its totality, it is necessary to break into the black box of the organization, a task to which disciplines such as sociology, socio-economics or management are better suited than economics itself. Penetrating the black box in this way puts the spotlight on the actors

---

[150] T. Greenhalgh, K. Stramer, T. Bratan, E. Byrne, Y. Mohammad, J. Russell (2008), *Introduction of shared electronic records: multi-site case study using diffusion of innovation theory*, "British Journal of Medicine" (Clinical research Ed.), Vol. 337, p. 1786.

[151] R. Biswas, A. Joshi, R. Joshi, T. Kaufman, C. Peterson, J.P. Sturmberg, A. Maitra, C.M. Martin (2009), *Revitalizing primary health care and family medicine/primary care in India – disruptive innovation?*, "Journal of Evaluation in Clinical Practice", Vol. 15, p. 873–880.

[152] J. Bridges, L. Fitzgerald, J. Meyer (2007), *New workforce roles in health care: exploring the longer-term journey of organizational innovations*, "Journal of Health Organization and Management", Vol. 21 (4–5), p. 381–392.

in innovation and on support functions (hotels, catering, laundering, transport etc.) that are also neglected. This underestimation of hospitals' non-medical functions is widespread and does not simply apply to matters related to innovation. For example, there is relatively little literature on the working conditions, competences and responsibilities of non-medical hospital staff, whereas the literature on these topics as they concern medical staff is extensive.[153]

One may conclude that organizational innovations in hospitals do not possess a great share in the main stream of research. Although the term "organizational innovation" is being used in the literature, it appears rather in a narrative context. There is no attempt to define it precisely and to make a distinction between organizational and other categories of innovations in hospitals. Organizational innovations are present directly in two out of four streams of research indicated above, but does not appear as a separate category.

2.1.1.4. SOME SUCCESS FACTORS

Being confronted with growing budgetary constraints and patients' expectations hospitals have adopted new policies, methods and technologies to change their processes, improve services, and support other organizational changes which are necessary for better performance. There are four areas identified in the literature which are considered as important in successful implementation of organizational innovations in hospitals and in health care in general:
– strategic leadership,
– competitive intelligence,
– management of technology,
– specific characteristics of the organization changing process.[154]

Space precludes more organized presentation of these four areas, so let us indicate just two issues: the role of chief officers in hospitals and the position of teams in the innovation processes in hospitals.

Chief executive officers (CEOs) play a leading role in implementation of innovations and changes in hospitals but as it is presented in the literature medical professionals, especially physicians influence this process considerably. Inquiries aimed at CEOs' and physicians' opinions about organizational innovations reveal that physicians are showing increased interest not only in surgical innovations[155] but in organizational innovations as well while CEOs are ambivalent

---

[153] M. Griffin-Cohen (2001), *Do Comparisons Between Hospital Support Workers and Hospitality Workers Make Sense? Report for Hospital Employee's Union*, Canada, October.

[154] M. do Carmo Caccia-Bava, V.C.K. Guimaraes, T. Guimaraes (2009), *Testing some major determinants for hospital innovation success*, "International Journal of Health Care Quality Assurance", Vol. 22 (5), p. 454.

[155] W.L. Biffl, D.A. Spain, A.M. Reitsma, R.M. Minter, J. Upperman, M. Wilson, R. Adams, E.B. Goldman, P. Angelos, T. Krummel, L.J. Greenfield (2008), *Responsible Development and Application of Surgical Innovations: A Position Statement of the Society of University Surgeons*, "Journal of the American College of Surgeons", Vol. 206 (6), p. 1204–1209.

about their changing role and respective responsibilities.[156] There is a growing literature indicating the increasing role of nurses in the innovation processes as well.[157]

While physicians and nurses voluntarily participate in innovation processes in hospitals, some categories of hospital employees are forced to join these processes too. Chief financial officers (CFOs) for example are forced to bring innovative ideas to the table and to act as change agents. This in turn creates quite a challenge for them because of their risk-averse nature.[158] One may argue that operational excellence – the natural domain of CFOs – rewards risk aversion. Risks are taken only if their outcomes and probabilities can be carefully calculated. Innovation, on the other hand, requires executives to try new and different things without knowing exactly what is going to happen. Operational thinking is rational, logical, and measured. Innovative thinking is sometimes not obviously rational, is almost intuitive, and requires the organization to take risks. How to balance this dichotomy remains the most demanding challenge CFOs face.

Consequently, all employees in hospitals are expected to participate in a change which is aimed especially (but exclusively) at adding value in such areas as: economy of contracts, delegation, administrative decentralization, incentives, risk avoidance, process re-engineering, health care continuity, competitiveness, leadership, information systems and client centeredness.[159] The incipient development of innovations reveals the need for changes in the style and characteristics of management structure (composition, functions, responsibilities).[160]

This in turn implies the necessity to create facet-specific climate for innovation and requires a perfect team work. Anderson and West showed how important is a group climate in fostering and implementing innovations in firms[161] and in British hospitals.[162] It was stressed that innovative teams of employees possessed the key role in the innovation processes. They showed that an innovation was originated and subsequently developed by a team into routinized practice within organizations.[163] Current innovation literature suggests that implementation into routine practice represents the end-point of an innovation's journey. Bridges et al. suggests that certain innovations may in fact continue to shift in nature even after this "end-point" and workforce plays a key role in it.[164]

---

[156] J. del Llano, J.F. Martinez-Cantarero, J. Gol, F. Raigada (2002), *Análisis cualitativo de las innovaciones organizativas en hospitales públicos españoles*, "Gaceta Sanitaria", Vol. 16 (5), p. 408–416.

[157] T.J. Polick (2000), *Professional Innovations: Lifting Up Lives*, "Journal of the American Psychiatric Nurses Association" (APNA), Vol. 6 (4), p. 133–134.

[158] M. O'Brien, *op. cit.*

[159] J. del Llano, J.F. Martinez-Cantarero, J. Gol, F. Raigada, *op. cit.*

[160] *Ibidem.*

[161] N.R. Anderson, M.A. West (1998), *Measuring climate for work group innovation: development and validation of the team climate inventory*, "Journal of Organizational Behavior", Vol. 19, p. 235–258; N.R. Anderson, G. Hardy, M.A.West (1990), *Innovative teams at work*, "Personnel Management", September, p. 48–53.

[162] M.A. West, N.R. Anderson (1992), *Innovation, cultural values and the management of change in British hospitals*, "Work and Stress", Vol. 6, p. 193–210.

[163] N. King, N.R. Anderson (1995), *Innovation and Change in Organizations*, Routledge, London.

[164] J. Bridges, L. Fitzgerald, J. Meyer, *op. cit.*

2.1.1.5. CONCLUSIONS

Although organizational innovations are not classified as a separate group in the literature on innovations in hospitals, they are present in nearly all of the streams of thought presented here and titled as: "innovation diffusion research", "a hospital considered as a firm", "a hospital as a set of technological and bio-pharmacological capacities", "a hospital as a data-processing machine", and "a hospital as a provider of complex services and healthcare system hub". This may suggest that organization innovation in hospitals creates an interesting and challenging field for further theoretical and empirical inquiry.

The literature shows that a success in implementation of innovation in hospitals largely depends on strategic leadership, competitive intelligence, management of technology, and specific characteristics of the organization changing process. It is broadly acknowledged in the literature that to create a specific climate for innovation and to engage all the professions in hospitals in innovative processes is the biggest challenge hospital managers face nowadays.

2.1.2. INNOVATION AND ORGANISATION IN THE HOSPITAL: A FRENCH PERSPECTIVE

2.1.2.1. INTRODUCTION

Economic literature has a long history of denouncing service activities and is quick to make metaphorical use of medical terminology. These activities have therefore suffered not only from certain more or less serious diseases (cost-disease, Solow's syndrome, etc.), but have also endangered and weakened the vital organs of the economic system, the manufacturing industries, the only real wealth generators and the only authentic innovative activities.[165,166,167]

The hospital service in some respects resists this diagnosis. The association of the terms innovation and hospital does not seem incongruous. On the contrary, innovation is considered an age-old activity that is constantly renewed in the hospital system. Nonetheless, existing work is heavily biased and systematically proposes technological innovation of a medical kind, when the hospital, as a provider of complex services, is a place of major organisational innovations.

The purpose of this chapter is, in the first instance, to review the challenges of organisational innovation in the hospital. In the second instance, we will highlight the diversity of this form of innovation. Finally, in the third instance, we will focus on the notion of network (in all its dimensions), which we consider one of the major forms of organisational innovation in the hospital.

---

[165] For a presentation and a critique of these myths see: F. Djellal and C. Gallouj (2007).

[166] B. Bluestone, B. Harrison (1986), *The Great American Job Machine*, Report for the Joint Economic Committee, Décembre.

[167] S. Cohen, J. Zysman (1987), *Manufacturing matters*, Basic Books, New York.

2.1.2.2. The challenges of organisational innovation in the hospital

The question of organisational innovation in the hospital cannot today be contemplated independently of certain general problems which orient the development of the hospital sector and the healthcare system as a whole. These problems (which we will refer to as "challenges") convey, from the point of view of organisational innovation, constraints that we must account for or work around, decisive factors that explain the emergence and orientation of innovation, and the objectives to pursue. Three major (closely correlated) challenges have for several years oriented the paths of innovation (and more generally change) in the hospital: a challenge of resources, a challenge of competition and a social or societal challenge.

2.1.2.3. A challenge of resources

In France, as in most OECD countries, healthcare costs have been constantly rising for a number of years. At the beginning of 2007, healthcare costs in France represented approximately 10% of GDP as opposed to under 6% at the beginning of the 70s.

Controlling these costs has become a major challenge in the economic and social policies of the different OECD countries. Since the end of the 70s in France, the authorities have been trying to establish methods for the administrative regulation of the healthcare system. The preferred methods aim to limit the rise in reimbursable costs, stop rising public hospital costs and control capacity in the provision of care.[168]

Resource constraints and regulatory constraints (which are closely linked) are thus at the origin of numerous organisational innovations in the hospital. For most hospital structures, in fact, this involves designing and implementing new organisational strategies. These strategies generally follow five principal axes: the search for new sources of funding, the expansion of the existing activity, the creation of new activities, the optimisation of processes and the rationalisation of procedures (rationalisation of logistic and administrative services, possibly by means of outsourcing and re-engineering practices) and experimenting with new forms of organising work and working time.[169]

2.1.2.4. A challenge of competition

For several years we have seen significant development in competition (or a sense of competition), whether within public or private sectors, between public and private

---

[168] B. Delaeter (1991), *La conduite du changement à l'hôpital public : principes dégagés de la démarche stratégique menée au CHRU de Lille*, « Cahiers Lillois d'Economie et de Sociologie », No. 18, 2ème semestre, p. 26–40.

[169] We should note that conversely, however, these resource constraints and controlling healthcare costs could also constitute not inconsiderable obstacles to introducing organisational innovation and more broadly speaking.

sectors and even with free practitioners.[170] Competitive pressure is heavily amplified by the financial constraints that now burden the institutions. It is also amplified by the emergence of large networks of "private promoters" on a market offering attractive future prospects. We have thus witnessed certain traditional public monopolies being challenged, such as those of specialist surgery or complex functional explorations.

This competitive pressure has a number of repercussions on organisational innovation. Firstly, it has led to a great incentive to acquire and master leading-edge technologies. For all hospitals, whatever their size, we are therefore seeing a race to acquiring the most comprehensive possible "technical armoury".[171] Next, we are observing increasing interest in the question of service relationship and quality of service, which become strategic tools in the competition game.[172] Faced with difficulties in improving the technical aspects of their activity, hospital management boards are focusing on the quality of hospital services, or rather improving the accommodation, comfort and the outfitting of the sites and the premises. Another strategy is competition through the range of services.[173] Thus, to "retain" (win the loyalty) or increase their "market share", institutions are tending to multiply the services they offer. Finally, competitive pressure also leads institutions to seek alternative organisational solutions to traditional hospitalisation.

Conversely, however, technological innovation also has an influence on the challenge of competition. Although technology is a central component to inter-hospital competition, it is also (increasingly) central to the rationale of inter-hospital cooperation. Facing pressure from trustees or for financial reasons, we see hospital cooperation in the acquisition of complex and costly equipment. Numerous innovative agreements for the shared use of complex technologies (scanners, MRI etc.) have been set up. Technology is also central to the creation of telemedicine networks and many more (we will return to this in section 3).

2.1.2.5. A SOCIAL AND SOCIETAL CHALLENGE

The social and societal challenge covers various dimensions: the transformation of demand, demographic change and certain now traditional health and social trends such as categorized patient management, particularly precarious populations.

For the last few years, the demand for medical care has experienced significant transformations. We have witnessed the appearance and development of true

---

[170] J.-C. Moisdon, D. Tonneau (1996), *Concurrence et complémentarité: stratégies de l'hôpital et de sa tutelle* [in:] A.P. Contandriopoulos, Y. Souteyrand (eds), p. 21–45.

[171] P. Chandernagor, J.P. Claveranne, M. Krichen (1996), *Le statut des équipements hospitaliers : stratégie(s) d'acteur(s) et ordre technicien.*

[172] B. Bonnici (1998), *L'hôpital : enjeux politiques et réalités économiques*, Notes et études documentaires, No. 5079, 15 Octobre, La Documentation Française, p. 205.

[173] J.-C. Moisdon, D. Tonneau (1996), *op. cit.*

"medical consumerism".[174] Users-customers (who are better informed but also more so co-producers) have become more demanding and exacting. As highlighted by Binst[175] "customer demands vis-à-vis hospitals are ever rising and becoming more general. It's not good enough just to be cared for, they must be very well cared for (and as quickly as possible), kept regularly informed of their illness and the course of the treatments put in place and respected for their culture, personality and their specific needs, all while being protected and cared for".

The demographic dimension is an important factor in hospital trends and its innovation capacity in general and organisational innovation in particular. The main challenge faced by the hospital is the inescapable ageing of the population. The increased weighting in the total population of the elderly has major consequences in the supply of healthcare and its different characteristics. On the one hand, the existing structures must be adapted to bring them into line with requirements. This adaptation generally includes, firstly, the conversion of short-stay beds into medium and long-stay beds. It also involves seeking out-of-hospital solutions, notably developing home care or home hospital care, particularly high-tech home care. Accommodating and providing support to the elderly has experienced numerous organisational innovations in recent years, both inside and outside the hospital.

The health and social dimension comes back to the need for the hospital to develop approaches tailored to specific population groups. The most significant examples of organisational innovations relate to precarious population groups. The ageing of the population and rising poverty have revived the social role played by the hospital, that was forgotten for a while.[176] Hospitals must create innovative solutions so as to better account for the specific needs of population groups of this type (see section 3).

2.1.2.6. INNOVATION ANALYSIS PERSPECTIVES AND THE PLACE FOR ORGANISATIONAL INNOVATION

Through an inventory of the literature, we have identified in previous works,[177] the different approaches or the way in which the question of hospital innovation is tackled. All things considered, we believe that the literature on innovation in the hospital could be split into four distinct groups.

Four groups or an analysis model for hospital innovation
The first group brings together all the work of the economists, who consider hospital services from the point of view of the *production function*, and who liken the hospital to a business. Contemplated dynamically, the hospital production function therefore conveys the involvement of technical change.

---

[174] B. Delaeter (1991), *op. cit.*

[175] M. Binst (1990), *Du mandarin au manager hospitalier*, L'Harmattan, p. 255.

[176] P. Volovitch (1998), *L'hôpital public en plein chantier*, « Alternatives Economiques », No. 155, p. 59–62.

[177] See F. Djellal, C. Gallouj, F. Gallouj, K. Gallouj (2004), *L'hôpital innovateur. De l'innovation médicale a l'innovation de service*, Masson, p. 11–12, 20.

The second group of work is extremely heterogeneous from the point of view of the disciplines in question, the theoretical approaches used within each discipline and the theoretical claims. The common point of all this different work focuses on what we will call *medical innovation*, which refers generically to the different types of technological (tangible or intangible) and biopharmalogical innovations in the field of healthcare. This work subscribes to what we propose to call the perspective of "a hospital as a technical and biopharmacological platform".

The third group comprises an ever-increasing group of work which contemplates the question of innovation in the hospital from the point of view of the introduction of *information systems*. The hospital does not, in fact, escape the invasive nature of disseminating ICT within the context of the new information paradigm. IT costs are constantly increasing in healthcare institutions, as is the hospital time given over to information processing. This group of work maintains close links with the following group and numerous works have insisted that ICT is a catalyst for organisational innovations.[178]

Finally, the fourth group favours the concept of the hospital product as *a complex service package* or as a "compack" in the sense of Bressand and Nicolaïdis. Here, we do away with a functional perspective (the hospital reduced to its healthcare function) and instead use an institutional perspective (the hospital as an organisation) and network perspective (the hospital as a node of a service network(s)). Innovation in the hospital should not be limited simply to medical innovation, or rather innovation oriented towards the "fundamental" service of the hospital: caring for the sick (in the strict sense). In other words we should not just consider drugs and tangible and intangible healthcare technologies. We should consider all forms of innovation that fall outside the strictly medical framework, or rather that stem from what management sciences sometimes call the "peripheral services", such as accommodation, catering, cleaning and even laundering services (these are but a few examples of a long and open list). We must also consider all the innovations relating to the general operation of the hospital, its internal organisation, its relations with its customers and their families, the organisation of external relations with other socio-economic players etc. The hospital is also a place of non-technological innovations, be they are service-related (new services) or organisation-related (new organisations) or both. This last group is the most recent and the leanest. One of the objectives of this work is precisely to contribute to the debate and research on the significance of innovations in the hospital that are not strictly medical and/or not strictly technological.

Organisational innovation and its forms

Accounting for organisational innovation in the hospital conveys a change in perspective (common in numerous other service activities including, most recently, public services where it was a veritable cultural revolution). This involves moving away from the technical perspective in favour of a perspective of service and service

---

[178] As recently as the 90s, Silver showed how the increased computerisation of medical and administrative files in the United States forced nurses to act as secretaries in performing certain administrative tasks.

relationship, internal and external, when dealing with the question of innovation. The patient is not just someone who is sick and must be cared for, but also the customer of a complex service, who must, along with his/her family, be satisfied.

Thus, innovation in the hospital is not just a black box (hospital as a production function). Neither is it now simply the sum of medical technologies that are more or less developed and spectacular, designed and/or used by a certain medical aristocracy (hospital as a technical and biopharmacological platform). Nor can it now be summed up as a sophisticated and sprawling information system (hospital as an information system).

To understand hospital innovation as a whole, we need to break into the black box of the organisation, an exercise to which sociology or socio-economics and management yield more easily than economics in the strict sense.[179] We admit, however, that we're not starting right at square one here. A number of works, essentially the case studies presented in specialist literature, implicitly adopt this perspective of being open to multiple aspects of hospital innovation, more specifically organisational innovation. This finding is a further sign of the frequent backwardness of theoretical reflection on professional preoccupations.

Academic works that study organisational innovation in the hospital can be characterised in different ways. Firstly, there are fewer of them and secondly, they place the emphasis on innovation within the realm of the care organisation or the care units.[180,181] Lastly, (relatively speaking), a good deal of the works tackle organisational innovation as a subordinated process, or rather most commonly as a consequence of introducing new medical technologies or information systems (ICT). For example, believes that the dissemination of technological innovations translates firstly into an increase in costs, before leading to organisational innovations susceptible of fully harnessing the new potential in productivity. This relationship of subordination is even more explicit in the works of Lamarque, who makes a distinction between central innovations and peripheral innovations. Central innovations (strictly medical) relate to diagnostic or exploratory technologies, and treatment, rehabilitation and prevention technologies, i.e. the trio: drugs, material resources (products and equipment) and techniques (procedures). Peripheral innovations are structural or organisational innovations oriented towards adapting the care organisation.

How to identify and define organisational innovations, however, is not always obvious. A number of authors have proposed "non-technological" hospital innovation typologies that highlight this difficulty. By subscribing to broad innovation perspectives, Anatole-Touzet and Souffir describe a veritable "system of innovation" in the hospital, which hinges around the following types of innovation:

---

[179] This break-in highlights the innovation players and support functions (accommodation, restaurants, laundering, transport etc.), also ignored.

[180] See E. Minvielle (1994), *Un changement sur ordonnance*, « Gérer et Comprendre », No. 35, p. 43–54.

[181] A. Barcet, J. Bonamy, M. Grosjean (2002), *Une innovation de service par la mise en réseau de services : réflexion sur une expérience dans les services de santé, 12ème conférence internationale du RESER*, Manchester, CRIC et PREST, 26–27 Septembre.

– technological innovations in the traditional sense of the term: bio-technologies, computerisation, new equipment etc.;

– service innovations defined as the implementation of new activities corresponding to changing hospital missions: such as outpatient activities, accommodating the underprivileged in medical and social terms, set-up of networks with town doctors or associations;

– organisational innovations: reorganisation of administrative and logistic sectors, evaluation of quality of care, development of therapeutic protocols, organisation of working time etc.;

– social and cultural innovations: development of training and action plans, programmes to improve working conditions etc.

This typology, which has the merit of recognising the multiple forms of innovation in the hospital, in a tradition we could qualify as Schumpeterian, suffers from the absence of a precise definition of each of the categories considered and how these categories overlap. Thus, as the proposed examples illustrate, the borders between service innovation, organisational innovation and social innovation are not clearly defined.

For our part, by adopting an open vision of organisational innovation (which better corresponds to professional practices), it appears to us that we can differentiate between five main categories of organisational innovation:

Organisational innovation (in the strict sense). On the one hand, this relates to all the experiments to modernise the organisation and the operation of the non-medical sectors in the hospital (service re-engineering, creation of new entities to set-up or take on new functions in the fields of catering, accommodation, trade, maintenance, management etc.). On the other hand, it relates to all the new care practices and forms of organisation. We cite, as an example, the formation of new clinical approaches within certain institutions, the "home hospital", the "day hospital", which have led to a net reduction in the duration of hospitalisation in France. Organisational innovations may be spin-offs (from technological innovations) or stand alone, as we have already highlighted.

Managerial innovation. This relates to new management techniques and methods: e.g. new accounting and financial techniques and procedures, new management practices such as the development of strategic approaches, the practice of segmenting customer bases, the implementation of total quality management approaches[182] for this last point, which analyse the conditions for implementing total quality management (TQM) in hospitals). The Programme for the medicalisation of information systems (abbreviated to PMSI) also falls in this category,[183] although it is part of information systems.

---

[182] See G.Y. Young, M.P. Charns, S.M. Shortell (2001), *Top Manager and Network Effects on the Adoption of Innovative Management Practices: a Study of TQM in a Public Hospital System*, "Strategic Management Journal", No. 22, p. 935–951.

[183] M. Naiditch, G. de Pouvourville (2000), *Le programme de médicalisation du système d'information (hospitalier) : une expérimentation sociale limitée pour une innovation majeure du management hospitalier*, « Revue Française des Affaires Sociales », No. 1, Janvier–Mars, p. 59–95.

Relational or service innovation. This relates to all innovations concerning the nature of the interface (relation or contact) between the provider and the customer/ user or his/her family: improving the quality of patient reception (and patient management) patients and their families, managing patient flow, reducing waiting times, accommodating the families of the patients etc.

Social innovation. Barreau (2002) defines social innovation as "the process that consists in modifying the rules of coordination and incentivisation on the basis of social negotiations and formal and informal undertakings". Social innovations therefore take the form of developing new attitudes concerning the organisation of work, the methods of exercising authority and the decision-making processes. We cite, as an example, experiments in internal communication[184] and even the development of part-time work and the planning of work schedules.[185]

External relations innovation. This type of innovation accounts for setting up certain new forms of special relations with the customers, suppliers, authorities and other institutions. Over the last few years, the hospital has opened out more and more to its environment. Opening out in this way aims to control costs and also facilitate the detection of changes and anticipate trends in demand and types of new requirements to be met.[186] External relations innovations (which have been encouraged by the authorities for some time) can take multiple forms that are more or less complex (depending on the number of players involved in the new relationship, the purpose of the relationship etc.).

The most simple external relations innovations therefore concern bilateral relations. We can cite the following examples (which aim either to reduce costs or exploit additional sources of funding): co-use agreements for complex equipment (either medical equipment or logistics equipment), agreements for the joint purchase of this type of equipment, mergers between institutions, the sale of services[187] to other hospital institutions or to businesses or organisations in other sectors. This activity is authorised by the law of 31 July 1991 which opens up the way to certain entrepreneurial activities by granting hospitals the status of public healthcare institutions, which is more permissive than their previous status of public administrative institutions. The service activities in question are diverse: catering, laundering, logistics, and also training, expertise, hire of premises for conferences or cultural activities etc.

The most complex external relations innovations relate to care networks. Here, we are witnessing the creation of increasingly varied care networks, be they formal or informal, integrated or non-integrated, ICT-based or non ICT-based etc. The network, which constitutes a major innovation in the hospital system can, to some extent, be analysed as an organisational innovation (category 1). The network, however,

---

[184] A. Bellemou, A. Fraigneau (1987), *La communication comme outil de management à l'hôpital*, « Gestions Hospitalières », No. 261–262, Décembre 1986–Janvier 1987, p. 763–766.

[185] M. Benedicto (1987), *Le temps choisi à l'hôpital de Béziers*, « Gestions Hospitalières », No. 261–262, Décembre 1986–Janvier 1987, p. 749–750.

[186] C. Cases, D. Beaubeau, M. Naiditch (2001), *Evaluer la capacité d'adaptation aux changements*, « Solidarité-Santé », No. 2, Avril–Juin, p. 67–69.

[187] We note that Le Berre et al. (1992) use the expression "hospital as a service provider" to identify this single activity.

is an organisational innovation of a particular type which is worth treating separately from traditional organisational innovation, if only for the reason that networks have a major impact on both the hospital system and, more generally, the care system as a whole. We could in some respect say that the "hospital as a service provider" is also, increasingly, the "hospital as a network (of healthcare and services)".

2.1.2.7. THE NETWORK AS A DOMINANT FORM OF ORGANISATIONAL INNOVATION

The notion of network, based on the diverse senses of the term, is, depending on many specialists, central to organisational innovation. Most network experiments (town-hospital networks, coordinated care networks etc.) are part of a combinated organisational innovation approach. Naturally, the analytical perspective here is an inter-organisational perspective. additions of elementary services (external) are multiple and often go hand in hand with stepping up and creating multiple structures for paths of innovation. Experiments with networks are diverse, depending on the number of players involved, the type of player, the objectives sought and the possible technologies used. Thus, hospitals "can constitute care networks specific to certain facilities, certain activities or certain diseases".[188]

The forefathers of the "town-hospital" networks are probably the gerontological networks and the HIV networks set up at the beginning of the 80s, essentially bringing together free practitioners and hospital physicians. Other networks have been set up around other medical or socio-medical fields: diabetes, hepatitis C, precariousness, perinatality. These networks can be set up at the point of intersection of different problems: this is the case, for example, of networks focused on perinatal issues and precariousness when caring for drug-dependent pregnant women and their children.

The networks, as we have already underlined, are more or less developed. They range from the simple co-purchase of complex equipment by several institutions or a co-use agreement for equipment (scanners, MRI), to more complex arrangements such as hospital mergers, the absorption of one institution by another or the creation, within the hospitals or nearby, of entities set up to forge links with general practitioners: gerontological and social units dedicated to general practitioners and welfare officers outside the institutions, "emergency medical units" (for minor emergencies), which are run and managed by external practitioners.

We propose now to develop the following three examples: town-hospital-clinic cooperation, public-private cooperation and home hospitalisation.

2.1.2.8. AN EXAMPLE OF TOWN-HOSPITAL-CLINIC COOPERATION

Barcet, Bonamy and Grosjean[189] offer a relatively refined analysis of an experiment to implement a town-hospital-clinic network designed to care (at home) for patients

---

[188] R. Dalmasso, J.-J. Romatet (eds) (2000), *L'hôpital réformateur de l'hôpital*, Eres, p. 158.

[189] A. Barcet, J. Bonamy, M. Grosjean (2002), *op. cit.*

(from hospital) affected by major diseases or major dependencies due to multiple diseases. At the origin of this experiment was the strategic wish to place patients at the heart of the care system, enabling them to retain a certain quality of life (particularly through better social insertion into their environment) and finally, from more of a management perspective, to optimise the occupation of hospital beds.

The experiment involved the creation of a network linking a hospital, clinics and the places of residence of the patients. The network in question mobilised a multitude of players under different rationales (trade and non-trade or public). These players, of varied statuses, first and foremost come under the rationale of care businesses (hospitals, clinics, doctors, nurses, laboratories etc.), but also under a social and political rationale (towns, various associations etc.) and lastly under industrial rationales (numerous manufacturers of medical goods and equipment).

By studying the conditions for extending the experiment, Barcet, Bonamy and Grosjean saw in this innovation the emergence of a new productive service model, which appears to be perfectly tailored to certain specific features of the world of the hospital and healthcare. This new model is in fact tailored to the question of a global service, to a combination of business areas and independent activities, to the development of accountability and to forging relationships between independent professionals. It allows for the effective management of the unknown and the unusual, while seeking the savings of a network (minimising coordination costs). Lastly, this model is tailored to the combination of a trade rationale and a public and/or association rationale.

2.1.2.9. EXAMPLES OF PUBLIC-PRIVATE COOPERATION

Numerous experiments on cooperation between public and private care entities are good illustrations of how a rationale of organisational innovation (from an inter-organisational perspective) is implemented. The Nord-Pas-de-Calais region of France appears to be particularly active in this field. Various "healthcare cooperation consortiums" have been set up in this region.[190]

Lens was the site of the region's first healthcare cooperation consortium. The arrangement involved a public hospital specialising in cardiac surgery and a large private clinic with a high cardiology component. This consortium has had undeniable success, with more than 400 operations carried out each year, and has contributed greatly to bringing down the long regional waiting lists.

A second cooperation consortium involving the Lille university hospital and a private clinic was set up in the field of hand surgery ("SOS mains"). The university hospital's hand surgery unit is thus located in a private clinic. The unit has 10 public beds and 10 private beds and a single team of physicians belonging to the public or private sectors, hand surgery and micro-surgery specialists. Hand transplantations, which are extremely complex procedures, are not therefore carried out in the university hospital, but in a private clinic as part of a healthcare cooperation consortium.

---

[190] These examples are from meetings with the ARH of Nord Pas-de-Calais.

Lastly, the Regional hospitalisation agency (abbreviated to ARH) of Nord Pas-de-
-Calais has favoured the mutualisation of interventional, diagnostic and therapeutic
cardiology within four public/private centres (Valenciennes first of all, then Lens,
Boulogne-sur-Mer and finally Roubaix). In a single technical platform, public and
private physicians treat patients presenting for interventional cardiology day and
night, including weekends. In accordance with professional standards, to be deemed
competent, a physician must carry out at least 100 dilations per year and a dilation
centre must carry out at least 400 dilatations per year, which is impossible individually but possible from the same technical platform. The exodus to Lille has therefore
been completely eliminated and the physicians have an excellent level of technical
expertise.

Home hospital care

Home hospitalisation (abbreviated to HAD) also follows a rationale of organisational innovation (contemplated from an inter-organisational perspective), since this
involves bringing together the world of the hospital and the home based on certain
technologies and methods.

In France, the first institutionalised HAD experiments date from the end of the
50s. (For a history of the creation of HAD[191,192]). The experiments involved the creation of two structures: *l'Hospitalisation à Domicile de l'Assistance Publique* (social
welfare home hospitalisation) and *Santé Service* (health service), set up by the cancer
specialists of the Gustave Roussy Institute for the purpose of caring at home for patients in remission who do not require sophisticated care or technologies.

The second phase of introducing HAD in France (at the end of the 60s) led to a net
increase in technological requirements or technological intensity (oxygen therapy,
haemodialysis etc.). Associations such as the *Association Lyonnaise pour la Lutte
contre la Poliomyélite* (Lyon association to combat Polio – abbreviated to ALLA)
and the *Association pour l'Utilisation du Rein Artificiel* (Kidney dialysis association
– abbreviated to AURA) played a vital role in this second phase.

At the beginning of the 80s, hospital paediatricians took an interest in this formula
in cases where it was beneficial for children and where a certain number of sophisticated technologies have emerged that could be set up at home, such as parenteral
feeding, renal dialysis, chemotherapy, venal drips etc.

In 1986, a ministerial circular encouraged the development of HAD in all hospital
institutions. Despite attractive prospects of "profitability",[193] however, this activity is
still relatively small-scale in France compared with other countries, particularly the
United States.

---

[191] See J. Bachimont (1998), *Les « soins hospitaliers à domicile » entre démédicalisation hospitalière et médicalisation du domicile*, p. 175–209.

[192] See M. Loriol (2002), *L'impossible politique de la santé publique en France*, Eres, p. 166.

[193] R. Dalmasso, J.-J. Romatet (eds) (2000), *L'hôpital réformateur...*

2.1.2.10. CONCLUSION

In this contribution, we have endeavoured to move away from the dominant paradigm in hospital innovation, which prioritises technological innovation in the strict sense of the term. We have seen that the hospital focuses overly on "innovation in equipment and medical practices", which relegates to second place the modernisation of other activities in the hospital, particularly aspects concerning the general running of the hospital and working conditions in the hospital.[194] Our contribution therefore aims to make non-technological innovation central to reflections, in particular organisational innovation. Put in other words, we aim to reconsider the relationship between innovation and organisation. By doing so, however, we must not be blinded to the conflicts and resistance that are con-substantial with it.

The organisational structure of the hospital can, in some cases, hinder the emergence and dissemination of innovation. The hospital is often viewed as a professional bureaucracy, whose main method of coordination is the standardisation of qualifications. It is a structure in which the key players (the hospital practitioners) are professionals with complex expertise, whose activity is characterised by substantial autonomy in identifying situations and implementing solutions. Their behaviour is individualist. They often have a tendency to disregard the needs, objectives and interests of the institution that employs them. They frequently identify more with their department, their discipline and their profession than with the hospital. Professional bureaucracy therefore suffers from coordination and control problems which are damaging to the phenomena of innovation and adaptation to the environment.

Furthermore, innovation is often a source of conflict between the different players, whether they belong to the medical or non-medical world. Innovation can, for example, put the physicians and the administration at loggerheads. This situation, however, can also manifest itself between the care units, within the care units and even horizontally or vertically between the different participants. As elsewhere, innovation in the hospital does not *a priori* receive the agreement of all the players in the organisation, just as it never receives a consensus of or definitive resistance. And of course there are always power games on the occasion of any innovation.[195]

2.1.3. ORGANIZATIONAL INNOVATIONS IN PRODUCTION OF HOSPITAL SERVICE

2.1.3.1. INTRODUCTION

The term 'innovations' referring to the service sector has been absent from the body of economic literature for quite a long time. It is different, however, with hospitals,

---

[194] G. Arbuz, D. Debrosse (1996), *Réussir le changement de l'hôpital*, « InterEditions », p. 248.
[195] N. Alter (1995), *Peut-on programmer l'innovation ?*, « Revue Française de Gestion », Mars––Mai, p. 78–86.

where the concept of innovation is not a novelty; on the contrary, it is believed that innovation is an activity that has been undertaken for a long time, constantly undergoing modernization in the hospital service system. This 'exceptional' character of hospitals may be interpreted in numerous ways. Hospital service or – more generally – medical service carries a certain positive connotation, which ranks high among the fundamental human needs. What is more, medical service is provided predominantly by players exercising 'scientific professions', i.e. professions of 'knowledge and research' that base their service on scientific knowledge, which they produce and distribute through the agency of teaching hospitals and various laboratories, including clinical ones.

In the service sector, hospital services occupy a special place in situations when no-one can question their usefulness for the public, their symbolic meaning in relation to life and death, or the fact that they make scientific research and innovations possible. It seems, however, that the effort made for the purpose of innovations goes unnoticed and, as a consequence, unappreciated in the literature on the subject. A substantial majority of publications emphasizes the introduction of new technological solutions by hospitals. This technological aspect is doubled by a professional factor. This is referred to as 'medical innovation', where doctors are the players.[196]

At this point, we will assume thesis that the notion of 'innovations in hospitals' perceived as introduction of new technologies, medications and medical knowledge is incomplete and, as a result, not fully understood by the hospital environment and the milieu.

Hospitals provide full service, which necessitates the participation of many different players devoting their work to various activities that are, of course, mainly medical, but also paramedical, logistical, and non-medical (finance and bookkeeping; hotel and restaurant service; organizational, technical, marketing, and PR services).

Such activities, processes of medical innovations as well as people who exercise different professions within the framework of these activities and processes deserve to be taken into consideration as a whole, all the more so, because they take part directly or indirectly in the realization of the hospital's main target, i.e. providing patients with medical care.

We aim at complementing the issues of innovations in hospitals with the elements they lack, mainly those of organizational nature.

2.1.3.2. TYPOLOGY OF HOSPITAL INNOVATIONS

At present, the issue of hospital innovations in Poland cannot be discussed separately from a certain number of general problems that affect the development of the hospital sector and the health care system as a whole. Those problems that are to be approached as challenges embody, from the point of view of innovations, the restrictions one needs to face, the determinants that explain the sources, as well as the direction of innovations and goals to be reached.

---

[196] More on this subject in C. Gallouj (1994), *Le prix de l'innovation hospitaliere*, « Gestions Hospitalières », No. 334.

For many years, four closely related challenges have defined the path followed by innovations, or, more generally, changes in hospitals:[197]
  – limited financial reserves,
  – competition,
  – social and communal challenges,
  – management and 'visible' results.

Limited Financial Reserves

In the EU member states, including Poland, health care expenditure constantly grows and will continue to do so. Bringing this expenditure under control has become a crucial challenge for economic and social policies in various countries which attempt to develop methods of administrative regulation of the health care system. The aim of such attempts is to limit expenditure of public hospitals and to control their ability to provide medical service.

Limited financial reserves and related rationing restrictions give rise to numerous innovations in hospitals. As a result, most hospitals aim at creating and introducing new strategies of development that can take one of five basic forms:
  – searching for new funding sources,
  – expanding the already existing activities,
  – optimizing processes, streamlining procedures (logistical, administrative, outsourcing, and reengineering),
  – experimenting with new organizational forms and working time.

Competition

In recent years, we have recorded a considerable development of competition within the public hospital service sector, the private sector, as well as between the two sectors. The pressure of competition builds up as a consequence of financial limitations weighing heavily on hospitals, as well as of enormous new private networks enticed by the market with good future prospects. As a result, we deal with the countering of traditional public monopolies such as, say, specialized surgery.

This pressure of competition has and will have a further wide influence on innovations. First and foremost, it stimulates acquisition and mastering of the newest medical technologies, i.e. the introduction of medical innovations into hospitals.

The practice in France shows that in areas with large numbers of hospitals competition between public and private hospitals has forced some hospital administrators to make heavy investments in equipment (different types of scanners, e.g. CAT scanners, ultrasound scanners) which consumes a considerable amount of funds and attracts more patients.

---

[197] F. Djellal, C. Gallouj, F. Gallouj, K. Gallouj (2004), *L'hôpital innovateur. De l'innovation médicale a l'innovation de service*, Masson, p. 11–12, 20.

What we are witnessing is a kind of a race for complete technical equipment.[198] We can also observe growth in importance of service relation and service quality, which become critical tools in the competitive battle. Indeed, as a consequence of facing difficulties in the improvement of technical aspects of their activity, hospital administrations focus on raising the quality of provided services, e.g. by enhancing hospital comfort as well as procedures concerning admission of patients, and modernizing hospital facilities. Yet another part of a strategy is competing by means of the range of provided services. Finally, competition between hospitals also makes them seek alternatives to traditional hospitalization.

But it works the other way round in that technological innovations have an impact on competition as well.[199] Indeed, if technology is a crucial element of competition between hospitals, it becomes an ever more important factor for a cooperation logic within hospitals, which, in turn, becomes a strictly organizational innovation.

Due to pressure from foundation authorities or out of financial necessity, cases of acquiring modern and costly equipment have been observed. Contracts on divided use of modern technologies (scanners, magnetic resonances) are being concluded. New technologies are also applied in centers where networks of telemedicine are developed, but they go beyond the development of networks too.

Social and Communal Challenges

The social and communal challenges are to be analyzed in the multidimensional manner considering:
– changes in demand for hospital service
– vital statistics
– evolution of medical care and social welfare, and particularly, of hospital service provided to a group on the verge of poverty.

The demand for medical care services has changed considerably in the last few years; a real medical consumerism, which constantly evolves, was also introduced in Poland. Patients (client – users) are not only better informed and more cooperative, but they also became more demanding. To meet such client-users' expectations has become a significant challenge faced by modern hospitals.

A demographic factor is yet another challenge for hospitals and its ability for innovation management and functioning. Hospitals have come to confront the inevitable phenomenon of aging society. Essentially, a growing number of the aged in general population significantly influences the supply of medical services and their nature. They consist in adjusting existent hospital structures to the level of need; in the initial stage, the adaptation includes replacement of short-stay beds with medium – and long – stay ones. Numerous solutions concerning the services outside hospital are considered. The ideas of nursing in home environment, or even hospital home care, particularly high tech home care, are being developed.

---

[198] L. Omnes (1996), *Choc technologique et mutation des organisations*, « Gestions Hospitalières », No. 354, p. 188.

[199] M. Duriez (1998), *Le role de la concurrence dans la conduite des systemes de sante en Europe*, « Hospitalisation Nouvelle », UHP, No. 254, p. 8–9.

Such solutions must be of systemic character and, in order to coordinate them, special coordination centers in hospitals are being created.

Such innovations inside and outside hospitals have already been tested in the EU member states for a number of years.

Challenges consisting in ensuring medical care and social welfare are closely connected with a necessity to develop an approach adjusted to particular groups of population. Aging of population constitutes one aspect; however, increase of the number of the poor is yet another issue which reminds us about the social role of hospitals, which tends to be avoided or unnoticed by the government. Hospitals are facing the challenge of developing the innovations supply within the mentioned framework, which will facilitate satisfying the needs of such a population.

2.1.3.3. ORGANIZATIONAL INNOVATIONS IN THE PROCESS OF MEDICAL PRODUCTION

Medical care establishments develop owing to the changing surroundings. Small operating blocks become centralized, whereas small, dispersed units of medical care services are grouped into larger organizations. Due to growing competition on the market of medical care services, hospital organizations are forced to secure their market position.

An operating block constitutes the most important and expensive sector in a great majority of hospitals. Its expenses consume more than 10% of hospital budget; moreover, points accumulated within ISA (Index of Synthetic Activity)[200] play a crucial role in the system. ISA point is a book value used for measuring hospital production. The financial aspect of the operating block is not the only crucial one. Other essential aspects include complexity of operating block functioning which results from qualitative and quantitative diversity of human and material resources, and limited financial reserves. When a need for optimization of finance and resources arises, players of the operating block are not prepared for it at all. In fact, the history of the operating block has always been culturally that of medical nature; it has always been directed at provision of medical care services and concentrated on surgical organization.

Nonetheless, the limited financial reserves require that operating blocks provide top quality medical services, control their expenses and minimize the time of work. The result is that operating blocks are confronted, in almost the same manner as industrial systems, with triple limitations including expenses, quality and deadlines. In order to meet the required criteria, not only medical, but rather objective management of production is to be applied. This can be accomplished by integration of new cultures and expert analysis from outside of the medical world. In the hereby chapter, the physical system of medical production was analyzed in the light of industrial production system.

---

[200] A. Macario, T.S. Vitez, B. Dunn, T. McDonald (1995), *Where are the costs in perioperative care? Analysis of hospital costs and charge for inpatient surgical care*, "Anesthesiology", No. 83, p. 1139–1140.

Exemplary applications of methods and tools of industrial management in hospital environment were presented. Finally, potential difficulties resulting from implementing management methods in operating blocks were outlined as well.

2.1.3.4. PHYSICAL SYSTEM OF MEDICAL PRODUCTION AND MANAGEMENT TOOLS

Production System

For any person outside the medical world, an operating block may seem a limited environment self-sufficient in its functioning, whereas inside the environment, a production process takes place which may imitate the production system of an enterprise. In fact, the production process consists of a number of tasks carried out by players in the same place and on the same patient. It starts the moment a patient has been brought in the operating block. The process may be divided into easily identifiable stages taking place one after another until the moment a patient has left the recovery room and, subsequently, hospital. This group of successive tasks constitutes the production process of medical care services, and occurs within physical production system represented by the operating block.

In the industrial environment, such a production process (technological card) consisting of the following activities (tooling, improving, packing) is realized by means of a physical production system. This system, in turn, consists of human resources (workers, technicians, executives) as well as material resources (warehouses, tools, logistics etc.)

The choice of organizational structure of production process is enabled by a function of various parameters among which the most important ones include product variety and quantity to be produced.

A brief description of industrial production systems will enable readers to understand which type of production they refer to, and will help to recognize similarities with the production of medical services in operating blocks.[201]

– *Mobile workshop* is a type of organization in which a product remains stationary, whereas resources ale movable. Such organization is suitable for the unit production in which it is difficult to move the product, as in the production of planes, ships, buildings etc.

– *Job shop* is an organization which groups resources in respect of their function: machines and workers are grouped on the basis of technological operations they are to perform (milling, denting…). This type of organization is adjusted to low-volume manufacture in enterprises producing diverse products (in cooperation with subcontractors).

– *Flow-shop*: resources are also grouped according to their tasks, but are organized in a permanent sequence. A good example of this organization is a process of

---

[201] S. Chaban, A. Guinet, N. Smolski, M. Guiraud, B. Luquet, E. Marcon, J.P. Viale (2003), *La gestion industrielle et la gestion des blocs opératoires*, Annales Françaises d'Anesthésie et de Réanimation, No. 22, p. 904–997.

assembly in the car industry. This type of organization is highly effective in the production of certain product groups and is characterized by a certain identical generic
range to which operations are assigned optionally.

– *Flow-shop-hybrid* is a type of *flow-shop* organization with a lot of items of the
same resource at different stages of production process. In that way at every stage of
production, the same task can be carried out by many machines.

Different organizations of production system can be identified in hospitals at the
level of medical wards or medical and technical laboratories. In fact, the production process in the operating block is analogous to the *flow-shop-hybrid* production
and takes place on two or three floors.[202] Every patient will pass the floor with an
operating room, the floor with a recovery room and, if need will be, the floor with
an intensive care unit. A patient makes use of one resource on every floor, and the
resources are numerous. Another example is the oncology ward which is a specialized unit. Patients who are to be admitted to it have to, prior to medical consultation,
undergo radiological and ultrasonographic examination, scanning and blood tests. If
the order of different stages of this process is not important, we find here a special
type of *job-shop* organization which is called *open-shop*. If one of the resources is
numerous, we deal with either the *open-shop-hybrid* or *job-shop-hybrid* organization. Identifying types of the production system of medical services is beneficial in
that it creates the possibility of applying tools used in managing industrial production to improve the management and productivity of organization of medical services in hospitals.

Operational Management Tools

Production management tools used in the production system can be adopted for
the objectives of hospital management, changing the degree of application, which
depends on the sector and country. If these tools turned out to be useful in managing
hospital supplies (of medications, materials), their application in managing operating
blocks is still limited.

Operational Scheduling

In a number of publications we find examples of implementing traditional techniques in order to create operational schedules.

For planning medical surgeries in a multidisciplinary block, Dexter *et al.*[203] suggest implementing heuristic methods in order to maximize the degree of room utilization. Such methods involve using solution-finding techniques based on a progressive
approach which takes into consideration changeable limitations such as unknown
duration of a surgery.

In contrast to heuristics, linear methods are suggested in [4] for creating schedules for operating blocks. Here, the reliable elements constitute the variables and

---

[202] A. Guinet, M. Legrand (1998), *Reduction of job-shop problems to flow-shop problems with
precedence constraints*, "European Journal of Operational Research", No. 86, p. 94–95.

[203] F. Dexter, A. Macario, R.D. Traum (1999), *Which algorithm for scheduling add-on elective
maximizes operating room utilization? Use of bin packing algorithms and constraints in operating
room management*, "Anesthesiology", No. 91, p. 1496.

include opening hours, overtime or dates of hospitalization and operation. The aim is to minimize changeable costs of utilizing operating blocks. There are also indirect techniques such as those presented in [6] whose role is to minimize factors such as extending closing hours of different operating blocks.

Operational Planning

Planning of surgeries consists in determining the order of planned operations per one day. In literature, many different concepts have been described depending on the aim which is to be achieved.

While analyzing a single operating block, one of the goals to be achieved is to reduce the lag time when the surgeon waits for the next surgery by reducing waiting time between two surgeries. This type of scheduling can be important in blocks where many surgeons who are not permanent workers of a given hospital operate on patients. In the case of post-operative rooms (POR), an analogy can be made to problems connected with managing production systems of *flow-shop-hybrid* type including two floors, which lead to techniques that aim at.

Flow Simulation

A complementary tool, potentially useful in managing the operating block, consists in a simulation of flows (a flow of products, information etc.), of reconstruction (or anticipation) of some aspects of the dynamic functioning of a production unit (or a future unit) of a given operating block (or a future operating block). It allows the choices in management strategies to be verified, e.g. the choice of scheduling which is aimed at operating rooms and which favors the cost of occupying these rooms, or the choice of scheduling which takes into account operating rooms and post-operative rooms (POR) [7]. The latter choice allows to find a classic problem in industrial management, i.e. moving the patient within the operating block, which is similar to the *flow-shop-hybrid* type including two floors.

In the same way, the simulation allows to estimate the influence of the staff's qualifications on the organization of operating blocks and post-operative rooms (POR) [8].

2.1.3.5. TRANSFER OF CURRENT MANAGEMENT TECHNIQUES FROM INDUSTRIAL SYSTEMS TO PRACTICES IN OPERATING BLOCKS AS AN INNOVATIVE UNDERTAKING

In recent years, numerous attempts have been made to transfer the tools and methods of industrial management to the management of medical care services in hospitals. In order to be adapted, the above mentioned tools created for the industrial world require certain analysis of various scheduling models.

Anglo-Saxon research team focused on Dexter's works publishes regularly in trade journals the results of implementing the tools for creating an operating schedule.[204,205]

In these journals, three models of operating schedule are presented:

– *Open scheduling* or *open booking* in which a certain program is proposed for each period of time, independently of all previous decisions. The schedule may be carried out chronologically as the information is delivered. A refined solution involves adding a negotiation phase between different players of the operating block. Scheduling is centralized in each case.

– Scheduling by prior assigning time blocks, i.e. *block scheduling*, consists in drawing an outline program which divides time blocks, within which surgeons or wards plan their operations. It is necessary therefore that the coordinator of the operating block has an employee at his disposal who is responsible for assigning time blocks, as closely to activities taking place in real time as possible, because that person decides on the amount of time and dates of surgical activities. In this case, the centralization of information is not necessary.

– In *modified block scheduling*, the concept of time block becomes flexible and can be extended. This technique is most frequently used in Anglo-Saxon countries. It allows a wider scope of freedom. The coordinators of operating blocks are able to manage time blocks on the basis of the course of a given operating schedule. The time for acceptance can be regulated according to the players' will and the person managing the information system.

The three aforementioned scheduling models may include three scheduling strategies; each of them is characterized by optimized goals inside the operating block. These strategies may be used for scheduled surgical wards as well as for surgical wards in outpatient's clinics.

– *Fixed hours system* aims at optimizing resources. Surgeries are scheduled only if they are finished before the operating block is closed, which creates the risk of not utilizing the operating room and postponing the operation until later.

– Contrary to the first strategy, the goal may consist in obeying the date chosen by a patient or by a surgeon, which may adversely affect the necessary flexibility of time schedule in order to favor work shifts in the operating block. The *anyworkday* schedule system is possible without postponing operations until later only if the rate of operating rooms being occupied allows the modification generally smaller than 80%.

– The intermediate strategy allows higher rate of operating rooms being occupied with postponing operations until later. Scheduling is not based on a patient's or surgeon's will but is carried out in order to reduce the time of waiting for an operation (*reasonable time system*).

---

[204] After: S. Chaban, A. Guinet, N. Smolski, M. Guiraud, B. Luquet, E. Marcon, J.P. Viale (2003), *La gestion industrielle et la gestion des blocs opératoires*, « Annales Françaises d'Anesthésie et de Réanimation », No. 22, p. 906.

[205] F. Dexter, A. Macario, R.D. Traum (1999), *Which algorithm for scheduling add-on elective maximizes operating room utilization? Use of bin packing algorithms and constraints in operating room management*, "Anesthesiology", No. 91, p. 1496.

Implementation

Description of the process of medical service production, selection of the model of operating programming and the choice of management tools is a result of the strategy and tactics adopted by hospitals. On the other hand, the expected results and the possibility of implementation depend on the participation of players and the organization of human resources. Restrictions and oppositions that are to be observed during the process of implementing organizational and structural changes were already noticed in industrial companies. In industrial companies, these restrictions and oppositions are numerous and varied; in hospitals, however, there are only two types of them as regards the management of blocks: insufficient information system and unadjusted culture.[206]

Information System

Efficient management of the operating block requires information system particularly adjusted for this purpose. The information entered has to correspond to the intended purposes which require the description of actions, supervision over the resources and patient flow as well as counting the rates referring to the functioning. An information system which refers to actions is different from the information system which is patient-oriented. It is necessary to design a program framework of the models such as the *modified block scheduling* type as well as to adapt and modify them. Managing authorities of hospitals become gradually aware of the positive effects of such systems.[207]

Culture of the Hospital Environment

Managing the production process is an element which prevails in the industrial production, but it is still not identified as a priority task within the operating block. This function is often entrusted to medical or paramedical staff which does not have time, sufficient qualifications or the will to fulfill this task. Rare trainings on the management of production expose the situation in the hospital environment. Important elements necessary in the managing of operating blocks may be defined as follows:

– Managing operating blocks is a responsibility of medical professionals. The industrial world succeeded in the 1980s due to the identification of various management functions; and so, operating blocks, in order to function properly, have to be managed by the staff that is properly trained and dedicated to their work.

– The techniques of managing operating blocks must include: elements determining success and the participation of medical players in their management, information concerning the activity, supervision, actions and the fulfillment of goals.

– Reasonable management of actions conducted in operating blocks should not be considered separately from the high quality work made possible due to its organization, prevention and minimization of risk connected with medical activity.

---

[206] F. Dexter, A. Macario (1996), *Applications of information systems to operating Rom scheduling*, "Anesthesiology", No. 85, p. 1232–1234.

[207] A. Macario, M. Vasanawala (2002), *Technology and computing in the surgical suite: key features o fan or management information system and opportunities for the future*, "Anesth. Analg.", No. 95, p. 1120–1121.

2.1.3.6. Conclusions

Optimization of the management of operating blocks is currently necessary to reduce the costs in the developed countries including Poland. Terms and tools originating in the production world may turn useful for the purpose of this innovative undertaking. As a result of organizational innovations, a new function emerges in hospitals – that of the block management.

2.1.4. Organisational standards of the endoscopic surgery ward

In contemporary endoscopy more and more significance gain endoscopic treatments performed in the ambulatory mode and their scope is constantly extending. To ensure proper conditions of the treatment, appropriate work organisation and suitable equipment are absolutely necessary. Unfortunately, only few wards dealing with endoscopic surgery meet those requirements.

On the basis of my own experience, I have determined the minimum criteria which should be fulfilled by such a ward. They have been divided into requirements concerning ward rooms, minimum necessary medical equipment, and the number and qualifications of the ward's personnel.

1. Medical apparatus – minimum equipment:
– 5 panendoscopes (including 1 small-calibre panendoscope),
– 3 colonoscopes,
– 2 duodenoscopes (at least 1 operating duodenoscope),
– 2 bronchoscopes
– 10 biopsy forceps for gastroscopes (required quantity dependent on the number of performed examinations: 1 pair of forceps per 1 examination every second day),
– 5 biopsy forceps for colonoscopes (required quantity dependent on the number of performed examinations: 1 pair of forceps per 1 examination every second day),
– swabs for smear tests,
– automatic, semi-automatic or manual washers.

2. Personnel – minimum qualifications:
– specialization in gastroenterology or gastrointestinal surgery,
– specialization in internal diseases, surgery or paediatrics with an additional confirmation of ability to perform particular procedures which was issued by the Polish Society of Gastroenterology or a regional consultant.

3. Minimum clinical experience of the unit in the following areas:
– diagnostic endoscopy in UGIB[208] – 1500 tests per year,

---

[208] Upper gastrointestinal bleeding.

– diagnostic endoscopy in LGIB[209] – 500 tests per year,
– diagnostic ERCP[210] – 200 tests per year,
– therapeutic endoscopy in UGIB – 500 performances per year,
– therapeutic endoscopy in LGIB – 300 performances per year,
– therapeutic ERCP – 400 performances per year.

4. Requirements concerning endoscopic equipment and decontamination process:
– only endoscopes allowing to achieve the level of high microbiological cleanliness (submersible endoscopes whose internal channels are brush accessible),
– only disposable or sterilizable accessories.

5. Other requirements:
– ensuring a possibility of moving the patient to an appropriate medical ward in any situations requiring hospitalization.

Premises conditions:
– Unit which is a separate organizational structure confirmed by a corresponding entry in the statutory and organisational regulations of the Health Care Centre.
– Treatment rooms assigned exclusively for the ward's needs – minimum 5 treatment rooms (separate rooms ezofagogastroduodenoscopy, colonoscopy, duodenoscopy, bronchoscopy, and endoscopy treatment room).
– Rooms assigned for taking care of the patient in the period of time directly preceding the diagnostic or treatment procedure.
– Rooms assigned for monitoring condition of the patient and nursing before a decision to discharge the patient is made.
– Rooms assigned for washers and of disinfection of endoscopes and endoscopic tools.

Required apparatus:
Endoscopic lab
– only automatic washing and decontamination of endoscopes – minimum 2 workstations for automatic washing and disinfection of endoscopes,
– obligatory equipment: minimum 1 ultrasonic washer, 1 diathermy for each treatment room nad argon beamer,
– not obligatory equipment: echo endoscopy set, laser,
– disposable tools recommended if available (otherwise use their multi-use equivalents),
– installations and facilities enabling access to medical gases,
– facilities enabling sterilization of endoscopic tools – autoclave or gas sterilizer (central sterilization),
– apparatus for monitoring basic life functions,

---

[209] Lower gastrointestinal bleeding.
[210] Endoscopic retrograde cholangio-pancreatography.

– C-arm X-ray machine,
– pathomorphology lab (access).

Personnel qualifications:
– senior registrar (supervisor) – specialist doctor with a surgery speciality,
– minimum 3 doctors specialised in endoscopy with at least 5-year experience,
– 6 nurses – after a full training obtained at endoscopy courses.

Cost components of gastroenterological endoscopy diagnostic and treatment procedures

The cost calculations whose purpose is to show the actual costs of the endoscopy procedures are based on analysing the data obtained from the hospital's accounts department. Data covers a period of 20 months.

All the costs (price components) have been included and these are the following:

1) Price component concerning cost of the medical personnel

a) It includes costs connected with remuneration of the personnel working at the endoscopy lab

2) Price component concerning cost of endoscopic tools and tools used for histopathological and cytological examinations

a) It includes the costs of purchasing endoscopic instruments such as tweezers, needles, and costs of histopathological examinations needed during the endoscopic procedures

3) Price component concerning cost of the medical equipment

a) It includes costs of depreciation of the endoscopic equipment, X-ray equipment, and other devices used during the endoscopic procedures

4) Price component concerning cost of medicines and liquids

a) It includes medicines and infusion liquids used during the endoscopic procedures

5) Price component concerning the running costs

a) It includes the hospital's running costs such as administration, laboratory, laundry.

Endoscopic tests – price list
Gastroscopic examinations:

1. Gastroscopy with a biopsy and histopathological examination, or applying a sonde – 200 PLN

2. Diagnostic gastroscopy incl. an urease – 150 PLN

3. Gastroscopy with a mechanical widening of the bore – 1,400 PLN

4. Gastroscopy with mucosectomy – 1,000 PLN

5. Gastroscopy with polypectomy – 750 PLN

6. Gastroscopy with a therapy treatment of vascular changes – 1,400 PLN

7. Gastroscopy with restoring patency or widening of the bore and installing self-expandable stents (excl. costs of the stents) – 1,700 PLN

8. Gastroscopy with laser/argon patency restoring – 2,000 PLN

9. Gastroscopy with removing a foreign body – 500 PLN

10. Gastroscopy with installing a gastrostome – 1,800 PLN.

Colonoscopic examinations:
1. Diagnostic colonoscopy – 300 PLN
2. Diagnostic colonoscopy incl. a biopsy – 450 PLN
3. Colonoscopy with a mechanical widening of the bore – 1,650 PLN
4. Colonoscopy with mucosectomy – 1,400 PLN
5. Colonoscopy with a standard polypectomy – 1,150 PLN
6. Colonoscopy with a complex polypectomy – 1,550 PLN
7. Colonoscopy with a therapy treatment of vascular changes – 1,650 PLN
8. Colonoscopy with restoring patency of intestine using laser/argon – 1,900 PLN.

Sigmoidoscopic examinations:
1. Diagnostic sigmoidoscopy – 200 PLN
2. Diagnostic sigmoidoscopy incl. a biopsy – 350 PLN
3. Sigmoidoscopy with a mechanical widening of the bore – 1,550 PLN
4. Sigmoidoscopy with mucosectomy – 1,250 PLN
5. Sigmoidoscopy with a standard polypectomy – 1,000 PLN
6. Sigmoidoscopy with a complex polypectomy – 1,350 PLN
7. Sigmoidoscopy with installing self-expandable stents (excl. costs of the stents) – 2,000 PLN
8. Sigmoidoscopy with a therapy treatment of vascular changes – 1,550 PLN
9. Sigmoidoscopy with restoring patency of intestine using laser/argon – 1,800 PLN.

Bronchoscopic examinations:
1. Diagnostic bronchoscopy – 150 PLN
2. Bronchoscopic treatment – 300 PLN
3. Bronchoscopy with taking specimens and with full diagnostics – 400 PLN
4. Bronchoscopic removal of tumours from the bronchial tree – 700 PLN.

Duodenoscopic examinations:
1. Diagnostic ERCP with a biopsy, removing the stents – 1,300 PLN
2. ERCP and PTC[211] performed for one patient to restore patency of the biliary tract – 3,500 PLN
3. ERCP of a high difficulty level (number of deposits over 3 or deposit with a diameter over 12 mm), mechanical lithotripsy, drainage of biliary or pancreatic tract – 2,600 PLN
4. ERCP of a standard difficulty level: replacing stents, removing deposits (number of deposits 1–3 and diameter of each not bigger than 12 mm) – 2,100 PLN
5. ERCP of a high difficulty level: removing deposits and installing traditional stents + cost of stents, treatment of pancreatic or duodenal cysts, treatment of chronic pancreatitis – 2,850 PLN
6. ERCP with installing self-expandable stents to biliary tract (excl. costs of the stents) – 2,400 PLN
7. Treatment and control ERCP: *sphincterotomy*, instrumental control of biliary or pancreatic tract – 1,650 PLN.

---

[211] Percutaneous transhepatic cholangiography.

Special examinations:

1. Photodynamic therapy of tumouric changes in the gastrointestinal tract – 5,000 PLN

2. Diagnostic endosonography of the gastrointestinal tract – 1,350 PLN

3. Puncture or drainage of cysts and abscesses with full diagnostics (excl. costs of the stents) – 600 PLN.

Due to the necessity of cooperation with radiologists, it is vital to locate the two labs, duodenoscopic and treatment, in the immediate vicinity of the ultrasound and radiological lab. Duodenoscopic lab should be equipped with its own **C-arm X-ray machine**. In both labs there should be tables for endoscopic examinations with a possibility of taking X-rays, pulse oximeter, and cardio monitor.

The other labs: bronchoscopic, diagnostic gastroscopy, and colonoscopic should function both as hospital and outpatient labs. All the room should constitute a functional unit with a centrally located apparatus washer. In the immediate vicinity of the washer there should be storage rooms for accessories, endoscopic equipment and medicines, dressing materials, stationery, needles and other kinds of small medical equipment.

Near the ward there should be an additional room for at least 5–6 beds to observe the patients after examinations with a possibility of monitoring the key life parameters after performing treatments with anaesthetization. This kind of examination needs also anaesthetic equipment.

All the endoscopic rooms should be equipped with access to medical gases, central suction, pulse oximeter. In four of them there should be **endoscopic diathermy** facilities, and in the fifth one there should be **argon diathermy**. Apart from that, the lab should be also equipped with **endoscopic laser** and **cryotherapy** equipment. Additionally, in the bronchoscopy lab there should also be a nebulizer and cardio monitor.

Patients should enter the lab rooms following registration at the reception with a possibility of computer data recording. All the set of the 6 computers used in the lab should work as a functional cluster thanks to their connection, by a central lab server, into an internal computer network. In the phase of designing the system, one should predict the possibility of storing and processing endoscopic pictures and full computer control of the registration process, storing and passing examination findings (hardware and software).

The following should be additional equipment of the central endoscopic lab:

1. portable gastro- and bronchoscopic set (to be used at the resuscitation ward),

2. echoendoscope – 1 piece,

3. set of insertion ultrasound probes,

4. therapeutic laser for PDT.[212]

To provide continual work of the central endoscopic lab, it is necessary to employ at least 4 fully-qualified doctors and 6 endoscopic nurses. It will enable a 24h availability of all the examinations performed in the endoscopic ward and running endoscopic emergency service.

Estimated cost of organising and setting up (accessories necessary for the period of 6 months) a central endoscopic lab in a hospital amounts to 3.5 million PLN.

---

[212] Photodynamic Therapy.

The ward could be expected to bring annual revenues of approximately 2.5 million PLN. After taking into account the expected lifespan of the equipment of 3–5 years, it means that the ward's income is sufficient to cover the costs of setting up the ward, keeping it in constant readiness, and maintenance costs.

This study analyses the possible income and expenses connected with functioning of a ward dealing with outpatient endoscopic gastrointestinal tract surgery. Although it is commonly known that medical procedures suffer from insufficient funds, the presented price list shows that, if applying realistic price calculations for endoscopic procedures, it is possible to achieve financial self-sufficiency of a ward dealing with outpatient endoscopic gastrointestinal tract surgery.

Future will inevitably bring diagnostic and therapeutic progress in endoscopy. It is not possible to avoid the increasing frequency of performing endoscopic treatments in the outpatient mode. However, inappropriate estimation of costs of medical procedures causes delays in development of the outpatient surgery in Poland.

It is absolutely necessary to make the decision-makers aware of the fact that the apparently higher costs of endoscopic procedures which enable appropriate and financially profitable functioning of the endoscopic gastrointestinal tract surgery wards will finally bring huge savings in expenses incurred currently for unnecessary hospitalizations of the patients.

2.1.5. ORGANISATION OF ONE DAY SURGERY CLINIC

2.1.5.1. INTRODUCTION

In May 2004 Poland joined the European Union and we started comparing a lot of areas in our country with the EU standards. We were interested in the challenges we were facing to meet the average level represented by the 'old' Europe and one of the most difficult tasks were the necessary changes in organisation of the health care system.

This paper is an attempt to present the initial situation in Poland in the so-called one day surgery and outlines the goals which should be aimed at.

The one day surgery treatments, just as the name suggests, are accomplished within one day. It means that admitting to hospital, surgery, and releasing the patient all take place on the same day – patient comes to the hospital in the morning, undergoes the surgery, and within a few hours after the treatment, accompanied by an adult person, they can go home. There should be a telephone at home just in case. Should any complications occur, there must be a possibility of bringing the patient to the hospital. A longer hospital stay is possible but it does not last longer than three days.

Surgeries performed in the one-day mode are a very advantageous type of operation treatments. Nowadays in the USA approximately 75% of all operation treatments are carried out in the one day surgery clinic mode. There are a number of unquestionable benefits the patient gets from undergoing treatment and anaesthetization within one day and these are the following:

1. No long contact with the adverse hospital environment, which means avoiding hospital infections.

2. No psychological stress connected with a long-lasting hospital stay.

3. No separation with home and family members – a psychological aspect.

4. Shorter waiting time for the planned surgery comparing to the typical surgery procedures.

5. Lower costs of stay and treatment compared to a typical operation treatment.

6. Quicker return to work.

In 2004 in Poland 1,818,771 surgery treatments were made including 894,685 general surgery treatments. At the same time in all the country there were barely 11,294 one day surgery treatments. This comparison clearly shows that one day surgeries constituted 0.620968% of all the surgeries contracted by the National Health Fund.

As you can see, we are still at the very beginning of the way which can take us closer to achieving standards comparable with other countries. For years 2004––2013 the National Health Plan assumes achieving such goals as: increasing efficiency of health care funding, shortening time of treatment and stay of patients at hospital wards, creating one-day beds to enhance development of the one day surgery and introducing mechanisms of directing patients to hospital wards only if it is absolutely necessary.

We should aim at setting up a network of one day surgery clinics which could contribute to a broader application of rules of this new surgery type in the Polish health care system. Below are the basic assumptions and requirements concerning organisation of a clinical one day surgery ward.

Qualifying conditions and contraindications against surgery in the one day treatment mode

Hospitalization time: 2 to 24 hours and medical supervision for 72 hours after the surgery including home visits.

Qualifications of the personnel providing service supervision by the ward's senior registrar doctors – minimum one specialist, other doctors during specialization nurses.

Premises conditions: bedded ward, operation block or operation room dedicated to the one day mode, dedicated rooms allowing to take care of the patient before the diagnostic or, treatment procedure, dedicated rooms allowing to monitor the patient's, condition and perform nursing care until a decision to release them has been made.

Medical apparatus: standard operation block equipment, anaesthesiological equipment, sterilization equipment, equipment allowing to follow the procedures.

Types of treatments performed as a one day surgery.

The patients who are operated on in one day surgery system are those who do not suffer from other serious health disorders and can boast a good general health condition. They must not be undergoing treatments against metabolic illnesses e.g. diabetes, hyperthyroidism or others like that.

In one day surgery system the following surgeries are performed (within particular specializations):

– vascular surgery: varicose veins of lower limbs, non-invasive and operating treatment,

– laparoscopic surgery: extraction of gall bladder, operations of biliary tract, operations of appendix, freeing adhesions, anti-reflux surgery, hernia repair surgery, diagnostics of abdominal cavity,
  – diseases of anus and rectum: varicose veins, fistulas, fissures,
  – operations of thyroid gland,
  – bone fractures,
  – oncological surgery: correction of protruding ears, removing skin birthmarks,
  – oncological surgery: teat, skin,
  – circumcising, removing phimosis, treating hydrocele,
  – thigh hernia, inguinal hernia,
  – removing exuberant scars, correcting scars,
  – removing isthmus of the wrist channels

2.1.5.2. WARD STRUCTURE

The organisational specificity of a ward dealing with one day surgery requires allocating the following functions within its structure:
  1. Waiting room, reception desk, doctor's surgery room, office administering flow of patients in the ward, discharging room.
  2. Preparatory rooms, rooms for anaesthetization procedures.
  3. Operation and treatment rooms.
  4. Rooms for anaesthesiological post-operation supervision.
  5. Hospital rooms for prolonged observation (up to 72 hours).
  6. Storage rooms for sterile medical equipment and dressing materials.
  7. Storage room for medical equipment.
  8. Room for washing and decontamination of the equipment.
  9. Room for preparing sets and preparing for sterilization.
  10. Anaesthesiological lab and storage room for anaesthetizing equipment and materials.
  11. Room for conferences, meetings, and seminars.
  12. Recreation rooms and dressing room for the personnel.
  13. Ward laboratory.
  14. Permanent access to the pharmacy.
  15. Manager's room.
  While designing the ward, it is crucial to keep the dirty and clean zones separate and avoid crossing of the dirty and clean flow of people and equipment. It is possible to achieve this organisation by dividing the ward into three zones: free access, restricted access and clean zone where access is possible only for clean equipment and personnel and which the personnel and patients can enter only after washing up and putting on clean protective clothing.

2.1.5.3. PERSONNEL

The hospital personnel can be divided into three groups: doctors, nurses and administrative staff. Each group has their own scope of responsibilities. Among the doctors there are both surgeons and anaesthesiologists. Together with the nurses they deal with direct patient service. A full ward efficiency is approximately 15 to 25 surgeries daily, which makes it necessary to employ 5–6 surgeons, 4 anaesthesiologists and 8 surgery nurses (instrumental and anaesthesiological nurses). There should also be 4–6 nurses working in the observation rooms after anaesthetization and looking after the patients staying longer at the ward.

The administrative personnel at the one day surgery ward plays a much more important role than at the traditional hospital wards. This particular group of staff have a direct contact with the people applying for treatments, register them, and are responsible for the right flow of patients at the ward. Patients leaving the ward will contact the administrative staff again as they will need to obtain the hospital discharge certificate and it is the administrative staff who will pass on to the patient the doctor's final recommendations. The administrative personnel's behaviour and performance will have a direct influence on the patient's judgements of the ward and quality of the medical service. The administrative personnel should consist of approximately 5 people.

2.1.5.4. WARD ROOMS

To achieve the biggest advantage of the employed personnel, it is advisable to incorporate three operating rooms into the ward. For three operating rooms there should be one additional room where patients can be anaesthetised before the surgery and two preparation rooms sale where the patient gets washed and changes the clothing.

Inside the anaesthesiological observation room there should be at least 5 stations for patients after anaesthetization. The ward should also possess 4–8 two-bedded rooms for patients staying at the ward for up to 72 hours.

As the ward combines both the medical care service and didactic functions, it should be equipped with internal closed-circuit television enabling observation of the surgeries by the students without violating the sterility discipline or the patient's privacy. It will also help keep records of the surgeries and possibly set up production of didactic films by the ward.

2.1.5.5. MEDICAL AND OFFICE EQUIPMENT

The ward should be equipped with three sets for full anaesthesia, three operating tables, including one with an X-ray facility. The operating rooms should possess a total of at least three laparoscope sets allowing to perform 3–6 laparoscopic surgeries daily.

To enhance an efficient flow of information and ensure good supervision over flow of the patients at the ward, it is necessary to equip the ward with computers and other IT equipment.

Setting up this kind of clinics will contribute to promotion of this new fast developing type of medical service. It will also allow medical universities to gain a strong position on the medical service market. Last but not least, one day surgery wards are usually financially profitable.

Medical universities should not ignore the situation when profitable specialisations and services are quickly privatized, and clinics are burdened with high costs of treating other types of patients. Setting up this kind of wards within the academic hospital structures will prevent the medical universities from being pushed out of profitable area of medical service. There are also no doubts about a necessity to initiate a didactic activity in this speciality which is brand new on our market.

Initiating scientific research in one day surgery at our medical universities should also lead to setting up new scientific centres developing an international cooperation in this area. At the moment in Poland none of the medical universities runs such a department.

2.1.6. INFORMATION SYSTEMS AND RISK MANAGEMENT IN HEALTH INSTITUTIONS. A PRACTICE-BASED APPROACH

2.1.6.1. THE METHOD AND OBJECTIVES

The basic research method has been the analysis of available literature and source documents, especially government regulations. The author has drawn on her own professional experience and hence the majority of the presented examples have been taken from her memos. The chief objectives of the paper are the following:

1) a description of the significance and role of risk management,

2) a presentation of the influence of risk management on the functioning of an organization,

3) a description of the relations between risk management and information management (including the advantages ensuing from computerization),

4) a presentation of the role of computer-based risk management,

5) a presentation of the practical methods of implementing appropriate risk prevention strategies.

2.1.6.2. THE THEORETICAL BACKGROUND

Many interesting research papers have been published recently. The author has taken them into consideration in the development of her own practical methods of risk management, for example:

1. J. Husson offered a conceptual model of *risk management* for *hospital* managers,[213]

2. I.M. Rodrigez indicated that "a *hospital* should take necessary steps for minimal *risks* such as ensuring delivery of best patient care and complying with safety regulations to avoid malpractice suits",[214]

3. G. Huby and J. Stewart suggested that participation *in* decision-making is linked to systems of *risk management* (staff had therefore little reason to trust patients' competence to manage and to take part *in* decision-making),[215]

4. W.J. Warfel examined the nature of the *hospital* medical malpractice liability exposure,[216]

5. S.Y. Huang claims that healthcare *information* technology can improve healthcare services quality,[217]

6. D. Naranjo-Gil and F. Hartmann explained how CEOs use management information system for strategy implementation in hospital.[218]

2.1.6.3. BRIEF OVERVIEW

It may seem trivial to state that risks exist everywhere in every hospital. Nevertheless, it should be made clear that risks in a hospital are in no way restricted to the hazards of advanced medical practice or to those related to the care of high-risk patients. First, medical practice in the hospital is a multidisciplinary activity. Second, hospital processes rely on a wide variety of skills, occupations and techniques, in a rather complex environment. As a consequence, risks – which often result from the fact that multiple negative causes can link together – permeate all domains of activity.

This is the reason why, in addition to medical risks, more and more specific risks are being taken into consideration: risks linked to water pollution (legionellose) or to air pollution (aspergillose), fire hazards, risks linked to accommodation and catering (e.g. a break in the cold chain of food supply), risks arising from Information Systems errors, risks in moving patients and equipment, and so on.

---

[213] J. Husson (2009), *Hospitals Looking for Performance: Methodological Outlook for New Hospital Risk Management*, "Gestion 2000", Vol. 26, Issue 5, p. 65–81.

[214] I.M. Rodrigez (2009), *Helping hospitals design appropriate risk management programs*, "Caribbean Business", 10/22, Vol. 37, Issue 42, p. S8–S8.

[215] G. Huby, J. Stewart, A. Tierney, W. Rogers (2004), *Planning older people's discharge from acute hospital care: linking risk management and patient participation in decision-making, Health*, "Risk & Society", Vol. 6, Issue 2, p. 115–132.

[216] W.J. Warfel, P.J. Mikolaj (2003), *Hospital Litigation: Risk Management Implications*, "CPCU eJournal", Vol. 56, Issue 4, p. 1–18.

[217] S.Y. Huang, W.H. Huang, Chia-An, S.Ch. Jiang (2010), *Critical factors of hospital adoption on CRM system: Organizational and information system perspectives*, "Decision Support Systems", Vol. 48, Issue 4, p. 592–603.

[218] D. Naranjo-Gil, F. Hartmann (2007), *How CEOs use management information system for strategy implementation in hospital*, "Health Policy", Vol. 81, Issue 1, p. 29–41.

As matter of fact, the hospital can also be viewed as a place of contractual commitments, where medical and catering services are provided to the patients, who themselves are in the care of the health institution. Since in this context objections may arise, or more seriously, disputes which could result in a lawsuit, as is more and more frequently the case, one has also to keep in mind the possible legal consequences when planning for risk management.

In a recent period, for example, a new concern has appeared, to prevent the substitution or even the theft of a patient's personal identity. A new activity has taken shape, now dubbed "identitovigilance" (i.e. patient identity watch).

Hospitals also routinely use costly equipments, whose failure, whether it is due to intentional damage or not, may have serious medical and financial consequences.

Thus, a very broad range of risks, when they materialize, do impact people (staff, patients, visitors) as well as property and equipments.

2.1.6.4. EMERGENCE AND DEVELOPMENT OF RISK MANAGEMENT

The emergence of an explicit Risk Management activity in the French Public Health System has been rather gradual, from a more or less clear awareness up to the current acknowledgment of a real necessity.

For many years, authorities in charge of fighting nosocomial infectious diseases (in France: "CCLIN – Comités Contre Les Infections Nosocomiales") have constantly drawn attention upon the occurrence of iatrogenic disorders and on the consequences these had for patients – hence, also on the circumstantial consequences for the nation and the institution itself.

In 2004 a French survey (ENEIS)[219] was performed in 292 Medical Care Units, throughout 71 various Health Institutions nationwide. It counted overall 450 "unwelcome incidents" for 35,234 hospitalization days (patient-days). At that time, this survey did fill a void, as no survey of comparable extent had been performed yet on this subject.

The emergence of Risk Management as a specific activity within the French Public Health System is in no way a fashion, but the result of a process of growing awareness. Today it is implemented as an extension and a generalization of management activities which had already existed during previous years, but only to contain the most obvious or the most threatening risks. It materializes the need and desire to prevent hazards that could be avoided from compromising the safety, the security and the performance of the Health System.

Without entering details, it remains of high significance that investigators have repeatedly deemed that one-third to one half of "seriously unwelcome incidents" (in fact, near misses) could have been readily avoided. The analysis of originating causes has further highlighted the primary role of poor organization and poor communication in these incidents.

---

[219] DREES (Direction de la REcherche des Etudes de l'Evaluation et des Statistiques) Enquête ENEIS Enquête Nationale sur les Evénements Indésirables liés aux soins en établissements de santé – Paris 2005.

Such conclusions have then led the DHOS[220] (Direction de l'Hospitalisation et de l'Organisation des Soins, a governing body of the French Public Health System) to demand that a true tracking system of unwelcome incidents be set up in each Health Institution, along with a periodic management summary of control data.

Today, the governing bodies of the Public Health System are considering a specific financial allowance for Risk Management in the budget planning of Public Health Institutions, which in a way acknowledges the cost-effectiveness and the key role in safety and security of this activity.

Supervising bodies feel rightly concerned with the overcosts linked to unwelcome incidents, since a significant part of those finally result in sending or sending back patients to the hospital, or in extending stays at the hospital.

Moreover, insurance premiums are on the rise, as are lawsuits, which become more and more frequent in case of dispute with patients or patients' families. This constitutes a strong incentive to crack down on the non-respect of procedures and to identify very high upstream the possible originating causes of unwelcome incidents.

Thus, in a span of few years, Risk Management has evolved from a vague concept of improved quality to the status of an absolute necessity, acknowledged at every level of organization and management.

2.1.6.5. IMPACT OF RISK MANAGEMENT ON THE ORGANIZATION

As we have already mentioned it above, the analysis of the originating causes of serious unwelcome incidents has highlighted poor organization as a key factor.

Does this really means that the traditional organization of Health Institutions should be entirely rethought and rebuilt to reap the benefit of an efficient Risk Management?

In this instance, one should bear in mind that, even though this kind of organization has been rightly criticized for some sluggishness, it has nevertheless succeeded in an acceptable day-to-day management of institutions where processes are complex and highly interwoven, with a variety of professions where each of them brings along its own techniques and concerns. Anyone can see for himself the number and diversity of actors in a patient's day at the hospital.

This mix of professions and this complexity constitute themselves a high risk factor, as they make it more difficult to strictly follow procedures, whether these pertain to medical protocols or to administrative processes, and as they make communication slower and more difficult.

For a number of years, well-tried and proven techniques of Risk Management have been in use in other sectors of the economy, for example in the nuclear power industry or in the aerospace industry. These techniques and the relevant concepts can be helpful to set up a reference framework for a Risk Management policy which would specifically suit Health Institutions.

---

[220] DHOS Direction de l'Hospitalisation et de l'Organisation des Soins – Ministère de la santé, de la famille et des personnes handicapées *Recommandations pour l'élaboration et la mise en oeuvre d'un programme de gestion des risques dans les établissements de santé* – Paris 2003.

However, importing such "not invented here" management techniques may prove tricky in professional circles who are highly aware of their specificity, obey specific regulations, possess their own reference concepts and even their own jargon, as is the case with the Public Health System.

In addition, in the Public Health sector, expectations are particularly high to drastically slash on the number of unwelcome incidents, whatever their origin, by implementing a Risk Management policy.

This is tantamount to say that this policy implementation is not an ordinary management action, which would simply proceed to minor adjustments in order to improve day-to-day operations. On the contrary, it involves a quantum leap, with strong implications on the very culture of the Institution. In other words, it requires an explicit management of change.

Implementing a Risk Management policy means that the senior management of an Institution should commit itself to this policy's success, by stating it clearly and by defining who will be accountable for decision making and for Risk Management operations.

A program which covers several years should be set up and made known to the whole staff of the Institution.

In particular, such a program:

1. Should of course meet official regulations pertaining to Risk Management,
2. Should in addition create within the Institution a proactive momentum integrated to everyday's professional practices,
3. Should specify the relevant roles and procedures needed at every management level for a continuous improvement of Risk Management.

It should not be forgotten either that the analysis which led to the decision to formally manage risks had from the very beginning highlighted that insufficient communication lay at the heart of unwelcome incidents.

In a more proactive style this means that the proper management of information and communications is a key success factor of Risk Management.

Therefore the system is needed which provides for:

– the collection and archiving of any relevant data, and the traceability of all events or incidents,
– information access and sharing for every professional with the need to know,
– relevant indicators to the general management to monitor security and Risk Management.

The first functionality, collecting and archiving information, when correctly implemented, will immediately allow learning from experience, which is the basic mechanism to foster change and quality improvement.

2.1.6.6. RISK MANAGEMENT AND THE INFORMATION SYSTEM
WHY USE THE INFORMATION SYSTEM'S CAPABILITIES FOR RISK MANAGEMENT?

Experience has widely shown that granting access to an up to date and relevant information to every professional is a key success factor in controlling the various processes in the hospital.

Too many safety failures are in fact a consequence of an incomplete adoption or knowledge of procedures and regulations, of the lack of communication between departments, individuals and professions, and of the lack of interest in fully understanding a number of alerts of real significance which had nevertheless been acknowledged in due time.

Most significant, the possession of information is often seen as a means of personal influence, hence so much hesitation as to sharing it or not, only to protect individual or local petty interests, though this may harm the patients and the Institution.[221]

Structuring and automating the Information System will drastically cut on this vulnerability. In some sense, an efficient Information System is a powerful instrument to force the evolution of professional mentalities.[222]

Functional requirements of Risk Management

A Risk Management System should have two key properties, vigilance and transparence.

Now, for a number of reasons we are going to expose hereafter, the human factor which makes it particularly uneasy to fulfill this requirement.

Vigilance

Before a risk materializes, i.e. before an accident happens or a serious dispute arises, most often there exists a rather long period of risk latency.

To analyze accidents after the fact requires, like every process of learning from experience, that as much data as possible be collected during this latency period. But the very fact that the risk is not readily apparent means that operators do not perceive it clearly, or even do not perceive it at all. If this is the case, why make the extra effort of collecting information or recording deviations from the nominal process, when everything seems under control?

Even if he keeps fighting sloppy work habits – which are usually described positively by expressions like "stick to the basics" or "be able to get by" – the best professional will eventually get weary of routine data collection or of reporting incidents which on the surface have no consequence. **This is one cause of ineffectiveness**.

Transparence

Transparence may also be jeopardized because of an erroneous understanding of hierarchy prerogatives.

It is not infrequent to hear that "the local hierarchy feels important to adapt instructions to local circumstances", this means however that in actual practice regulatory instructions are not circulated in the same way and at the same time in all departments.

---

[221] D. Brissaud (2006), *Mise en place d'un Système d'Information de Gestion des Risques en Etalissement de Santé (SIGR)* – Thèse professionnelle, Mastère spécialisé – École Centrale de Paris.

[222] GMSIH Groupement pour la Modernisation du Système d'Information Hospitalier *L'identitovigilance* – Paris 2003.

Data collection, and more important, incident reporting is hampered by the natural fear to report facts that could open peer criticism or give rise to admonishments from senior management, let alone trigger a legal dispute. In such circumstances, a local hierarchy may deliberately block the upwards transmission of reports. Operators just forget that transparence and non indulgent reporting are ultimately required to protect them.

Such unwillingness to report is frequently compounded by a cultural lack of cooperative habits in the workplace. This definitely weakens any attempts to monitor processes in full transparence. A total paralysis of the reporting system cannot be excluded. **This is the second cause of ineffectiveness**.

Fundamental benefits of computerization

To meet the above requirements of vigilance and transparence, an effective Risk Management System should provide the means to firmly guide those operators who would be tempted to yield to subjectivity when following Risk Management procedures.

What is at stake is to have at one's disposal a system which is able to **untiringly** collect, follow-up and process any relevant data **without any bias**.

A computerized system will have the following properties:

Tireless

A computerized system does not subjectively feels that "no risk exists" or that "the current situation is under control". It does not forget to execute a task or does not skip one because "there is something more important to do". **It just does what it has been programmed for**.

Tirelessly, it collects whatever data it has been requested to collect, even seemingly minor ones. Tirelessly, it will ask for reports or declarations in due date, it will chase up late reporters and it will eventually record the lack of report itself, which in some way still constitutes a follow-up of activity.

The system does not lose patience, it just repeats its requests until they are fulfilled.

Incorruptible

A computerized system cannot be cowed into censoring reports and even less into recalling or cancelling data which has already been entered.

Since information is captured at the closest, where incidents do happen, it reflects the actual situation in the field and it cannot be altered by transmission through successive hierarchy levels.

Immune to dispute or controversy

The system specifications have been set up in due time by consensus or by a majority decision, with senior management approval.

Once implementation and acceptance tests are over, it becomes difficult to challenge the system's legitimacy and its output without launching a public debate with closely argued points.

Impersonal and unbiased

Documents of general interest whose circulation is compulsory cannot anymore be held on to, in order to meet ulterior motives.

Document circulation reaches all departments and all individuals at the same time, so no one, whether a whole department or a single individual, can complain about being underprivileged.

With the computerized collection of data, all departments are exposed to the same traceability requirements. No one can say he is under excessive scrutiny.

Interactive

A computerized system can acknowledge the submission of reports, declarations and collected information. The individual who made a declaration can be granted personal access rights to do the follow-up of his declaration and to be kept informed, if applicable, of what decisions where taken thereafter.

Reactive and flexible

The system makes it possible to retrieve and analyze a huge quantity of data on demand, with dynamically defined sorting criteria, even if this data was entered into the system a long time ago.

It is no longer possible to discard a request from the senior management or from governing bodies simply by explaining that "data has been lost, it can no longer be retrieved".

Analysis is fast and automatic, it is no longer possible to delay it by saying "this is too complex, there is too much data to browse, we cannot bear this extra workload".

Supportive of well defined standards

A computerized system fosters the standardization of procedures and documents. Although it is flexible enough to be tailored to the specific needs of each department and of each profession, when it comes to Risk Management proper, it requires a standard vocabulary and standard procedures from every operator.

In time, this common language will ease inter-department communication and foster **the emergence of a common culture of Risk Management**.

In addition, information is stored using a limited number of standard formats, which eases **data cross-analysis**.

To summarize this, it is easy to see that the main contribution of computerization is more about performance and dependability than about the introduction of some sort of new functionalities. Dependability simply makes it possible to seriously say for certain that risks are managed.

Computerization is an efficient work around to eliminate the troubles of the human factor. With the support of a computerized system, intermediate levels of management can really focus on their true local managerial role, and the senior management is re-empowered into its prerogatives of decision making and policy making – in this case, the Risk Management policy.

Last but not least, the system guarantees a fair sharing of information and a fair treatment to every individual and to every department in sharing responsibilities towards risks.

2.1.6.7. OBJECTIVES AND FUNCTIONALITIES OF A COMPUTER-BASED RISK MANAGEMENT SYSTEM

Since the 90's, there has been in France a strong drive for Health Institutions to streamline their activities and to provide a better service to patients and to their families.

Much progress has been accomplished in the field of Information Systems, especially for patient care.

Another type of evolution has been initiated by the demand of the Administration to incorporate medical matters into data processing at large. Information Systems are now able to process the full range of data pertaining to every process of patient care, and to track every physical flow in relation to the production of medical care.

In order to improve the ability to monitor, assess and control this production, there is now a trend to develop systems which can guarantee the traceability of all activities and which ultimately will provide a true representation of these activities by consolidating all collected data.

A major objective of these Information Systems is to record all activity data in relation to a given patient:

– Diagnostic and medical prescriptions.
– Nursing care and following results.
– Medical treatments, lab tests and check-ups carried out for this patient, test results and data entered at lab registration time.
– Personal medical data.
– Administrative data.
– Admission, leave and transfers.
– Prescribed and administered medications, test tube tracking etc.

These data will be consolidated in turn to provide the following high-level information, more readily usable to prevent incidents and to provide guidance to decision makers:

– monitoring control panel, to analyze medical and nursing activity,
– procedures follow-up,
– system-aided medical decision making,
– incident follow-up.

This last point clearly shows that some existing functionalities in Health Institutions Information Systems will also exist in Risk Management Systems, however with a somewhat different focus.

But one cannot extrapolate, and believe that Health Institutions Information Systems are already a full superset of a Risk Management System. This would be a purely theoretical and abstract view, without consideration of the actual data processing capabilities of a given Information System at a given point in time.

It would not take into account the specific priorities of Risk Management and the necessary management of change – heightening the awareness and educating professionals, implementing the organizational structures etc. – which **must** take place before one can seriously say that Risk Management is operational.

Ensuring the global consistency of an Information System is not an easy task. One has to answer the following questions:

1. How to determine which information data should be tracked and how to define them precisely
2. How to perform the real-time collection of these data
3. How to tackle the problem of missing activity reports
4. How to implement traceability.

In addition, there are still a number of problems in relation with:

1) the selection of the appropriate hardware and software,
2) projects deployment,
3) the specific culture of health professionals in the workplace.

Of course, some similitude exists between problems met with the development and deployment of a computer-supported Health Information System and what can be foreseen in the implementation of a Risk Management System.

Clearly, any experience gained with the deployment of a Health Institution Information System will benefit to the deployment of a Risk Management System.[223]

The challenge the governing bodies of the Public Health System have now to take up is to comply with more and more demanding health security requirements.

The number and complexity of production processes in the hospital, the way they rely on each other, the number of operators in a given process, the diversity of professions, all this creates a high concentration of various risks. This means that every actor in these processes is – and has to be – involved in the improvement of health safety and of property and equipment security.

As a consequence, **a strategy for change is needed at all management levels** in a Health Institution. The central question is: "How to improve, for each actor, the visibility of threatening risks, in order to improve in turn decision making processes?".

Building a dedicated information and communications subsystem to manage risks will clearly be a determining factor of success. Such a system should offer the following functionalities:

1. Support all kinds of data collection, event tracking and data archiving needed to correctly identify risks,
2. Ease information access and sharing for each professional involved in risk management,
3. Provide to each professional the necessary equipment and computing power to access various centralized alerts about drug watch and technology watch,
4. Elaborate relevant reports the aim being that each professional improves his own knowledge and awareness of the threats and vulnerabilities which may be of concern to his own practice, and that countermeasures be widely circulated.

---

[223] J.T. Reason (1997), *Managing the Risk of Organizational Accidents*, Ashton Publishing, Aldershot (UK).

2.1.6.8. IMPLEMENTATION STRATEGY

A computer-based Risk Management System: opportunities and threats

An existing deployment of modern computer-based tools throughout all departments obviously create favorable circumstances, especially if the staff has developed habits of locally entering into the systems of all reports, patient file data and test results. Users should have no reluctance in consulting on-line reference material at their disposal and in using workflow tools and electronic mail.

The fact that doctors and senior managers may already have some familiarity with modern datamining or ERP software will help the successful adoption of a computer-based Risk Management System.

But these only are desirable prerequisites. The true key success factor is a culture in the workplace which favors multidisciplinary collaborative work.

On the other hand, one may expect irrational, but very real hesitations in adopting a computer-based Risk Management System if some departments – or some organization levels – have only to be partially exposed to computer-based tools or to weakly interactive systems.

Difficulties may also be expected, in some cases, because of the conservative stance of some doctors or of some department heads who are not prone to give a significant role to cooperative work among departments or professions.

Because of this possibility of structural sluggishness and of reluctance at some key points within the organization, the strategy which is most likely to succeed is to implement and enforce computer-based tools progressively, starting with those departments which are ready to accept without fuss to use them. One can reasonably expect that both the example and the visible subsequent benefits will persuade less enthusiastic actors to finally enroll into the new system.

Step-by-step process

The proposed strategy should follow the following steps:

Clearly state the key role of incident reporting

The link should be made with policies of quality improvement at large, with safety and security policies and even with sheer well-being in the workplace Emphasis should be brought on the senior management's commitment to Risk Management, while explaining what is at stake, what are the new rules of the road and also what kind of external driving factors may exist : the evolution of professional best practices, what other comparable institutions are doing and how official regulations evolve.

Involve every professional

In order to incorporate previous individual experience and to take into account any special circumstances, professionals should be encouraged to comment on the proposed procedures and on the forms they will use. Incorporating these opinions will ease the adoption of the future system.

Clearly define roles and responsibilities

The fact that individual responsibilities have been established (e.g. for the system as a whole, for improvements, for analyzing results, and so on) and approved by the senior management defuses conflicts and discourages questionable initiatives. It makes clear the operational supervising role the intermediate management should always have had.

Guarantee confidentiality

It is of the utmost importance to guarantee the confidentiality of collected data and to restrict the disclosure of the identity of individuals, whether they are directly involved in an unwelcome incident itself or involved in its reporting.

It may be useful in this context to stress again the fact that the implementation of a Risk Management System originates from a decision of the institution's senior management.

Protecting the confidentiality of data and the identity of individuals does not forbid, however, to use these same case data for the purpose of alerting or teaching.

Clearly state operational rules

From the very beginning, which actions and attitudes are acceptable and which are not should be made clear.

In this circumstance, the senior management should not forget that it is vested with real prerogatives of authority, and in addition that it represents locally the governing bodies of the Public Health System.

This however does not mean that reaching as wide a consensus as possible in these matters is not desirable.

Foster mutual trust

A clear distinction should be made between the factual description of unwelcome incidents and fault investigation.

Everyone must understand that the purpose of the system is to protect both the patients and the staff. It is in no case implemented to replace or assist the senior management and the governing authorities in blaming faulty individuals.

Understanding this is a key component of the "cultural environment" necessary for the system to be successful on the long run.

Encourage the emergence of "places of information sharing"

Holding systematic debriefing meetings when unwelcome incidents are detected is typically an action which falls in this category.

Meetings should be held in a collaborative atmosphere, without any sort of prejudice, particularly about individuals. The main purpose of such meetings is to keep a professional eye on an unwelcome incident, and in severe cases, to control the emotional burden which may be felt by the involved professionals.

Making errors should primarily be viewed as something which can be avoided by a coordinated preventive action.

2.1.6.9. Conclusion

One lesson to be learned from this experience with the French Public Health System is that it is of the utmost importance to start from existing professional practices and to explain the purpose and operation of the system, in relation with the existing concepts and vocabulary of the various departments. This approach should be as sincere as possible.

Forcing the pace is useless and would forbid the much wanted "cultural change" necessary to develop Risk Management successfully within Health Institutions.

A second lesson to be learned is that uncertainties brought in by the human factor cannot be overlooked. This is why right from the start, the forms to be used and the procedures to be followed should be computer-based. When planning for this implementation with the support of an Information System, dependability and ergonomic are highly preferable to any kind of functional sophistication.

Finally, it must be recognized – and told to the widest audience – that risks within the hospital are far from being restricted to advanced surgery and medical practice, such as thoracic and cardiac surgery, or the treatment of HIV patients. Risks – and this includes the most severe possibilities, major accidents or threats to life prognosis – mostly materialize by linking together multiple negative causes, and such causes may be appear in every process step, in every department. To speak seriously of risk control is meaningful only when the staff in its totality has received a proper education in this domain and has effectively adopted the relevant security and safety rules.

2.2. MANAGEMENT OF HOSPITALS

2.2.1. The application of the process-oriented management concept in improving the productivity of hospital operation

2.2.1.1. Introduction

In the times after the hustle and bustle of reengineering and the promises this method of increasing management productivity brought, there is now time for another change in the organisational psyche, described as "horizontal thinking" or "process thinking". Business Process Management (BMP) is not a simple consequence of reengineering – it is rather the realisation of the fact that value for the client is created as a result of the processes realised, which cross the traditional organisational structures. This report is an indication of the place the Process Management can take in medical organisations and also, whether there is at all a place for a business-like way of thinking in them. The research conducted shows, that medical organisations identify themselves with service and production companies to a greater and greater extent, drawing new experiences from them, applying the same tools of management productivity improvement. The rapid growth of the interest in quality management systems in hospitals has additionally caused a change in perceiving the patient as a client. Not only the productivity of the therapeutic process, but also the quality and patient's satisfaction have started to play an important role in diagnostic and therapeutic processes.

From the point of view of management, also the treatment process itself has undergone significant changes. So far, the role of the hospital manager was to organise the human and material resources properly, in order to enable the medical professionals to fulfil their obligations towards the patients. Today the healthcare managers are faced with totally new tasks, such as proper process management, organising cooperation with medical entities in order to optimise own costs, increase the productivity of treatment and also of management.

In order to reach these aims, the experience of process management, which was already applied and checked in industrial and service companies, is used more and more often.

2.2.1.2. CHARACTERISTICS OF THE PROCESS APPROACH

It is possible to risk a statement that the first dimension of process approach in management is the understanding of what elements of an organisation and its component acitivities influance one another and, thanks to that, of how they form a comprehensive management system. In the first half of the 1990s, process management used to be presented as a revolutionary organisational innovation,[224] allowing to view a company in a cross-cutting (transverse) manner. It was initially associated with quality management and flow management, however, with time, it proved that process management is directly connected with the process of responding to market needs. The fact that it is the process management which creates the value in the eyes of the clients and owners seems obvious today but it was not noticed until the 1990s.

Many experts dealing with the issue of process management have suggested different definitions of the process. The most important ones include:

– Process is a set of activities within a company, performed in order to provide the client with a certain service or product (Hammer and Champy),

– Process is a specific organisation of activities in time and space, with well-defined data and results, and with a clearly-defined input and output (Davenport),

– Process is a purposeful chain (sequence) of events happening one after another and constituting stadia, phases and stages of development or transformations (Encyklopedia Powszechna PWN).

All of the above definitions indicate that a process is understood as a sequence of activities conducted with the aim to transform the input state into the output state, with simultaneous application of necessary resources and with the aim to satisfy the expectations of the client.

---

[224] M. Hammer, J. Champy (2001), *Reengineering the Corporation: A Manifesto for Business Revolution*, HarperCollins Publishers, New York, p. 216.

It should be noted that according to process approach, the satisfaction of client's needs is necessary, so, concentrating on the area of quality management, it requires also activities which lead to recognition of those needs, which makes it necessary to introduce process approach together with integrated quality management systems or as a result of activities resulting from such implementations.

Organisational processes should be analysed, assessed and improved first of all with respect to values they bring for the clients. It is obvious in organisations whose target are external clients, however, a special approach is required in the case of organisations which concentrate on internal clients. Taking into consideration mutual relations and influence of processes, as well as the expectations of internal clients, which may often be contradictory, we should view an organisation as a whole. Distinguishing different processes does not mean that shall be realised in isolation from the rest.

We are, therefore, speaking of a process approach characterised by the following factors:[225]

– there is a requirement to define the connections among all the processes and their mutual influence,

– there is a necessity to translate organisational aims into the aims of specific processes,

– the main emphasis is put on processes which are the most important ones for an organisation with respect to added value.

An advantage of the process approach is above all the current supervision over connections between specific processes in the system of processes, as well as supervision over their arrangement and mutual influence. In order to supervise the processes and introduce activities enhancing their productivity and efficiency, it is necessary to identify them precisely. Then, by means of statistical, verifying and cognitive methods, it is possible to indicate the weak points of a process or elements that require instant implementation into the process. Process approach makes it possible to fully understand an organisation, it shows all the correlations within it, and thanks to supervision, it shows critical points, which influence the final product, client satisfaction and financial performance of the organisation.

2.2.1.3. PROCESS MANAGEMENT IN A HOSPITAL

It seems easy to transfer the process approach into the realm of medical organisations becasue on the one hand (which has been already mentioned before), hospitals are more and more eager to use industrial and service organisations experiences, and on the other hand, they have an exceptionally developed orientation for satisfying client needs. A separate issue is how they realise these needs and what is the level of client satisfaction that they obtain; nevertheless, the fact that they have such an orientation is incontrovertible.

---

[225] P. Grudowski (2004), *Metodyka zarządzania procesami w małych firmach. Wdrażanie, nadzorowanie i doskonalenie procesów*, "Problemy Jakości", No. 36, May, p. 33–36.

The empirical research conducted in hospitals on the area of Lower Silesian Province within the research entitled "Reorganisation of cost accouting for the needs of hospital management"[226] has shown that process management is not applied there at all or the applied elements of process management do not reflect the real structure of providing health services. It can be stated that the identification of processes as an activity imposed by quality management or some finance management models is conducted improperly and they cannot be fully applied for management purposes. Typical examples of mistakes made by managers include:

– division of processes into operational and support ones, without prior identification of all processes realised within a hospital, as a result of which only some processes are described,

– no indication of sites where the processes are to be realised or only partial indication (e.g. admitting a patient in the admission room, with a total omission of the emergency ward),

– omission of out-patient processes, realised in outpatient hospital clinics,

– omission of key processes required for the functioning of a hospital (e.g. performing surgeries, conservative treatment in different conditions) with simultaneous multiple indication of processes which are support ones from the point of view of an organisation (eg. supervision over the infrastructure, supervision over the equipment),

– creating process maps based on subjective perception of an organisation,

– not including within the medical processes maps such processes as laboratory and imaging diagnostics, preventive care, dietetics, hotel services,

– not taking into consideration the variety of processes and of the necessity to modify according to different health conditions of patients (the so-called trajectory of treatment process[227]).

These observations are even more surprising if we take into account the fact that the proper identification of processes is key in introducing innovations within the area of management accounting, quality management and controlling. It is impossible to create maps of processes, to develop a transversal structure of management without an introductory and proper identification of processes occurring within a hospital.

The attempts of introducing a process approach in French hospitals resulted in a collision of the following areas: the variety of processes realized by a health care facility, methods of treatment of patients and changeability of each type of treatment.[228] These observations are identical to the problems present in Polish hospitals, however one can notice a difference in approaching the issue – the French managers attempt to implement the managing of processes in their hospitals. It is extremely difficult to

---

[226] The project of "Reorganisation of cost accouting for the needs of hospital management" is conducted by the Jagiellonian University in Cracow on the basis of a contract with the Polish Ministry of Science and Higher Education.

[227] J. Stępniewski (2009), *Funkcja produkcji usług w szpitalu*, Materiały konferencyjne, "Komunikacja i jakość w zarządzaniu", Uniwersytet Jagielloński, Kraków 6–7.11.2009.

[228] J. Kimberly, E. Minvielle (2001), *The Quality Imperative. Measurment and Management of Quality in Healthcare*, Imperal College Press, London, p. 36.

isolate all the activities that are a part of the diagnostic-therapeutic process, but this does not mean that the realization of the process approach should be abandoned. Each patient goes to a hospital with different health problems, with different expectations as to the medical staff. The way of treating patients is determined by specific medical, biological, psychical and physical determinants. It is possible to discern a regularity within these factors as to the fact that patients with a similar health condition decide to use the same medical procedures, human and material resources. If so, then these conditions are sufficient for the process approach to be used also in the area of hospital management. It should also be stated explicitly that the way in which a patient is treated is never a subject of an intervention of administrative employees – it is always created by medical professionals – even though it is described by a process of granting medical care. This remark is essential, since in the course of the discussion on the introduction of process approach in hospitals dissenting voices can be heard which criticize the integration of the 'grey'[229] part of the hospital into a diagnostic-therapeutic process.

It is not difficult to notice that process management is the onset of introducing such innovative solutions like for example: hospital controlling, which, in turn, may be a perfect tool for building of the competitive advantage. The health managers seem to not notice that when the conditions for competition are limited (on the market of health care services), its efficiency may be decisive if we take the future of a given facility into account.

In American hospitals the conception of competence-based competitiveness is getting more and more popular. This kind of competitiveness shows how essential it is to specialize in specific medical procedures.[230] In this case one can talk not only about specialization based on the scale-effect, but rather about a group of factors such as experience, the ability to learn from one's own mistakes, an increased ability to specialize within specific medical activities, a larger number of patients allowing the unit costs to be lower.

The introduction of process management in the medical organization is connected with one more problem of a definitional character. The earlier-defined process is understood by the medical professionals in a completely different way who treat it as a group of activities occurring between physicians and patients.[231] Such an approach eradicates all the processes in which the physicians do not intervene, as well as those taking place during the treatment process and among physicians (consultations). The medicalised definition of a process rules out non-medical processes that accompany the process of granting health care services, that are directly connected to them and according to the classical approach they are an element of a transversal understanding of organization.

---

[229] The 'grey' part are the administrative workers, whereas the 'white' part are the medical professionals, nurses and people who are engaged into granting medical services (e.g. diagnosticians, therapists).

[230] M.E. Porter, E. Olmsted Teisberg (2006), *Redefining Health Care – Creating Value-Based Competition on Results*, Harvard Businnes School Press, Boston, p. 122.

[231] A. Donabedian (1980), *The Definition of Quality and Approaches to Its Management*, Health Administration Press, Chicago, p. 54.

The fact that professionals rarely draw from their experience of organization management, and treat their work very seriously, may be an explanation of this problem. According to many of these professionals, it is their work that is the essential part of the hospital's existence and one could say that all the other areas (i.e. organization management, process management) are not as significant to have any extraordinary values ascribed to them. Luckily since the birth of process management, that is the second half of the1990's, a lot has changed in the medical organizations and the process management has been slowly starting to fit in not only within the management area, but also in the process of granting of medical services.

2.2.1.4. UNDERSTANDING OF THE PROCESS MANAGEMENT

Traditional organizational structures that are used in the majority of organizations reflect only the functions of individual persons in a given organization. Processes that are realised in such an organization are much different from functions and activities connected with the structural organizations, because the majority of processes are not realised in one unit, and sometimes not even in one organizational section. These processes are characterised by the fact that they intersect the organizational borders and are especially susceptible to the so-called ,narrow throats' among different organizational units. Here one can find delays, a poor flow of information or a disfunctional organization. It is also worth mentioning that the labour-saving actions and decisions made up by individual units may lead to the worsening of the entire process if one does not realise what may result from the further course of processes.

An additional burden of the process management is the fact that are oriented onto this management model one can constantly observe an increase of hierarchical structures, which significantly contradicts the definition of the process. It seems that the organization which introduces the process management should be concerned not with creating new levels of management, but with creating new transversal and lateral structures that would allow it to properly identify the actions within individual processes, reduce irrelevant actions and simultaneously diagnose the customers' needs, as well as being responsible for those needs. This structure should be as flattened as possible – unfortunately the reality shows that it is not.

It is worth paying attention to the fact that the process-owner plays an important role here. It is such a person who is responsible for the effect of the entire process and has appropriate qualifications and competence to coordinate its realisation. This person also has appropriate knowledge on the process and is able to identify its course and can introduce proper changes.

The fact that numerous modern conceptions make use of (at least in fragments, if not entirely) the ideas of process management shows how effective and essential a conecption it is. Many common elements can be found in such conceptions as Business Process Reengineering, Lean Management, and also Total Quality Management.

The most important common features of these conceptions (in accordance with the model of process management) are:[232]

– analysis of the processes connected with satisfying customers' needs and their systematical upgrading with the simultaneous creation of values for the customer,

– the need for team-work aiming at the betterment of processes, their introduction and schoolings,

– constant improvement, learning new skills and experience exchange,

– flattening of hierarchical structures, decentralisation of decisions, changing of the organisational culture and the system of values,

– constant surveillance of the flow of processes and introduction of corrections in order to increase the effectiveness and their functioning.

The above-shown features of the process management are not the only ones that can be identified in the presented conceptions, however a synthetic presentation of these areas proves the significance of the methods of the process management.

2.2.1.5. CONCLUSION

The process management is a relatively new approach toward organising and it is not to be found everywhere yet. Taking into consideration the fact that in recent years the health care sector in Poland has been ignoring almost every organisational innovation without having decided to introduce almost any new management model, one should say that the development of the conception of managing of the process in hospitals is of significant importance from the point of view of both, effectiveness of management and the patients' treatment.

The studies show that hospitals have never had and will never have an enthusiastic approach towards new management conceptions, because medical professionals do not think that any changes in this area are necessary. They expect increased effectiveness from managers which would translate into higher remuneration and more satisfaction from their work, however without knowing what the tools should be to introduce the change, they often are very suspicious of any change. Process management is this tool that also in the health care sector would allow to change the very essence of the organisation functioning reducing the hierarchy to the level of processes occurring in a hospital.

Polish hospitals there is to this day a structure of departments, clinics and wards, which makes the administration, technical support grow, the processes double and the effectiveness constantly decrease, both medical and managerial. Every change aiming at pointing at a process and ascribing its owner, leading a patient through all medical procedures according to his/her health needs and expectations will not only cause the satisfaction grow on the outer and inner clients' side, but most of all it will allow to eliminate the irrelevant actions, the actions that are double, and it will make

---

[232] M. Winiarz (2004), *Zarządzanie procesami i jego rola w dynamicznych koncepcjach zarządzania*, Materiały konferencyjne, I Ogólnopolska Konferencja Kół Naukowych "Nowoczesne koncepcje zarządzania", Świebodzice, 21–22.10.2004, p. 6–7.

the functional structure easier, which will prevent mistakes resulting from the wrong flow of information.

Unfortunately, a limitation of the influence zones of some of the medical professionals, an inner dependence of those zones, and, as a result of the reduction of hierarchical structures also losses of work posts will be a challenge for managers, which will be the side effect of management process. However, it does seem that the goal that can be reached in the course of introducing of the process management in hospital is of bigger importance than the costs of this introduction.

2.2.2. FUNCTIONING OF HOSPITALS AFTER COMMERCIALIZATION

2.2.2.1. INTRODUCTION

Changes in health service are of utmost importance for the society and, because of the Government's plan B regulations which give the possibility of commercialization of public hospitals, they are also essential issues for both practice and theory of public management. When making decisions which initiate potential commercializing undertakings in health service, it is worth referring to the case study of some hospitals that have been functioning as capital associations. One of such examples is „Szpital Powiatowy"Ltd in Golub-Dobrzyn which in 2001 underwent a pioneer transformation from a public hospital into a commercial company managing a nonpublic hospital with 100% share of District Office in Golub-Dobrzyn. The aim of this paper is the description of working process in the "Szpital Powiatowy" Ltd. in Golub-Dobrzyn.

The method of *case study* assumes that if some definite regularities in individual cases appear, they do not constitute accidental occurrences and their thorough and multilevel analysis may complete or replace a thorough statistic material. The method has been used in the sciences of management for a long time although it is neglected in Polish literature on the subject. According to the representatives of the management sciences who are interested in the research methodology, the case study should become the main method of verifying and creating new aspects in this field of knowledge.[233] The value of *case study* is that it allows to present a real situation of a hospital in a descriptive way and explain the relations which are too complicated to be identified with survey research. Also it presents truly the processes of transformation in a hospital, allowing to draw vital conclusions, as it has happened in this case. The data for *case study* may come, among others, from such sources as:[234] records, archival data, interview, direct observation, active observation. The description of the case was created after many meetings and interviews with former managers of the hospital and District Office representatives, also with former and present representatives and administra-

---

[233] K. Lisiecka, A. Kostka-Bochenek (2009), *Case study research jako metoda badań naukowych*, "Przegląd Organizacji", No. 10, p. 25.

[234] R.Y. Yin (2003), *Case Study Research. Design and Methods*, Sage Publications, Thousand Oaks–London–New Dehli, p. 85–97.

tive workers of the company. Archival and current records of the District and company were analyzed. The above mentioned research proceeding has been completed with a context analysis, which concentrated on the norms on widely-understood system of health service in Poland and the changes in it. Also the competitive environment in which the described company worked and works, has been analyzed.

2.2.2.2. CHARACTERISTICS OF TRANSFORMATION PROCESS

The hospital in Golub-Dobrzyn was open in February 1971. The public hospital existed in Golub-Dobrzyn since 1.08.1998[235] after its transformation and it worked as a budget unit subjected to the Voivod of Torun. In January 1999 in accordance with the Act of October 13th, 1998 article 47 – regulations on reforming public administration[236] the duties of the founding body were taken over by Golub-Dobrzyn District. In 2001 The Schedule of Public Hospital Reorganization in Golub-Dobrzyn[237] was amended. It assumed that the hospital workers, District Office, local government and a strategic investor would be the founders of the company. On account of the hospital commercialization plans the necessary administrative and legal actions were taken.[238] The liquidation of the public hospital took place and the hospital, i.e. „Szpital Powiatowy" – as a limited liability company with 100% share of District Office, its founding body in Golub-Dobrzyn came into being in 2001 as the result of the commercialization. „Szpital Powiatowy" Ltd. replaced the public hospital in Golub-Dobrzyn[239] (actually the liquidation finished December 31st, 2006).

Seed capital was 100,000 PLN. The company was registered in National Executive Committee on June 27th, 2001. At the same time the hospital run by the company was recorded as a nonpublic hospital on the decision of Regional Center for Health Service Organization and Economics.[240] On September 1st, 2001 „Szpital Powiatowy" Ltd. started its statutory activity. It was not indebted as District Office had taken a bank loan secured against the assets of the former public hospital to pay off its debts. The bank loan secured against the assets of the former public hospital

---

[235] Public Health Care Center Statute passed in 1999 – Resolution No. VIII/86/99 of Golub--Dobrzyn District Council of November the 3rd, 1999.

[236] Dz. U. No. 133 of 1998, item 872 with subsequent amendments.

[237] *Scheme for Health Protection in Golub-Dobrzyn District. The Schedule of Public Hospital Reorganization in Golub-Dobrzyn, 2001.*

[238] Resolution No. XVIII/151/01 Golub-Dobrzyn District Council of 19th February, 2001 on introducing the process of restructuring of the public hospital in Golub-Dobrzyn. Resolution no XX/168/01 Golub-Dobrzyn District Council of 9th April, 2001 on the liquidation of the public hospital in Golub-Dobrzyn. Resolution No. XX/169/01 Golub-Dobrzyn District Council of 9th April, 2001 on establishing a limited liability company, as a set-up agent for the public hospital in Golub--Dobrzyn. Resolution No. XXIV/199/01 Golub-Dobrzyn District Council of 10th September, 2001 changed Resolution No. XX/169/01 by replacing the word 'public' with the word 'non-public.'

[239] Resolution No. XX/168/01 Golub-Dobrzyn District Council of 9th April, 2001 on the liquidation of the public hospital in Golub-Dobrzyn.

[240] Decision of Regional Centre for Health Service Organisation and Economics of 11.09.2001 (WOOiEZ/III/D/589/2001).

and the fear of poor management leading to a potential property loss made it impossible to hand the property over to the commercialized company. Because of the lack of resources to pay off the public hospital debts, its liquidation was extended until December 31st, 2006.[241] To make the hospital work the company commissioned the public hospital as a subcontractor for the signed neurological center and tool a lease of its equipment until December 31st, 2006, spending 227,426.40 PLN in total. In addition „Szpital Powiatowy" Ltd. had a lease on fixed property: the buildings and land and movables, mainly medical equipment, up to 2008. As it did not possess the fixed property and movables of its own the depreciation was not possible and the investment activity was hindered. The situation increased profits (lack of depreciation) and taxes at the same time, so 'withdrawing' money from the company because of higher taxes. The positive result in the company was not high on account of the way the services were priced in the contract negotiated with NFZ (National Health Fund) for many accounting periods. It was rather growing up because of NFZ payments for 'over-realization' at the end of the year, which hindered or even unabled a rational investment activity. As the profit of 2002 was especially high, the owner imposed a lease fee for the buildings, which was supposed to become 'an anti-tax shield.' The money gained that way was to have been re-invested in those buildings, owned by District Office. But District Office finances were not good and it was commonly believed that the situation had been caused by the debts of the public hospital so the re-investment was never realized. As a consequence, instead of creating 'an anti-tax shield', the withdrawing money from the company was redirected to fund the budget of District Office. Until the end of 2009 the company had lost 2 million PLN while the fixed property had not often been renovated since 1971, which resulted in its depreciation and put the further functioning of the hospital under question.

According to the August 27th Act on health services paid from public resources, NFZ does not pay for hospital buildings renovations or medical equipment purchases,[242] which should be done by the founding body (i.e. the owner) , District Office in case of „Szpital Powiatowy" Ltd. in Golub-Dobrzyn. Such regulations on health service financing obviously did not encourage 'investments' because District Office was not engaged in funding its own property, having rented it to the company. And the company did not have the money for investment as its services were paid by NFZ. NFZ is of the opinion that if a nonpublic hospital sings a contract on 24-hour medical service it cannot undertake commercial activities.[243] It cannot provide commercial medical service in the same range as defined in the contract with NFZ. It would be against the rights of servicees to the health service funded with public money.[244] Both the contract with NFZ and the hospital's scope of operation

---

[241] Resolution No. XX/48/03 Golub-Dobrzyn District Council of 30th October, 2003 on the change of the resolution on the liquidation of the public hospital in Golub-Dobrzyn.

[242] Dz. U. No. 210 of 2004, item 2135, art. 117.

[243] D. Sikorska (2009), *Kontrakt z NFZ nie pozwala szpitalom na odpłatne zabiegi*, "Gazeta Prawna" 16 czerwca.

[244] Z. Kubot (2009), *Komercyjne usługi medyczne szpitali*, Wydawnictwo Specjalistyczne Kramer, Wrocław, p. 27.

was impossible to be changed without investment, practically made it unable to provide commercial services and benefit from those. The company without a fixed property could not apply for a bank loan not presenting a pricey guarantees whereas the owner disagreed on issuing a guarantee, because of the existing accounting regulations (actually a guarantee meant freezing the resources) and a bad financial condition.

On June 30th 2008 due to the owner's commercialization concept, the following items were contributed to the company: the fixed property – 12,348 m² of land and 5,618 m² of buildings (the main building, a porter's lodge with garages, the hospital storehouse, the storehouse of flammable materials, the oxygen plant, greenhouse), worth 7,170,000.00 PLN and the movables, estimated at 1,221,500.00 PLN.[245] After that contribution the company held a lease on the land of 4,112 m² and the buildings of 2,005 m² (the building of Pneumonopathy and Tuberculosis Ward, 8-box garage, administration and hotel building, the dissection theater, opthalmologic clinic, a garage).[246] In July 2008 the decision to market „Szpital Powiatowy" Ltd.'s shares was made.[247] Finally, the privatization was not carried out because of an unsatisfactory sale price.

The subjects interested in buying indicated the over-valued property of the company. When the privatization was not carried out at the end of February and the beginning of March 2009, the Board of Trustees decided to change the Board of the company in relation to the concept change on functioning and developing of the hospital. The new Chairperson was responsible for working out the scheme.

The Ministry of Health Regulation (November 10th, 2006) on the medical and sanitary requirements concerning the health center's rooms and equipment, makes it obligatory to improve the conditions in all hospitals until 2012. Therefore a special Adjustment Programme for „Szpital Powiatowy" Ltd. in Golub-Dobrzyn was prepared in 2008 and then it was supplemented with a project of windows change, central heating installation change, fire-fighting installation improvements, renovations and equipment purchase for total 6,341,341.81 PLN to take place from 2009 to 2012. The investments will be realized thanks to the assets from the Regional Operational Programme of Kujawsko-Pomorski Voivodship (65%) and the company's own assets (35%) on the basis of the project no RPKP.030200-04-023/08, titled „The purchase of medical equipment and adjustment of the hospital buildings for using it and meeting the standards defined by the mandatory legal regulations." In 2008 an application was

---

[245] Notary Deed, Notary's Office in Golub-Dobrzyn, Rynek 28, Paweł Flis a notary, Repetytorium A No. 2345/2008.

[246] Resolution No. XX/119/08 Golub-Dobrzyn District Council of 28th April, 2008 on approval of proprietorship of the premises contributed to the company „Szpital Powiatowy" Ltd. in Golub-Dobrzyn. Resolution No. XXI/124/08 Golub-Dobrzyn District Council of 26th May, 2008 on approval of proprietorship of the movables contributed to the company „Szpital Powiatowy" Ltd. in Golub-Dobrzyn.

[247] Resolution No. XX/121/08 Golub-Dobrzyn District Council of 26th May, 2008 on establishing the regulations on commercialization of the company „Szpital Powiatowy" Ltd. in Golub-Dobrzyn by divesting of the company. Resolution no 63/85/08 Golub-Dobrzyn District Council of 4th July, 2008 on appointing the Board for Negotiation on divesting of „Szpital Powiatowy" Ltd. in Golub-Dobrzyn.

filed but it was only in 2009 when the inventorying, renovation planning, tendering and securing the assets as the company's contribution, were executed by the new Board.

2.2.2.3. EMPLOYMENT IN 2001–2009 AS THE MAIN COST-INCURRING FACTOR

Before commercialization the public hospital in Golub-Dobrzyn underwent restructuring based on „Restructuring Schedule for 1999–2000". It included the restructuring of employment, housing and service providing conditions, also the restructuring of work management and the range of service offered. The employment in all hospital was reduced from 599 jobs in 1997 to 297 jobs and 45 contracts on January 1st, 2001. The overtime and extra jobs were cut in most departments of the hospital. The work-time control and permanent employment, civil law contracts, also as subcontracts, were introduced. The minimum norms for employing middle medical staff in shift work system were decided. Cleaning teams were created on the basis of currently employed cleaners and hospital attendants. The human resources policy was oriented towards the expanding to the range of services and more efficient use of current resources. Despite the previous restructuring of employment, the further process of restructuring continued along with commercialization. It resulted in reducing it from 275 permanent contracts, 45 civil-law contracts, 4 free-for-task agreements to 229, 41 and 6 respectively. The changes in employment in „Szpital Powiatowy" Ltd. in Golub-Dobrzyn are presented in Table 13.

Since the commercialization in 2001 the employment in „Szpital Powiatowy" Ltd. in Golub-Dobrzyn increased systematically reaching: 249 permanent contracts, 52 civil-law contracts and 7 free-for-task agreements in 2003. It was reduced in 2004 but from 2005 to 2009 it was growing again regularly. The fact, along with the increase in other expenses of the company, determined all activities concerning the concept of employment rationalizing, which has been drawing to an end. Table 14 shows the share of the work costs, the amortization, the costs in total and the work costs constitution of standard costs reduced by the amortization in „Szpital Powiatowy" Ltd. in Golub-Dobrzyn in 2001–2009.

Table 13. The changes in employment in „Szpital Powiatowy" Ltd. in Golub--Dobrzyn in 2001–2009

Year	Employment contracts	Civil-law contracts	Free-for-task agreements
31.08.2001	275 workers	45	4
01.09.2001	229 workers/ 226 jobs	41	6
2002	246 workers/ 239.19 jobs	46	7
2003	249 workers/ 242.08 jobs	52	7
2004	233 workers/ 227.71 jobs	59	7
2005	235 workers/ 231.52 jobs	59	7
2006	236 workers/ 232.9 jobs	63	10
2007	244 workers/ 241 jobs	67	11

| 2008 | 244 workers/ 239.35 jobs | 69 | 15 |
| 2009 | 247 workers/ 242.95 jobs | 77 | 19 |

Source: Author's analysis based on the documentation of „Szpital Powiatowy" Ltd. in Golub-Dobrzyn.

Table 14. The share of the work costs, the amortization, the costs in total and the work costs constitution of standard costs reduced by the amortization in „Szpital Powiatowy" Ltd. in Golub-Dobrzyn in 2001–2009

Shares	2001	2002	2003	2004	2005	2006	2007	2008	2009
Work costs share in total costs in (%)	61.14	59.32	60.35	59.29	59.30	61.38	65.63	65.63	65.93
Amortization costs share in total costs in (%)	0.00	0.84	1.5	1.91	1.38	1.31	1.16	4.58	5.45
Work costs share in standard costs reduced by amortization in (%)	61.14	59.82	61.28	60.44	60.13	62.20	66.40	68.78	69.73

Source: Author's analysis based on the documentation of „Szpital Powiatowy" Ltd. in Golub-Dobrzyn.

The increase in the share of work costs in total costs and those reduced by amortization became another reason for making a decision on rationalizing the employment system.

2.2.2.4. CHANGES IN ORGANIZATION STRUCTURE IN 2001–2009

In 2001–2009 the changes in the organizational structure of „Szpitala Powiatowego Ltd. w Golub-Dobrzyn[248] were made gradually:
– 31.12.2001 closing the Dental Ward and Electrocardiography Room,
– 01.01.2002 establishing the Cardiology Ward, the Emergency Room (OIOM in Polish) and Rehabilitation Ward,
– 01.01.2004 setting up the Emergency Rescue Team in Kowalewo-Pomorskie, the Allergy and the DDH (Developmental Dysplasia of the Hip) Clinics;
– 05.08.2005 establishing a department responsible for ISO, introducing quality management system,
– 01.01.2008 opening the Urology and Oncology Clinics, also establishing the Pain Management (Algiatry) Clinic.

---

[248] The author's analysis based on the documentation of the company.

In relation to the new concept of the hospital's activity and development, the schedule of changes in organization structure of the company was prepared in 2009. It started with the introduction of new regulations on public procurement. Next, the hospital began preparing for the ISO audit, which was successful and „Szpital Powiatowy" Ltd. in Golub-Dobrzyn received ISO 9001:2008 certificate of hospital treatment, emergency medicine, out-patient specialist counseling, physiotherapy, visual diagnostics, analytical and bacterial laboratories. The instructions concerning office work and company's papers repository management were introduced. Also the new organizational regulations were developed and the employment by-law was modified. To ensure security a position of a crisis and sensitive information protection manager was established and appropriate procedures were adopted. A commercial lawyer was employed to make the Board's activity more professional. Bearing in mind patients safety, the epidemiology department was reinforced by placing it in the sector of the treatment vice-director's powers (the company's Chairperson and NZOZ Manager at the same time has higher economic education). The employee who had administered the network was asked to develop full-scale computerizing of the hospital. The finance-accounting department was restructured into the sector of the vice-director for finance and projects department. A newly-established sales and marketing department was placed in the sector of General Director's authority. Having analyzed the market, a daily Center POZ with a affiliate department was established to provide thorough medical care to patients, combining the departments and the nurse attendance (a head nurse's post was reduced). Thanks to that the hospital, as the only one in the Golub-Dobrzyn District, would have a 24-hour (i.e. daily, nightly and open on free days) POZ department, which would increase the offer of medical service to patients, letting win patients' loyalty. In the future a pharmacy is going to be open. Also after signing the contract with an out-supplier, a CAT scan was installed on the premises of the hospital which reduced the frequency of taking the patients to other hospitals. After appropriate analyses the hospital kitchen remained and its modernizing was planned, also to be used commercially.

2.2.2.5. FINANCES IN 2001–2009

Within 2001–2009 each financial year the company had a positive financial net balance. There was a big fluctuation in the amount of profit, especially in the early years of the company's activity. Its first year brought 5,673.85 PLN net profit. The sales profitability (counted as the net profit related to sales net income) was only 0.17%. However, the fact that the hospital balanced after the years of loss generated by the public hospital ZOZ proved the process of restructuring efficient. The company's second year closed with nearly 200,000 PLN net profit and the gross financial result at 294,000 PLN net (the income tax rate was 28% then).The profitability of sales was 1.73% at that time. In the following years – until 2005 the net financial result did not outgrow the values achieved in 2002 only because of being financed by Kasa Chorych (the future NFZ) to a lower degree. 2003 was the most difficult year in the company's history, as the income from Kasa Chorych fell by 5.83% in comparison with 2002. The costs were cut significantly, including personnel, which allowed to avoid the financial loss (the net profit was only 1,539.79 PLN). Between 2006 and 2009 the income was rising gradually again. In 2008 a shareholder contributed a part of the previously rented premises to the company (including the main building of the hospital). The value of the contribution was 8,391,500.00 PLN. The financial balance in 2008 was determined by the NFZ payments for over-the-limit services and the possibility of amortization deduction after the contribution. In 2009 the company's financial result was positive again despite the lack of NFZ over-the-limit services payments.

2.2.2.6. CONCLUSIONS

There were many inconveniences to the hospital after the commercialization, influencing its finances and investments. The hospital functioning in that way is regarded as a Corporate Income Tax bearer. Corporate Income Tax Act[249] introduced remission for the income of those payers whose activity is connected with health care (art. 17.1 par. 4), but it did not apply to companies (art. 17 par.1c point 1). The hospital as a limited liability company did not receive any help in clearing of debts. The Act on public support and restructuring of public health care centers went into effect in 2005.[250] It concerned the financial restructuring of public hospitals ZOZ, including: public obligations, bond by bill, individual claims of employees on the basis of art.4a of the Act on the negotiating system of payments rise, which appeared from January the 1st, 1999 to December the 31st, 2004. It allowed to apply for an appropriation-in-aid to support the employment restructuring, changes in organizational structure of the hospital and other activities to improve both its economic situation and the quality of services (art. 40 par. 1). The Act mentioned above was for public health care centers only. In 2006 the company applied for a grant from PFRON to support the project in 'Scheme For Reconciling Differences Among Regions' – part A included providing equipment for rehabilitating the disabled. Unfortunately the application was rejected by National Disabled Persons Rehabilitation Fund (PFRON) in Kujawsko-Pomorski District in Torun because it could not be granted to non-public health care centers. It is more difficult for „Szpital Powiatowy" Ltd. in Golub-Dobrzyn to receive any EU financial support because non-public centers' input in the European projects is paid by their own means (the need to get a credit) while public centers receive the means from the local government budget. „Szpital Powiatowy" Ltd. in Golub-Dobrzyn was not competitive for medical staff as far as the prices were concerned in the analyzed period of time. The payments were lower than in other companies at that time. The competitors in the medical market acted as public hospitals and offered higher salaries, running up debts. It resulted in losing medical staff by „Szpital Powiatowy" Ltd. in Golub-Dobrzyn. There were not enough employees and lower efficiency. It was not until 2009 along with the 'Plan B' when the local District had the opportunity to

---

[249] Dz. U. No. 54 of 1991, item 654 with subsequent amendments.
[250] Dz. U. No. 78 of 2005, item 684.

apply for a refund of some of the liabilities it had taken. In case of the Local District in Golub-Dobrzyn it is about 2 ml zl. The shareholder is going to use the means for the modernization of the buildings rented to „Szpital Powiatowy" Ltd. in Golub-
-Dobrzyn for medical purpose.

BIBLIOGRAPHY

1. Ahern M. (1993), *The softness of medical production and implications for specifying hospital outputs*, "Journal of Economic Behavior and Organization", Vol. 20.
2. Alter N. (1995), *Peut-on programmer l'innovation ?*, « Revue Française de Gestion », Mars–Mai.
3. Anatole-Touzet V., Souffir W. (1996), *Innovation technologique, organisation du travail et gestion des compétences*, « Gestions Hospitalières », Mars, No. 354.
4. Anderson N.R., Hardy G., West M.A. (1990), *Innovative teams at work*, "Personnel Management", September.
5. Anderson N.R., West M.A. (1998), *Measuring climate for work group innovation: development and validation of the team climate inventory*, "Journal of Organizational Behavior", Vol. 19.
6. Arbuz G., Debrosse D. (1996), *Réussir le changement de l'hôpital*, « InterEditions ».
7. Argoud D. (2000), *Politique d'hébergement et innovation : les petites unités de vie pour personnes âgées*, « Revue Française des Affaires Sociales », No. 1, Janvier–Mars.
8. Bachimont J. (1998), *Les « soins hospitaliers à domicile » entre démédicalisation hospitalière et médicalisation du domicile*.
9. Banks A. (2007), *Innovations in postoperative pain management: continuous infusion of local anesthetics*, "Association of periOperative Registered Nurses Journal" (AORN Journal), Vol. 85 (5).
10. Barcet A., Bonamy J., Grosjean M. (2002), *Une innovation de service par la mise en réseau de services : réflexion sur une expérience dans les services de santé, 12ème conférence internationale du RESER*, Manchester, CRIC et PREST, 26–27 Septembre.
11. Barreau J. (2002), *Les services publics français et l'innovation sociale* [in:] Djellal F., Gallouj F. (eds).
12. Bellemou A., Fraigneau A. (1987), *La communication comme outil de management à l'hôpital*, « Gestions Hospitalières », No. 261–262, Décembre 1986–
-Janvier 1987.
13. Benedicto M. (1987), *Le temps choisi à l'hôpital de Béziers*, « Gestions Hospitalières », No. 261–262, Décembre 1986–Janvier 1987.
14. Biffl W.L., Spain D.A., Reitsma A.M., Minter R.M., Upperman J., Wilson M., Adams R., Goldman E.B., Angelos P., Krummel T., Greenfield L.J. (2008), *Responsible Development and Application of Surgical Innovations: A Position Statement of the Society of University Surgeons*, "Journal of the American College of Surgeons", Vol. 206 (6).

15. Binst M. (1990), *Du mandarin au manager hospitalier*, L'Harmattan.
16. Biswas R., Joshi A., Joshi R., Kaufman T., Peterson C., Sturmberg J.P., Maitra A., Martin C.M. (2009), *Revitalizing primary health care and family medicine/primary care in India – disruptive innovation?*, "Journal of Evaluation in Clinical Practice", Vol. 15.
17. Blank J.L., Van Hulst B.L. (2009), *Productive innovations in hospitals: an empirical research on the relation between technology and productivity in the Dutch hospital industry*, "Health Economics", Vol. 18 (6).
18. Bluestone B., Harrison B. (1986), *The Great American Job Machine*, Report for the Joint Economic Committee, Décembre.
19. Bonafini P. (2002), *Réseaux de soins : réforme ou révolution*, « Politiques et Management Public », Vol. 20, No. 2, Juin.
20. Bonnici B. (1998), *L'hôpital : enjeux politiques et réalités économiques*, Notes et études documentaires, No. 5079, 15 Octobre, La Documentation Française.
21. Bressand A., Nicolaïdis K. (1987), *Les services au cœur de l'économie relationnelle*, « Revue d'Economie Industrielle », No. 43.
22. Bridges J., Fitzgerald L., Meyer J. (2007), *New workforce roles in health care: exploring the longer-term journey of organizational innovations*, "Journal of Health Organization and Management", Vol. 21 (4–5).
23. Brissaud D. (2006), *Mise en place d'un Système d'Information de Gestion des Risques en Etalissement de Santé (SIGR)* – Thèse professionnelle, Mastère spécialisé – École Centrale de Paris.
24. Burke D.E., Menachemi N. (2004), *Opening the black-box: measuring hospital information technology capability*, "Health Care Management Review", Vol. 29 (3).
25. Campbell G.M., Briley T. (2008), *Bundled redesign: transformational reorganization of acute care delivery*, "Critical Care Nursing Clinics of North America", Vol. 20 (4).
26. Cases C., Beaubeau D., Naiditch M. (2001), *Evaluer la capacité d'adaptation aux changements*, « Solidarité-Santé », No. 2, Avril–Juin.
27. Chaban S., Guinet A., Smolski N., Guiraud M., Luquet B., Marcon E., Viale J.-P. (2003), *La gestion industrielle et la gestion des blocs opératoires* « Annales Françaises d'Anesthésie et de Réanimation », No. 22.
28. Chandernagor P., Claveranne J.P., Krichen M. (1996), *Le statut des équipements hospitaliers : stratégie(s) d'acteur(s) et ordre technicien*.
29. Cohen S., Zysman J. (1987), *Manufacturing matters*, Basic Books, New York.
30. Dalmasso R., Romatet J.-J. (eds) (2000), *L'hôpital réformateur de l'hôpital*, Eres.
31. Danjoux N.M., Martin D.K., Lehoux P.N., Harnish J.L., Zlotnik Shaul R., Bernstein M., Urbach D.R. (2007), *Adoption of an innovation to repair aortic aneurysms at a Canadian hospital: a qualitative case study and evaluation*, "BMC Health Services Research", Vol. 7 (182), 15 November; retrieved on March 8, 2010 from: http://www.biomedcentral.com/1472-6963/7/182.
32. Decision of Regional Centre for Health Service Organisation and Economics of 11.09.2001 (WOOiEZ/III/D/589/2001).

33. del Llano J., Martinez-Cantarero J.F., Gol J., Raigada F. (2002), *Análisis cu-alitativo de las innovaciones organizativas en hospitales públicos españoles*, "Gaceta Sanitaria", Vol. 16 (5).

34. Delaeter B. (1991), *La conduite du changement à l'hôpital public : principes dégagés de la démarche stratégique menée au CHRU de Lille*, « Cahiers Lillois d'Economie et de Sociologie », No. 18, 2ème semestre.

35. Dexter F., Macario A. (1996), *Applications of information systems to operating Rom scheduling*, "Anesthesiology", No. 85.

36. Dexter F., Macario A., Traum R.D. (1999), *Which algorithm for scheduling add--on elective maximizes operating room utilization? Use of bin packing algorithms and constraints in operating room management*, "Anesthesiology", No. 91.

37. DHOS Direction de l'Hospitalisation et de l'Organisation des Soins – Ministère de la santé, de la famille et des personnes handicapées *Recommandations pour l'élaboration et la mise en oeuvre d'un programme de gestion des risques dans les établissements de santé* – Paris 2003.

38. Djellal F., Gallouj C., Gallouj F., Gallouj K. (2004), *L'hôpital innovateur. De l'innovation médicale a l'innovation de service*, Masson.

39. Djellal F., Gallouj C. (2007), *Introduction à l'économie des services*, PUG.

40. Djellal F., Gallouj F. (2005), *Mapping innovation dynamics in hospitals*, "Research Policy", Vol. 34.

41. do Carmo Caccia-Bava M., Guimaraes V.C.K., Guimaraes T. (2009), *Testing some major determinants for hospital innovation success*, "International Journal of Health Care Quality Assurance", Vol. 22 (5).

42. Donabedian A. (1980), *The Definition of Quality and Approaches to Its Management*, Health Administration Press, Chicago.

43. DREES (Direction de la REcherche des Études de l'Evaluation et des Statistiques) Enquête ENEIS Enquête Nationale sur les Evénements Indésirables liés aux soins en établissements de santé – Paris 2005.

44. Duriez M. (1998), *Le role de la concurrence dans la conduite des systemes de sante en Europe*, Hospitalisation Nouvelle, UHP, No. 254.

45. Dz. U. No. 54 of 1991, item 654 with subsequent amendments.

46. Dz. U. No. 78 of 2005, item 684.

47. Dz. U. No. 133 of 1998, item 872 with subsequent amendments.

48. Dz. U. No. 210 of 2004, item 2135, art. 117.

49. England I., Stewart D., Walker S. (2000), *Information technology adoption in health care: when organisations and technology collide*, "Australian Health Review", Vol. 23 (3).

50. Gallouj C. (1994) *Le prix de l'innovation hospitaliere*, « Gestions Hospitalières », No. 334.

51. Garcia-Goñi M. (2006), *Diferencias y similitudes antre los procesos de adopción de innovaciones tecnológicas y organizacionales en los hospitals*, "Gaceta Sanitaria", Vol. 20, Suppl. 2.

52. GMSIH Groupement pour la Modernisation du Système d'Information Hospitalier *L'identitovigilance* – Paris 2003.

53. Greenhalgh T., Robert G., Bate P., Kyriakidou O., Peacock R. (2004), *How to Spread Good Ideas: A Systematic Review of the Literature of Diffusion, Dissemination and Sustainability of Innovations in Health Service Delivery and Organization*, NCCSDO, London.
54. Greenhalgh T., Stramer K., Bratan T., Byrne E., Mohammad Y., Russell J. (2008), *Introduction of shared electronic records: multi-site case study using diffusion of innovation theory*, "British Journal of Medicine" (Clinical research Ed.), Vol. 337.
55. Griffin-Cohen M. (2001), *Do Comparisons Between Hospital Support Workers and Hospitality Workers Make Sense? Report for Hospital Employee's Union*, Canada, October.
56. Groenewegen P.P., Hutten J.B. (1989), *Improving primary health care through technological innovation*, "Health Policy", Vol. 13 (3).
57. Grudowski P. (2004), *Metodyka zarządzania procesami w małych firmach. Wdrażanie, nadzorowanie i doskonalenie procesów*, "Problemy Jakości", No. 36, May.
58. Grutters J.P.C., Joore M.A., van der Horst F., Stokroos R.J., Anteunis L.J.C. (2008), *Decision-Analytic Modeling to Assist Decision Making in Organizational Innovation: The Case of Shared Care in Hearing Aid Provision*, "Health Services Research", October, Vol. 43 (5), Part I.
59. Guinet A., Legrand M. (1998), *Reduction of job-shop problems to flow-shop problems with precedence constraints*, "European Journal Operational Research", No. 86.
60. Hammer M., Champy J. (2001), *Reengineering the Corporation: A Manifesto for Business Revolution*, HarperCollins Publishers, New York.
61. Harrison M.I., Kimani J. (2009), *Building capacity for a transformation initiative: system redesign at Denver Health*, "Health Care Management Review", Vol. 34 (1).
62. Hebert M.A. (1998), *Impact of IT on health care professionals: changes in work and the productivity paradox*, "Health Service Management Review", Vol. 11 (2).
63. Huang S.Y., Huang W.H., Chia-An, Jiang S.Ch. (2010), *Critical factors of hospital adoption on CRM system: Organizational and information system perspectives*, "Decision Support Systems", Vol. 48, Issue 4.
64. Huby G., Steward J., Tiery A., Rogers W. (2004), *Planning older people's discharge from acute hospital care: linking risk management and patient participation in decision-making, Health*, "Risk & Society", Vol. 6, Issue 2.
65. Husson J. (2009), Hospitals *Looking for Performance: Methodological Outlook for New* Hospital Risk Management, "Gestion 2000", Vol. 26, Issue 5.
66. Jerome-D'Emilia B., Begun J.W. (2005), *Diffusion of breast conserving surgery in medical communities*, "Social Science and Medicine", Vol. 60.
67. Kimberly J., Minvielle E. (2001), *The Quality Imperative. Measurment and Management of Quality in Healthcare*, Imperal College Press, London.
68. King N., Anderson N.R. (1995), *Innovation and Change in Organizations*, Routledge, London.

69. Kinneman M.T., Hitchings K.S., Bryan Y.E., Fox M.A., Young M.J. (1997), *A pragmatic approach to measuring and evaluating hospital restructuring efforts*, "The Journal of Nursing Administration", Vol. 27 (7–8).

70. Kubot Z. (2009), *Komercyjne usługi medyczne szpitali*, Wydawnictwo Specjalistyczne Kramer, Wrocław.

71. Lamarque D. (1984), *L'innovation médicale et les dépenses de santé*, « Gestions Hospitalières ».

72. Lau F., Penn A., Wilson D., Noeworthy T., Vincet D., Doze S. (1998), *The diffusion of an evidence-base disease guidance system for managing stroke*, "International Journal of Medical Informatics", Vol. 51.

73. Le Berre R., Barralon J.L., Lepin J.L., Saby M., Vilain M. (1992), *L'hôpital prestatairede services*, «Revue Hospitalière de France», No. 5, Septembre–October.

74. Lee R.H., Waldman D.M. (1985), *The diffusion of innovations in hospitals. Some econometric considerations*, "Journal of Health Economics", Vol. 4 (4).

75. Lisiecka K., Kostka-Bochenek A. (2009), *Case study research jako metoda badań naukowych*, "Przegląd Organizacji", No. 10.

76. Loriol M. (2002), *L'impossible politique de la santé publique en France*, Eres.

77. Macario A., Vasanawala M. (2002), *Technology and computing in the surgical suite: key features o fan or management information system and opportunities for the future*, "Anesth. Analg.", No. 95.

78. Macario A., Vitez T.S., Dunn B., McDonald T. (1995), *Where are the costs in perioperative care? Analysis of hospital costs and charge for inpatient surgical care*, "Anesthesiology", No. 83.

79. Minvielle E. (1994), *Un changement sur ordonnance*, « Gérer et Comprendre », No. 35.

80. Moisdon J.-C., Tonneau D. (1996), *Concurrence et complémentarité : stratégies de l'hôpital et de sa tutelle* [in:] Contandriopoulos A.P., Souteyrand Y. (eds).

81. Naiditch M., de Pouvourville G. (2000), *Le programme de médicalisation du système d'information (hospitalier) : une expérimentation sociale limitée pour une innovation majeure du management hospitalier*, « Revue Française des Affaires Sociales », No. 1, Janvier–Mars.

82. Naranjo-Gil, D., Hartmann F. (2007), *How CEOs use management information system for strategy implementation in hospital*, "Health Policy", Vol. 81, Issue 1.

83. Newhouse J.P. (1992), *Medical care costs: how much welfare loss?*, "Journal of Economic Perspectives", Vol. 6 (3).

84. Notary Deed, Notary's Office in Golub-Dobrzyn, Rynek 28, Paweł Flis a notary, Repetytorium A No. 2345/2008.

85. Nystrom P.C., Ramamurthy K., Wilson A.L. (2002), *Organizational context, climate and innovativeness: adoption of imaging technology*, "Journal of Engineering and Technology Management", Vol. 19.

86. O'Brien M. (2008), *Leading innovation in a risk-averse healthcare environment*, "Healthcare Financial Management", August, Vol. 62 (8).

87. Omnes L. (1996), *Choc technologique et mutation des organisations*, « Gestions Hospitalières », No. 354.

88. Paré G., Trudel M.C. (2006), *Knowledge barriers to PACS adoption and implementation in hospitals*, "International Journal of Medical Informatics", Vol. 76 (1).
89. Pascal Ch. (2003), *La gestion par processus a l'hôpital entre procédure et création de la valeur,* « Revue Française de Gestion », No. 5/146.
90. Polick T.J. (2000), *Professional Innovations: Lifting Up Lives*, "Journal of the American Psychiatric Nurses Association" (APNA), Vol. 6 (4).
91. Porter M.E., Olmsted Teisberg E. (2006), *Redefining Health Care – Creating Value-Based Competition on Results*, Harvard Businnes School Press, Boston.
92. Public Health Care Center Statute passed in 1999 – Resolution No. VIII/86/99 of Golub-Dobrzyn District Council of November the 3rd, 1999.
93. Ravichandran T. (1999), *Redefining Organizational Innovation: Towards Theoretical Advancements*, "The Journal of High Technology Management Research", Vol. 10 (2).
94. Reason J.T. (1997), *Managing the Risk of Organizational Accidents* – Ashton Publishing – Aldershot (UK).
95. Resolution No. XVIII/151/01 Golub-Dobrzyn District Council of 19th February, 2001 on introducing the process of restructuring of the public hospital in Golub-Dobrzyn. Resolution No. XX/168/01 Golub-Dobrzyn District Council of 9th April, 2001 on the liquidation of the public hospital in Golub-Dobrzyn. Resolution no XX/169/01 Golub-Dobrzyn District Council of 9th April, 2001 on establishing a limited liability company, as a set-up agent for the public hospital in Golub-Dobrzyn. Resolution No. XXIV/199/01 Golub-Dobrzyn District Council of 10th September, 2001 changed Resolution No. XX/169/01 by replacing the word 'public' with the word 'non-public.'
96. Resolution No. XX/48/03 Golub-Dobrzyn District Council of 30th October, 2003 on the change of the resolution on the liquidation of the public hospital in Golub-Dobrzyn.
97. Resolution No. XX/119/08 Golub-Dobrzyn District Council of 28th April, 2008 on approval of proprietorship of the premises contributed to the company „Szpital Powiatowy" Ltd. in Golub-Dobrzyn. Resolution No. XXI/124/08 Golub-Dobrzyn District Council of 26th May, 2008 on approval of proprietorship of the movables contributed to the company „Szpital Powiatowy" Ltd. in Golub-Dobrzyn.
98. Resolution No. XX/121/08 Golub-Dobrzyn District Council of 26th May, 2008 on establishing the regulations on commercialization of the company „Szpital Powiatowy" Ltd. in Golub-Dobrzyn by divesting of the company. Resolution No. 63/85/08 Golub-Dobrzyn District Council of 4th July, 2008 on appointing the Board for Negotiation on divesting of „Szpital Powiatowy" Ltd. in Golub-Dobrzyn.
99. Resolution No. XX/168/01 Golub-Dobrzyn District Council of 9th April, 2001 on the liquidation of the public hospital in Golub-Dobrzyn.
100. Rodriguez I.M. (2009), *Helping hospitals design appropriate risk management programs*, "Caribbean Business", 10/22, Vol. 37, Issue 42.
101. Rogers E.M. (1983), *Diffusion of Innovations*, Free Press, New York.

102. *Scheme for Health Protection in Golub-Dobrzyn District. The Schedule of Public Hospital Reorganization in Golub-Dobrzyn, 2001.*
103. Sikorska D. (2009), *Kontrakt z NFZ nie pozwala szpitalom na odpłatne zabiegi,* "Gazeta Prawna" 16 czerwca.
104. Stępniewski J., *Funkcja produkcji usług w szpitalu,* Materiały konferencyjne, "Komunikacja i jakość w zarządzaniu", Uniwersytet Jagielloński, Kraków 6–7.11.2009.
105. Toner M., Tompkins M.R. (2008), *Invention, Innovation, Entrepreneurship in Academic Medical Centers,* "Surgery", Vol. 143 (2).
106. Volovitch P. (1998), *L'hôpital public en plein chantier,* « Alternatives Economiques », No. 155.
107. Warfel W.J., Mikolaj P.J. (2003), *Hospital Litigation: Risk management Implications,* "CPCU eJournal", Vol. 56, Issue 4.
108. Wejnert B. (2002), *Integrating Models of Diffusion of Innovations: A Conceptual Framework,* "Annual Review of Sociology", Vol. 28.
109. West M.A., Anderson N.R. (1992), *Innovation, cultural values and the management of change in British hospitals,* "Work and Stress", Vol. 6.
110. Winiarz M., *Zarządzanie procesami i jego rola w dynamicznych koncepcjach zarządzania,* Materiały konferencyjne I Ogólnopolskiej Konferencji Kół Naukowych "Nowoczesne koncepcje zarządzania", Świebodzice, 21–22.10.2004.
111. Yin R.Y. (2003), *Case Study Research. Design and Methods,* Sage Publications, Thousand Oaks–London–New Dehli.
112. Young G.Y., Charns M.P., Shortell S. M. (2001), *Top Manager and Network Effects on the Adoption of Innovative Management Practices : a Study of TQM in a Public Hospital System,* "Strategic Management Journal", Vol. 22.

Part III

HUMAN RESOURCE, PATIENTS' RIGHTS AND QUALITY SERVICE OF HOSPITALS

3.1. HUMAN RESOURCE OF HOSPITALS

3.1.1. Perspective of personnel function development in Polish hospitals

3.1.1.1. Introduction

Changing environment of the sector of health care entities brings new challenges for these organizations. Concentrating on material aspects of the issue will not allow them to seize the chances or to measure the risks coming from their surrounding. It is necessary to concentrate on intangible capital management, involving human capital above all. Such challenges are considered as: an ageing society[251] with the increase in health care demand as a consequence, shortage in medical personnel both of senior and middle ranks,[252] or bigger requirements of patients for better current and perceived quality of medical service.

The indicated rationale determine the need for both analysis and diagnosis of the way personnel function is implemented in Polish health care entities because their competitiveness depends on the effective system of human resource management, as it is presented in the literature or results from the observation of health care entities undertakings.[253] In the context of the significance of personnel function implementation, the article aims at indicating the way the personnel function is implemented in the sector of Polish health care entities and showing the possibility of personnel function development.

---

[251] A. Pocztowski (ed.) (2008), *Zarządzanie talentami w organizacji*, Wolters Kluwer Business, Kraków, p. 11–34.

[252] A. Austen, A. Frączkiewicz-Wronka, M. Majowska (2008), *Odpływ profesjonalistów medycznych – postulowane narzędzia jego ograniczenia*, "Zarządzanie Zasobami Ludzkimi", No. 2, p. 13–16.

[253] J. Jończyk (2008), *Diagnoza i ocena wybranych elementów zarządzania zasobami ludzkimi w jednostkach sektora usług medycznych*, "Zarządzanie Zasobami Ludzkimi", No. 2, p. 39.

The data from the research, which was done in independent public and non-public hospitals, have been used to describe the way the personnel function is implemented in those hospitals. In her conclusions, the author of the article concentrated on stating the instructions for improving the implementation of the personnel function in the surveyed organizations.

3.1.1.2. PERSONNEL FUNCTION IMPLEMENTATION IN HEALTH CARE ENTITIES IN POLAND

While presenting the way of the implementation of personnel function in Poland, it is worth considering the data from both public and non-public hospitals. In case of public health care entities, so called independent organizations in health care sector we can observe personnel function implementation at the administration level. With regard to the data analyzed by the author in her PH.D. theses[254] and the contemporary attitude to bearing personnel function, called *human resource management* one may notice several aspects of the situation.

Firstly, treating people as the source of a differential advantage appears only in the management force declarations and not in the truly implemented actions. The hospitals systematically focus on solving operational problems concerning human resources management. There is no strategy for molding human capital. The organizations really rarely take on the challenge to build a personnel strategy, being a coherent configuration of aims, procedures, plans and schemes which would enable to achieve and keep a differential advantage with its source – human capital. The surveyed hospitals focus mainly on material resources, regarding them as the source of potential success although both theoretical and practical health care management show the connection between the quality of medical service and the quality of human resources providing the services.

Secondly, only fragmentary vertical integration between the strategies of the surveyed public entities and the aims in the sphere of personnel management has been noticed. The hospitals have defined their strategic aims of personnel management, even stating them in their statues. However, they have not put them into the partial objectives concerning particular functions of human resources management. What is more, there has been no long-term planning, which should result from the agreed aims of personnel management. The existing 12-months plans (schemes) are built on the basis of current demands. Thus we may assume that vertical integration between the entities' strategies and their personnel strategies is only peripheral. In the surveyed hospitals the horizontal integration among particular functions of personnel management does not exist. Each sub-system of human resources management acts

---

[254] Research was done in independent public healthcare entities, hospitals, whose founding agent in Marshall Office of Malopolskie Voivodship. There were four hospitals altogether. The methods used in the research were as follows: case study, data analysis (hospital documentation), questionnaires with the managing staff, surveys among the employees of the hospitals.

separately not influencing other sub-systems. Functioning of employees' appraisal system that is not combined with any other sub-system may serve as an example. The results of the employees' appraisals are only archived.

Thirdly, in the surveyed hospitals, human capital is rather seen as a cost of the business and not a valuable ingredient of the assets, which should be properly cared for. It is proved by the fact that the hospitals do not have any plans on systematic development of human resources and the development is only a consequence of current needs. Actually, in case of the senior and middle medical personnel, the hospitals do not have a serious influence on the way their personnel improve or acquire their skills. There are no procedures for directing careers or projecting aftermath plans. So the development of competence by medical personnel, especially the senior one, must be regarded as independent of organizational requirements.

Fourthly, managers play their roles as assigned to them in the literature only scantly. The roles are: a contributor of knowledge, behavior, attitude, values and a trainer. Organizational limitations do not allow them to serve the roles of knowledge creators or agents of change. It should be noticed that all final decisions on personnel management are made by the General Directors of the surveyed hospitals. Yet all managers suggest solving any personnel problems, which may not, but usually is accepted by the Directors. For this reason the hospitals are sometimes called 'the head of hospital's state.'

Fifthly, management of organization culture does not exist in any of the hospitals. The lack of transparent personnel policy, coherent systems of personnel management, the loss of motivational function, employees' appraisal or payment system causes that the management staff have insignificant influence on shaping the norms, values or attitudes for the employees. Therefore the hospitals are helpless in coping with the negligent employees, as the results of the research show, relying on the questionnaire presented to the respondents during the empirical stage of the research. It also shows that there is unpleasant atmosphere, many ludicrous conflicts appear and the information, even the important one, is censored. All the activities undertaken in the hospitals only correct the employees' negative attitudes and they do not shape the organizational culture, which would further support the implementation of the strategy planned.

Sixthly, the labor relations in the analyzed entities are not individualized. Majority of employees is employed on the basis of a contract for an indefinite period and is paid according to the standards resulting from the collective wage agreement – Payment Regulations. Only one of the hospitals has introduced contracts for almost all specialist doctors who provide varied medical services (not only duties).

Seventhly, personnel departments in the hospitals are perceived as administrative departments, not strategic partners taking part actively in creating personnel policy which would let the human capital become the source of a differential advantage. Pro-client orientation of the personnel departments is limited to administrative support for other organizational departments. Practically the personnel departments are administrative experts, interests integrators, home counselors on the labor law. The departments in the research do not provide outsourcing service.

All the arguments mentioned above, resulting from the analyses for Ph. D. theses, prove the thesis that the attitude to personnel function in the surveyed hospitals is closer to administrating personnel than human resources management. The synthesized assessment of the approach to implementing personnel function in the analyzed health care entities in shown in Table 15.

To learn about the practice of HR management in non-public health care entities, the author carried out a research project of the Ministry of Science and Higher Education on the implementation of personnel function in non-public health care entities. Diversified set of research instruments were used in the project: literature study, interview questionnaire, analysis of source materials. Because of the wide range of the results of the research, the author focused on the analysis of the data collected from the surveys carried out in 54 non-public units of health care sector (at 17% turn).

Table 15. The synthesized assessment of the approach to implementing personnel function in the analyzed health care entities

Treating people as a differential advantage	**Failed** – declarations of managing staff not implemented in reality
Strategic integration	**Partly fulfilled** – strategic aims of the organization integrated with the strategic aims of personnel management; strategic aims of personnel management not putting them into partial aims; no horizontal integration among the systems in the HR.
Perceiving human capital as a valuable ingredient in the assets that is worth being invested into	**Failed** – perceiving the employees as the employment expenses, absence; HR development based on meeting current demands; development of medical personnel competence independent of the requirements of the organization resulting from the strategy of the organization
Active participating of managers in the process of HR management	**Partly fulfilled** – managers perform only some roles described in the thematic literature; final decisions on personnel are centralized – made by the Directors of the hospitals
Managing the organizational culture	**Failed** – activities correcting specially negative attitudes of employees, not shaping the organizational culture in the way it could support organizational strategy
Individualization of labor relations	**Failed** – collective labor relations; no individual solutions; the hospital in Tarnow offers specialist doctors contracts for the whole range of medical service
Orientation towards the inner and outer clients	**Partly fulfilled** – personnel departments are perceived as administrative support; no strategic orientation in personnel departments activities; no orientation to outer clients

Source: The author's analysis.

In the research it was essential to define whether the analyzed units had management strategy which indicated the strategic aims and methods of their implementing. It turned out that almost half of the analyzed hospitals had the strategy of management either in the form of a formal document or in some informal form. 7 out of 54 units were just working on that strategy and 24 out of 54 did not have such strategy (Picture 4). The companies, which declared the organizational strategy, mentioned among the aims: keeping the contract with National Health Fund, providing high quality medical care, possibilities of a company's development (buildings, equipment, range of activities), opening new departments, taking over other public and non-public hospitals, maintaining the high quality of providing service along with gaining financial profits, offering new services, continual improvement of employees' qualifications (plan of trainings), securing personnel needs for the following year, winning new patients, renewing the accreditation or introducing a new system of quality management, opening new wards, introducing subscription to packages of medical services, providing corporation and individual moderately rich clients with services, building the first multi-specialist hospital in Poland, hospital care development, health insurance sale, local development, providing medical service of high quality thanks to systematic improvement of competence, setting trends and standards in health care as the market leader, maintaining the key position in the medical service market, expanding the chain of health centers and hospitals in Poland, propagating the system of workers' health programs (subscriptions) and health insurance, introducing modern techniques of picture diagnosis, development of tele-medicine.

Picture 4. Business strategy in the units

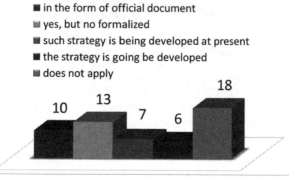

Source: The author's analysis.

In relation to identifying the organizational strategy it was significant to describe whether the analyzed units had the strategy of HR management. After the analyses of data it was decided that only ten hospitals had such strategy in formal or informal form. Seven hospitals were just working on that strategy and further seven hospitals were going to work on that. 30 out of 54 units did not have such strategy (Picture 5).

The organizations which declared the HR management strategy indicated the following aims of personnel function: winning specialists in the fields which would allow to expand the activity, matching personnel to the structure of the company, winning and keeping qualified employees (especially those with II degree of specialization), keeping up a good atmosphere in work which ties the employee with the company, clear and legible system of employees' appraisal, interesting program of trainings for employees, job evaluation, job satisfaction, creating an effective system of measurement task completing, combining the budgeting and the motivational systems, organization and work time optimization within current formal-legal regulations, keeping an employment of the repetitious group of workers, keeping loyalty towards the company by motivational programs, introducing most effective organizational structure of the company, building organizational culture by implementing the system of company's value (promoting proper attitudes and behaviors), cooperation with highly-qualified medical staff, scheme of trainings and development of personnel, building careers, introducing innovative HR instruments adapted to the needs of a large and modern medical company.

Picture 5. The HR management strategy in the units

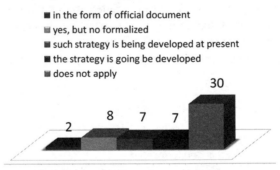

- in the form of official document
- yes, but no formalized
- such strategy is being developed at present
- the strategy is going be developed
- does not apply

Source: The author's analysis.

The main task of the sample survey research was to gain the information on the way human resources management was practically implemented, in other words to find out whether there were procedures for HR management either formal or informal. As the data analysis showed, most units decided on making the adaptation and planning trainings procedures formal – 15 out of 54. 14 out of 54 formalized employees' appraisals. Only 4 out of 54 formalized planning careers. In case of informal procedures workers' adaptation process was the most essential. Next there were the procedures of hiring, selecting and trainings planning. The fewest number of organizations had unwritten procedures for managing employees careers.

To sum up the analysis of the functioning of formal and informal procedures for the HR management it is important to notice (Picture 6).
- majority i.e. 32 out of 54 units had the procedure for hiring employees,
- majority i.e. 32 out of 54 units had the procedure for employees selection,
- straight majority i.e. 44 out of 54 units had the procedure for adaptation,
- majority i.e. 29 out of 54 units had the procedure for employees' appraisal,

– straight majority i.e. 34 out of 54 units planned employees trainings,
– minority i.e. 16Out of 54 planned employees careers,
– straight majority i.e. 28 out of 54 units had fitted payment solutions.

Picture 6. Having or lacking the HR management procedures

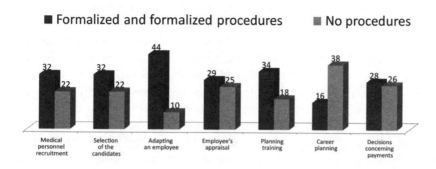

■ Formalized and formalized procedures   ■ No procedures

Source: The author's analysis.

The data concerning the condition of human resources management practice in non-public health care entities show that the level of implementing personnel function in those units was more advanced than in public units. Mainly it results from the fact that there were straight majority of procedures for the HR management in those units. What is more, the analysis of the questionnaires carried out among the managing personnel shows that the issue of HR management was regarded as strategic and the HR department was in the top rank of the organizational hierarchy. In addition the organizational culture was created by an adequate motivational system in those units. In spite of all these positive signs of the development in implementing personnel function in non-public hospitals it must be pointed out, without doubts, that it is still not satisfying. The source of financing medical services and the competence of managing staff should be regarded as the main obstacles for the function. And so, the more dependent upon the public payers the unit is, the less developed the personnel function implementation is. Also if the unit is managed by a person with medical qualifications only, the practice of HR management works worse than in the units which are managed by a professional manager.

3.1.1.3. CONCLUSIONS

Ageing society, outflow of senior and middle personnel, rising competition in the medical service market or bigger requirements of clients (patients) are the main challenges for the public and non-public units of health care sector to be met. Yet the effective management of the health care company in the context of the challenges requires not only effective tangible capital management but also intangible one, such as human capital. It results from both the specific process of providing a medical service and the type of approaching challenges. So:

1. Ageing society means the increase in the demand for medical service and personnel that could cope with it,

2. Shortage in medical personnel means difficulties in keeping and winning medical personnel,

3. Rising competition in the market means the pressure for improving widely understood quality of medical services.

In the context of the challenges and the level of implementing personnel function in the analyzed hospitals, a set of instructions seems to be worth mentioning. They would improve the system of human resources management in the hospitals. Firstly, it is essential to create the strategy for management of health care sector. The strategy should indicate long-term aims concerning the range of the service provided, the group of clients or main financing source (public or non-public means). It should take into account the aims against the HR management, which would allow for integration of activities within the personnel function. Taking it into account in the organization strategy puts the HR management strategy in certain frames and also lets it integrate.

Secondly, along with the strategy for management of organizations in health care sector, the units should concentrate on working out the strategy for the human resources management. But it requires a thorough analysis of personnel function, its environment above all.[255] Within the HR management strategy, understood as a coherent configuration of activities for long-term aims, building rules, plans and programs to create and benefit from human capital of the organization, which guarantees achieving and keeping a differential advantage,[256] it is necessary to create partial strategies. The classification of sub-strategies of HR management most often met in the literature[257] is based on the criterion of function and divides the sub-strategies into:[258]

– sub-strategy of defining the demand for employees,
– sub-strategy of hiring and selecting,
– sub-strategy of motivating,
– sub-strategy of development,
– sub-strategy of reducing employment,
– sub-strategy of appraisal,
– sub-strategy of creating organizational culture.

---

[255] B. Buchelt (2008), *Metodyczne aspekty projektowania strategii personalnej w jednostkach sektora usług medycznych*, "Zarządzanie Zasobami Ludzkimi", No. 2, p. 43–59.

[256] A. Pocztowski (2007), *Zarządzanie zasobami ludzkimi. Strategie – procesy – metody*, PWE, Warszawa 2007, p. 53.

[257] We can read about other personnel sub-strategies in: M. Juchnowicz (ed.) (2000), *Strategia personalna firmy*, Difin, Warszawa; O. Lundy, A. Cowling (2000), *Strategiczne zarządzanie zasobami ludzkimi*, Oficyna Ekonomiczna, Kraków; H. Król (1999), *Strategie personalne organizacji*, "Humanizacja Pracy. Zarządzanie Zasobami Ludzkimi", No. 1–2; T. Listwan (1999), *Strategie personalne* [in:] R. Krupski (ed.), *Zarządzanie strategiczne. Koncepcje, metody*, Wydawnictwo AE Wrocław, Wrocław.

[258] A. Lipka (2000), *Strategie personalne firmy*, Wydawnictwo PSB, Kraków, p. 28.

Thirdly, indicating the strategic domain of personnel function with setting adequate strategic aims of personnel function it should be combined with working out a set of specific activities in the HR management. As all the activities connected with personnel management in the organization should be 'fitted,' it is not possible to indicate effective solutions for each organization active in medical service sector but general basis for projecting such activities may be:

1. Creating the condition and structure of employment according to the predictions on provided services,

2. Broadening recruitment criteria beyond these required by law, e.g. personality profiles, competence profiles,

3. Projecting and introducing the system of employees' appraisal based on the quantity and quality criteria, e.g. competence,

4. Planning training in compliance with the profile of the business and development in marketing activity,

5. Rewarding employees according to their contribution to the organization at market rate verification.

In conclusion, it is worth underlining that the way personnel function is implemented currently, especially in public units does not contribute to creating and gaining a differential advantage. The fact is that the awareness of human capital significance in the hospitals in medical service market has been changing, the development of personnel function in these business entities can be expected in the future.

3.1.2. INTERPERSONAL AND INTERGROUP COMMUNICATION PROCESS IN THE HOSPITALS

3.1.2.1. INTRODUCTION

Every member of the existing societies, regardless of the geographical location, nationality or sex, while coming into interpersonal or intergroup contacts, employs the stereotypes concerning the perception of other people which has the influence on the quality of those contacts. The stereotypes simplify the communication processes and they are present in the daily life of each of us.

Stereotypes are applied in the course of the daily interhuman interactions and they play in many situations a role in the perception of others. They provide instructions which enable the formation of the interactions with the doctors, nurses, waiters, accountants, professors, children, schizophrenics, people suffering from depression, the shy, as well as with the family, acquaintances etc.[259] Interhuman contacts, especially the first meeting of two persons, compose the most vivid and typical example of

---

[259] W.G. Stephan, C.W. Stephan (2007), *Wywieranie wpływu przez grupy. Psychologia relacji*, Gdańskie Wydawnictwo Pedagogiczne Sp. z o.o., Gdańsk, p. 16.

the use of stereotypes in the adversary's perception. Basing the deliberations on the $4x20^{260}$ rule, including the rules and stages of non-verbal perception of other people, we may notice the elements important for the interhuman contacts and their order. The first stage refers to the statement "he sees me". The attitude of the person is established on the basis of, among others, the walk, looks and posture.

And so when we see a smiling person we can establish, even when we have no hints concerning the non-verbal character, that this person is open, good-natured and, above all, that he/she has a positive attitude towards the external contact. We can also be in possession of the information about the profession the given person performs. There are some professions which evoke negative connotations, (e.g. a party activist or an owner of a small shop[261]). Our attitude towards a person performing this type of profession may change. Also other criteria (such as lifestyle, sex, age, social background, religious confession, education etc.) may have the influence on our attitude towards an adversary. By the posture of the person we may assess their attitude, if they are open or reserved. An open attitude is characterised by an upright posture with feet directed outwards. The posture of a reserved person, in turn, will be stooping with legs directed inwards. These are very vivid examples of existing stereotypes. However, they do not take into account the fact that the person's posture may result from illnesses and their perception from an incomplete non-verbal lexicon, as well as from the situational and background context.

A similar situation concerns the successive elements taken from the 4x20 rule, so successively: facial expressions, the perception of intonation and verbal argumentation as well as making a favourable impression on the speaker. In the first case the most important aspect concerning the perception of the adversary are the eyes and the mouth, which *should be analysed collectively not separately.*[262] There is a saying used by the society and it tells us that the eyes are the mirror of the soul. If the speaker will perceive a given person only through the prism he/she will succumb to the stereotype and, at the same time, obtain a wrong or incomplete result.

Nevertheless, an important aspect connected with the perception of other people is their ability or disability to intonate and express oneself. Many people do not care about this aspect although it is important to formulate simple messages by distinguishing the most vital components of the content. An example of such a person may be a head who prepared the scenario of his/her speech very carefully with a view to strengthening the worker's motivation, but forgot to practice it beforehand or did not reckon that it was necessary. As a result of this oversight the content of the speech was exhibited in a wrong way, i.e. the influence on the workers was not maximised. The fourth cognitional stage refers to the so called full, entire impression, other people's perception of our person. In this part additionally the aspect of the argumentation of our needs, the expectations and the *profits* which may be gained from our person is added. To put it simply, we have to learn *the best way to sell ourselves.*

---

[260] J. Stępniewski (2005), *Jak opanować sztukę negocjacji. Przewodnik praktyczny*, Wyd. Wyższej Szkoły Zarządzania i Marketingu w Sosnowcu, Sosnowiec, p. 19–20.

[261] http://www.cbos.pl/SPISKOM.POL/1999/K_032_99.PDF, 09.03.2010.

[262] One of the rules of the non-verbal interpretation informs us that a set of gestures and not single gestures shpuld be subject to interpretation.

3.1.2.2. Causes and rules governing the formation of stereotypes

Stereotypes become most evident when they are negative, excessively generalised or false, because in such cases they destructively affect interactions. Their influence may be damaging as they shape our expectations regarding other people's behavior. If those expectations are negative, we start to expect undesirable behaviours on the part of members of a strange group. If, in addition, they are excessively generalised, we anticipate that the majority of "strangers" will behave in the same way.[263]

Stereotypes are a kind of phenomenon which is categorised for the ease of association. We can perceive them in two ways, that is, top-bottom, as well as bottom-top. What does it mean? Perceiving persons that form a given group, we concentrate on those features that they share and that distinguish them from others. There may also be a situation in which we ascribe a given group features that characterise it and ascribe those features to the group's representative by means of calque.

It is a significant problem that each of us easily 'sticks' a stereotype on another person. On the other hand, it is more difficult to get rid of something we should call an external description.

People often make a spontaneous classification on the basis of easily noticeable physical features.[264]

Figure 1. Ultimate mistake of attribution

	One's own group	Stranger group
Positive results	Internal attribution (e.g. great abilities)	External attribution (e.g. a lucky chance)
Negative results	External attribution (e.g. bad luck)	Internal attribution (e.g. lack of abilities)

Source: W.G. Stephan, C.W. Stephan (2007), *Wywieranie wpływu przez grupy. Psychologia relacji*, Gdańskie Wydawnictwo Pedagogiczne Sp. z o.o., Gdańsk, p. 24.

The formation of stereotypes that consists in perceiving two groups on the basis of a feature characteristic for both of them. That feature will be perceived positively in the case of one's own group, while in the case of a strange group it will be perceived in a negative way. Such phenomenon is called labeling.[265] An example of it may be the workers of two companies which do and function very well. In the case of evaluation of one's own achievements one will pay attention to high skills of workers and executives. We will notice that our market competitors employ people who 'cheat' or simply are lucky.

---

[263] W.G. Stephan, C.W. Stephan (2007), *op. cit.*, p. 16.

[264] See: C. Stangor, L. Lynch, L. Duan, B. Glass (1992), *Categorization of individuals on the basis of multiple cocial features*, "Journal of Personality and Cocial Psychology", No. 62, p. 207–218.

[265] W.G. Stephan, C.W. Stephan (2007), *op. cit.*, p. 22.

Biased labeling concerns not only intergroup relations but also takes place while interacting with particular members of a strange group.

A very important element in the formation of stereotypes is their structure which consists of so-called knots[266] of several types. These include defining features (which determine the members of a group), characteristic features (ascribed to a given group) and examples (which confirm or deny a stereotype), respectively. The processing of information in a network of stereotypes usually starts with an activation of the knot for a defining feature.

The activation expands automatically on the group knot and a given person is identified as a member of a particular group. For example, a person in a café, wearing white blouse and black trousers may be mistaken for a waiter etc.

Emotions related with the group label are particularly interesting. If those feelings are in a greater part negative and if they lead to a negative assessment of a group, one may say that a given person is prejudiced against this particular group.

With reference to the results of research,[267] one may think that during the intergroup interactions, the emotional features informing the public opinion about a group are automatically stimulated and accessible to be used, in order to form expectations, attitudes, behaviours and further comments.

A person in a bad mood notices a negative behaviour of another person and remembers it even better, as a result of which, a negative stereotype is maintained. In case of a person in a good mood, a contrary situation takes place.[268]

3.1.2.3. STEREOTYPES IN INTERGROUP AND INTERPERSONAL RELATIONS

In case of the intergroup relations, the worst situation is a formation of a negative stereotype, which constitutes the great power allowing to maintain and intensify stereotypes in relations and intergroup perception.

It is assumed that any rivalisation increases hostility, whether it refers to individual, or intergroup relations. The situation in hospitals may be an example, where the whole personnel is not satisfied with remuneration, but only in case of a medical group, the financial situation has improved. The rivalization between groups for the limited and valuable supplies entails the intensification of mutual prejudices. Competition for welfare causes hostility between groups, and, in extreme cases, it ends with a conflict, an open war.

There is no doubt that many various groups directly compete for social and material goods.[269] The majority group defines the common inequality concerning the

---

[266] See: D.E. Rumerlhart, G.E. Hinton, J.L. McClelland (1986), *A general framework for parallel distributed processing* [in:] D.E. Rumerlhart et. al. (ed.), *Parallel distributed processing*, MIT Press, Cambridge, p. 45–76.

[267] W.G. Stephan, C.W. Stephan (2007), *op. cit.*, p. 30.

[268] See: J.P. Forgas, G.H. Bower (1986), *Mood effects on person-perception judgments*, "Journal of Personality and Cocial Psychology", No. 53, p. 53–60.

[269] R.A. LeVine, D.T. Campbell (1972), *Ethnocentrism: Theories of conflict, ethnic attitudes, and group behavior*, Wiley, New York.

division of goods as just and fair, becoming involved in discriminating behaviours, in order to protect one's privileged position.

It was proven that the increased competition is accompanied by legislations protecting the privileges of elites.[270]

Four factors affecting the level of interpersonal and intergroup interaction are as follows:
- an interaction based on cooperation,
- an equal status of the members of interaction,
- an individualized contact,
- an official support of a contact.[271]

Were the above-mentioned conditions fulfilled in the context of the contact of the representatives of different groups at work, at school, in recreation centers or in any other environments, it would result in the improvement of intergroup relations. In turn, M. Hewstone and R. Brown stated that treating a member of a different group as an identity, and not as the representative of a group, may not influence the perception of the whole population, but only the individual point of view. The context of a situation or an environment is also a very important issue here. The factors, increasing the clarity of division of an own and a foreign group and which are also conducive to identifying oneself with an own group, stimulate the so-called "I" of a group. There is also the opposite of described dependence between an individual and a group level. Each of us concentrates on one of them, simultaneously the attention on the good of the other person is decreased. A human being perceives others as similar, if they share the same group label, and they consider people as not similar, if they have a different label.

Many different mechanisms are responsible for maintaining the group stereotypes, among others the rule of putting as little effort as possible. It refers to the situation when a man is inclined to persistently believe in one's first, simple generalization, as long as it is possible. It was proven in the research of G. Allport.[272]

3.1.2.4. FUNCTIONING OF THE COMMUNICATION PROCESS BASED ON STEREOTYPES IN HOSPITALS

Fulfillment of a few conditions is fundametal for the communication process to take place. Firstly, at least two people must take part in it – a Sender and a Recipient. Secondly, there must be a message carrying some content and it must be sent in one direction. Thirdly, communication process is based on communication channels, through which contact is maintained. Drawing No. 2 presents exemplary interpersonal communication process. However, apart from the subject and the object of communication, errors and disruptions may occur. They are also marked on the drawing.

---

[270] S. Olzak (1992), *The dynamics of ethnic competition and conflict*, Stanford University Press, Stanford.

[271] W.G. Stephan, C.W. Stephan (2007), *op. cit.*, p. 77.

[272] *Ibidem*, p. 125.

Analysing the process on the Sender's part, the Sender formulates the content of the message. Then he encodes it and sends it to the Recipient through the information channel. In the case when Recipient has no problems with decoding the content, information is understood in 100 percent.

Figure 2. Simplified process of interpersonal communication.

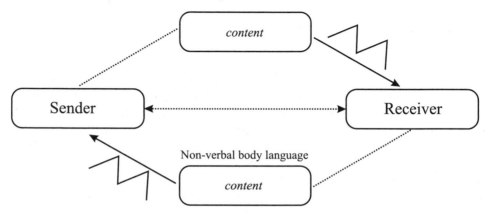

Source: Self-study based on J.Stankiewicz (1999), *Komunikowanie się w organizacji* (*Communication in an Organization*), Wyd. Astrum, Wrocław, p. 44–48.

However, in communication process errors and disruption may arise. They may be external or internal. External errors and disruptions may be caused by noise, distance between interlocutors or perceiving the interlocutor on the base of deep-rooted stereotypes. Internal errors and disruptions in turn include errors in pronunciation (lisping), phonetic errors and using the language, which the interlocutor does not know.

An example of such communication process may be the communication taking place in hospitals: both in groups and at the individual level. While investigating both types of communication it is noticeable that stereotypes have a great influence on relations between the groups in hospitals. Therefore, our deliberations will focus on identification of relations in the groups.

The research was conducted in four hospitals in the administration units in Lower Silesia Province (Dolnośląskie) and Wielkopolskie Province during two months – from January till March 2010. The author of the research used three research methods: survey forms, observations conducted by respondents in the given environment as well as reviews with health service workers. The results show that positive relations exist among the following professional groups: nurses (including midwives) – doctors, doctors – nurses, administrative workers – doctors, technical workers – doctors, administrative workers – technical workers and technical workers – administrative workers. It is significant that the doctors are perceived in a positive way by other professional groups. However, the only group perceived positively by the doctors are nurses. Negative relations, in turn, concern only the nurses. Among all professional groups functioning in hospitals, technical workers are the most isolated group. There are many stereotypes functioning in hospital environment. These stereotypes are placed in the table 16.

Table 16. Negative stereotypes in different professional groups in hospitals.

	doctors' features	nurses' features	administrative workers' features	technical workers' features
doctors about:		– they do not have enough professional knowledge, – they are an auxiliary service, – they are the white staff in a hospital, – they are helpful.	– it is not clear what they do, – there are too many of them, – they organise the functioning of the hospital in a wrong way.	– they are useful but they do not know much, – they exist, – they are useful from time to time, – I do not know them.
nurses about:	– they earn a lot, – they do not respect nurses, – they have extensive knowledge, – they are very friendly.		– it is not clear what they do, – they take money for nothing, – they are cadgers.	– there are too many of them, – when they are needed they are not where they should be, – I do not know them.
administrative workers about:	– they earn a lot, – they are very nice and friendly, – together with the nurses they form a closed group, – they have extensive professional knowledge.	– they act superior, – they want to impose their own decisions on others, – they do not understand our job.		– they perform their duties.
technical workers about:	– they earn a lot, – they are very nice and friendly, – together with the nurses they form a closed group, – they have extensive professional knowledge.	– they act superior, – they want to impose their own decisions on others, – they do not respect us.	– they perform their duties well, – there are too few of them, – they are the so-called white-collar workers or office workers, – they are ineffective.	

Source: Own analysis on the basis of quantitative and qualitative research.

Each professional group perceives its own features in a positive way, whereas if the same feature is ascribed to another professional group, it may be regarded as something negative in reference to this foreign group. And so, doctors perceive themselves as an educated group, which, due to the nature of the profession, constantly increases its qualifications. However, this feature, when it is ascribed to nurses, is perceived by doctors as a negative one. They often wonder why nurses study and state that their basic education is enough in their job and to perform their duties.

Figure 3. Description of intergroup relations in hospitals

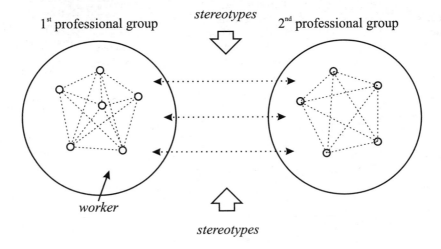

Source: Own analysis on the basis of quantitative and qualitative research.

Interpersonal relations in hospitals depend on intergroup relations, which are influenced by stereotypes.

The following figure presents a typical intergroup relation in hospitals, where different groups communicate in intragroup and interpersonal systems reflecting the stereotypes that arise from the way a given group is perceived.

3.1.2.5. SUGGESTIONS OF IMPROVING THE INTERGROUP RELATIONS IN HOSPITALS WITH THE APPLICATION OF STEREOTYPES

Relations between groups can be improved by means of leading to structuralized interactions which include interpersonal or intergroup contact. In order to create more beneficial stereotypes, the connections between the knot regarding a given group and knots representing positive features should be strengthened or created.

In order to reduce the influence of some disadvantageous stereotype, the connections between the group knot and negative features can be weakened. Another method is to create subtypes for a given category, the subtypes being connected with less negative information.

Three conditions have to be fulfilled in order to add a positive feature by means of a direct experience: the behaviour connected to a given feature should be encoded, an inner atribution should be made, and the given feature should be connected to a group knot.[273]

In order to modify a stereotype a man has to have at his disposal sufficient cognitive resources that enable the transfer of data related to the stereotype.[274]

That means that a given situation cannot require much cognitive effort. The author who bases on literary deliberations and research analysis in hospitals, offers 3 alternative methods whose aim is to improve the intergroup and interpersonal relations.

The first method called 'a pattern for others' refers to actions whose aim is to seek a person in a group whose attitude and actions are viewed as positive by foreign professional groups. On this basis the positive image of the group in the surroundings will be built by modifications or neutralization of the negative stereotypes. The weak side of this method is persuasion of the group to perceive others through an ideal worker. This method is difficult to introduce when there are very negative relations, especially personal.

The delivery of the data to people about the actions of individual members of a foreign group influences the opinions on individual people, and the social categories are brought to the background.[275]

Figure 4. Modification of stereotypes by means of individual patterns

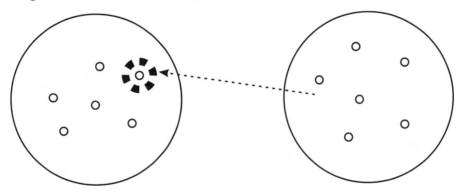

Source: Own analysis based on quantitative and qualitative research.

The method called 'overgroup team' serves to improve the intergroup relations and its aim is to create overgroup teams that would contain the representatives of all professional groups. Then, the most important factor influencing the improvement of perceiving other groups would be to create a team whom the workers could identify with, and create friendly relations inside of such a team. A leader would be an essential element of this group who would unite the team. The weak side of this method might be a wrong selection of employers as a result of which the negative stereotypes

---

[273] *Ibidem*, p. 39.

[274] D.T. Gilbert, G. Nixon (1991), *The trouble of thinking: Activation and application of stereotypic beliefs*, "Journal of Personality and Social Psychology", No. 60, p. 509–517.

[275] W.G. Stephan, C.W. Stephan (2007), *Wywieranie wpływu przez grupy. Psychologia relacji*, Gdańskie Wydawnictwo Pedagogiczne Sp. z o.o., Gdańsk, p. 81.

about the representants of different professional groups would strengthen and would even be preserved.

According to S. Gaertner and J. Dovidio the improvement in the intergroup relations might be achieved thanks to such a reorganisation of the cognitive representations of the own and foreign group so that instead of the two perceived group an image of one, a superior category would emerge.[276] If a man is capable of the recategorization of his/her own personality to the superior group, his/her attitudes in relations with the reprentants of the ex-group should improve.

Figure 5. Modifying stereotypes by creating overgroup teams in hospitals

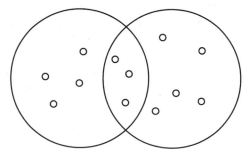

Source: Own analysis based on qualitative and quantitive research.

In the last method called 'lack of group differences' based on the 'struggle' against the negative stereotypes the actions are directed at removing any outer artefacts differentiating the representants of given groups from one another. In case of hospitals that would mean for the doctors and nurses to stop wearing white uniforms, for the auxiliary staff to stop wearing blue uniforms and for the administrative workers to stop wearing their own clothes. Hospitals should take banks as an example on how to dress – there are enforced rules of dressing, as well as to what colours and cut they may wear. The disadvantage of this method is that the employers might be resistant to changes, because they destroy the hierarchy and order in hospitals.

Figure 6. Modifying stereotypes by removing professional groups

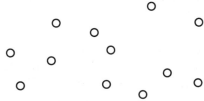

Source: Own analysis based on qualitative and quantitative research.

---

[276] S.L. Gaertner, J. Mann, J.F. Dovidio, A. Murrell, M. Pomare (1989), *How does cooperation reduce intergroup bias?*, "Journal of Personality and Social Psychology", No. 59, p. 692–704.

3.1.2.6. CONCLUSIONS

Hospitals belong to the category of units, where regardless of the character and range of activities it is extremely important to create positive intergroup and interpersonal relations. The three aforementioned methods of neutralising or improving the negative stereotypes show that there are ways in which it is possible to change the attitude of professional groups among one another. It could have an ifluence on the better organisation and effectiveness in hospitals.

3.1.3. ETHICAL ASPECTS OF COMPETITIONS ON MANAGING POSITION OF HOSPITALS

3.1.3.1. INTRODUCTION

Economic and political changes, which took place in the last two decades, affected health care delivery sector as well. These changes included, most of all, different ways, in which health care units were managed. Competitions for managerial positions are one of the most important accomplishments of democracy. How these competitions are conducted in public health care units can be observed since the regulations, which govern them came into effect.[277,278,279,280,281] Legislation relieves, to a certain extent, public health care units of working out recruitment and selection procedures for managerial positions. As a result, these procedures are often nothing else but formally executed guidelines of law. This reveals how imperfect they are, but most of all, shows a total lack of individual approach to their most important resource – people in managerial positions. It is skills of these people, which determine, to a great extent, success of a health care unit.[282] Competition, in a common understanding, is a procedure, the

---

[277] B. Buchelt-Nawara (2006), *ZZL w jednostkach sektora usług medycznych* [in:] H. Król, A. Ludwiczyński (ed.), *Zarządzanie zasobami ludzkimi*, Wyd. PWN, Warszawa, p. 645–647, 662––663.

[278] Dz. U. Nr 91, poz. 408 z dn. 30 sierpnia 1991 r. Ustawa o Zakładach Opieki Zdrowotnej.

[279] Dz. U. Nr 44, poz. 520 z dn. 17 maja 2000 r. Rozp. MZ: W sprawie wymagań, jakim powinny odpowiadać osoby na stanowiskach kierowniczych w zakładach opieki zdrowotnej określonego rodzaju..

[280] Dz. U. Nr 30, poz. 30 z dn. 29 marca 1999 r. Rozp. MZiOS: W sprawie kwalifikacji wymaganych od pracowników na poszczególnych rodzajach stanowisk pracy w publicznych zakładach opieki zdrowotnej.

[281] Dz. U. Nr 115, poz. 749 z dn. 19 sierpnia 1998 r. Rozp. MZiOS: W sprawie szczegółowych zasad przeprowadzania konkursu na niektóre stanowiska kierownicze w publicznych zakładach opieki zdrowotnej, składu komisji konkursowej oraz ramowego regulaminu przeprowadzania konkursu.

[282] D. Kunecka, B. Karakiewicz (2010), *Procedury konkursowe na stanowiska kierownicze w ZOZ-ach. Co dalej?* [in:] I. Rudawska, E. Urbańczyk (ed.), *Studia i materiały Polskiego Stowarzyszenia Zarządzania Wiedzą* (25), Wyd. Bel Studio, Bydgoszcz, p. 165–166.

aim of which is to select a winner or winners from a group of applicants, who comply with certain criteria. Failure to file entry of at least two candidates within a given time limit results in a competition being cancelled. This is the only circumstance, in which an organizer's commitment to select the best candidate is logically impossible and ineffective. A competition being organizer's irreversible commitment to award the best candidate can be cancelled only if the procedure is found to contain irregularities or if an organizer or a candidate resort to dishonest practices.[283] In such a case, a legislator assumes at this stage an amendment to a definition of a competition allowing the procedure to take its formal course, even if there is no a rival candidate. This is what makes a competition imperfect as it creates conditions to eliminate those, for whom decency is not an alien and empty term.[284] As an observer of nursing environment and a participant in discussions about legitimacy to run competitions only for the sake of fulfilling a formal duty of a legislator, the author makes an attempt to describe ethical aspects not pertaining to the evaluation of a formal course of competition procedures with regard to compliance with regulations of competition procedure under the applicable legislation. She assumes that research findings will allow to gain yet another argument for starting a debate not only within nursing environment but also among management or to undertake firm steps with a view to altering the existing legislation.

3.1.3.2. OBJECTIVES

The objective of the study was to seek the opinions of candidates participating in a competition procedure (candidates for the post of ward nurse), organized in hospitals in Szczecin, to which public health care units are obliged by a statutory requirement.[285] A strong emphasis was put on the ever-present ethical aspects, being subject of numerous discussions not only within nursing environment, which holds a critical and negative opinion[286] of the competition proceedings.

3.1.3.3. MATERIAL AND METHODS

The study was conducted in hospitals in Szczecin, in which due to different reasons, (end of tenure, retirement, resignation) managers planned to run competitions from March 2009 to March 2010 for the posts of ward nurses. All five managers from the mentioned hospitals agreed to participate in the study. Research material consisted of 40 questionnaires filled in by candidates for the posts of ward nurses participating in 19 competition procedures. A majority of respondents were women (38 persons),

---

[283] Wikipedia. Free Encyclopedia. Competition, [online: 11.04.2010 r.] http://pl.wikipedia.org/wiki/Konkurs.

[284] W. Filipowicz, *Białe konkursy w szarych odcieniach*, [online: 11.04.2010 r.] http://www.tvnwarszawa.pl/33026,51818663,Bia%B3e_konkursy_w_szarych_odcieniach_cz_II,artykul.html.

[285] Dz. U. Nr 91, poz. 408 z dn. 30 sierpnia 1991 r. Ustawa o Zakładach Opieki Zdrowotnej.

[286] Niezależne Forum Pielęgniarek i Położnych: *Konkursy Tak czy Nie*, [dostęp online: 11.04.2010 r.] http://www.forum-pielegniarek.pl/viewtopic.php?f=22&p=1034.

with 2 men being in a minority of this group, which confirms a phenomenon of feminization of a nursing profession. Here is a candidates' profile with respect to their age: there was 1 person below 30, the age range of 31–40 was represented by 8 persons, the most numerous group of 23 was represented by respondents aged 41–50 and 8 persons aged over 50. A majority of respondents were married (26 persons). Given that the study was conducted on candidates for managerial posts, a relative uniformity with respect to education should be expected, pointing to higher education which prevails. However, the findings indicate diversity, characteristic of the whole of the group, which may be puzzling. As a result, 17 respondents were high school graduates (13 persons graduated from a medical high school, 4 from a medical training college), 23 persons had University diplomas (11 Bachelors and 12 Masters) including 4 persons with University diploma unrelated to nursing profession.

The questionnaire used in the study consisted of 16 questions about the course of a competition procedure, laying emphasis on a professional ethic (access to information, independent nature of committee members, criteria for selecting the best candidate). The obtained findings were presented in percentage terms on the basis of the opinions of nurses/candidates for the posts of the ward nurse. Moreover, the chi – square (X test was used in further statistical analysis). The study was conducted from March 2009 to December 2009.

3.1.3.4. FINDINGS

Findings were presented in tables to expose particular elements, which were studied by means of a questionnaire.

Selection of staff is of strategic importance for a smooth functioning of every organization. It seems to be particularly important when it comes to managerial posts. Crucially important is ability to point to a source, from which a candidate was taken: external or internal.[287,288,289] Types of sources preferred by health care units included in the study are presented in table 17. The data show how the information about initiating competition proceedings was obtained.

Table 17. The way of obtaining information about initiating proceedings

The source of information	N	%
Advert in a dedicated magazine	1	2.5
Advert in other magazine	4	10
Bulletin board in Health Care Administration Office	15	37.5

---

[287] J. Jończyk (2008), *Zarządzanie zasobami ludzkimi w zakładach opieki zdrowotnej*, Difin, Warszawa, p. 129–130.

[288] G. Bartkowiak (2008), *Dobór personelu medycznego* [in:] M. Dobska, K. Rogoziński (ed.), *Podstawy zarządzania zakładem opieki zdrowotnej*, Wyd. PWN, Warszawa, p. 341–345.

[289] G. Bartkowiak (2009), *Psychologiczne aspekty zarządzania zasobami ludzkimi w zakładach opieki zdrowotnej*, Wolters Kluwer Business, Warszawa, p. 185–188.

Information passed orally	Personnel	4	10
	Head nurse	8	20
		3	7,5
Other, e.g. Nurse Chamber Website		5	12,5

The way information is obtained by respondents indicates that they prefer internal sources. A majority of respondents concluded that the manner of diffusing the information about initiation of competition proceedings was accurate. 31 respondents held such a view. Those, who found it inaccurate (5 respondents), or did not have any opinion, opted for a change of the source.

Furthermore, it is worth taking a note that a majority of respondents (32 persons), are current employees of health care units, in which competition proceedings were ongoing. 11 out of 28 employees working on the wards were ward nurses, whose tenure expired but were not entitled to retirement. In the case of 5 such employees, the post was entrusted to them again for a period of three years owing to a fact that there was not any rival candidate in the competition.

In view of a fact that a selection process of committee members, who hold an interview with candidates on the date provided for by the legislation, starts as early as in a planning stage of the course of a competition, the respondents were asked if they knew any members sitting on the committee, both on a private as well as professional level. The question seems to be well-grounded as a make-up of the said committees is often subject to various discussions. In both cases, the committee was found to be lacking objectivism with respect to candidates for the post of ward nurses, whom the committee members had known before. The obtained findings are presented in the table 18.

One person did not answer any question. The person, who was asked about a professional acquaintance with the committee members, won a competition. The respondents did not point to the answer, which would confirm the committee's subjectivism or non-objectivism. However, it should be pointed here, that most respondents chose not to answer this question – 5 persons altogether, 2 of which did not have a rival candidate and 4 persons answered: 'I have no opinion.'

Table 18. Candidates' acquaintance with members of the committee prior to a competition

	Yes, with all of them			Yes, with more than 50% of committee's make-up			Yes, with less than 50% of committee's make-up			No, I did not know anyone		
	N	%	Including candidates, who won (N)	N	%	Including candidates, who won (N)	N	%	Including candidates, who won (N)	N	%	Including candidates, who won (N)

Profes-sional level acquaint-ance	6	15	5		14	35	5		12	30	5		7	17,5	3
Private level acquaint-ance	0	0	0		6	15	3		11	27,5	7		22	55	9

With respect to a formal course of the procedure, in most questions, respondents pointed to answers, which indicated satisfaction. It is confirmed in the question:'Was the make-up of the committee right?', to which 35 respondents gave a positive answer. It remains debatable, though, that 5 respondents who gave a negative answer or no answer at all, did not win any competition. A group's similar unanimity could be observed in the case of a question about a neutral character of a location, in which the interview was held. 35 respondents found the location neutral or it did not matter to them. However, with respect to a question about formal requirements, 38 respondents assessed that they were complied with. 2 persons abstained from answering this question.

The most essential part of the study was reflected in the question pertaining to a subjective evaluation of the studied criteria, which played a decisive role in selecting a candidate for a post of the ward nurse. The respondents could point to several answers, however, 3 of them did not give any at all. In the opinion of 20 respondents, professional qualifications play a crucial role in selecting a candidate for a given post. However, a statistical analysis of the gathered data, done with chi-square test (χ^2) did not confirm that. Moreover, the respondents pointed to a professional experience as an important criteria in selecting the best candidate (13 respondents gave such an answer). In order to study a level of correlation between a previous experience on the post of the ward nurse and a positive result in the ongoing procedure, chi-square (χ^2) test was applied, too. The coefficient of probability of $p=0.014$ allows to recognize a statistically important correlation between studied phenomena. The obtained result should become a powerful argument in favor of public debate on introduction of necessary changes to the existing procedures of recruitment and selection of candidates for managerial posts in public health units. It should serve not only as a tool to comply with the applicable laws but first of all as a tool of selection of the most appropriate candidate. It should take into account a contribution of a previous employee with a successful work history, which can be verified by his/her superiors and workmates. The easiest solution is to relate this stage to a periodic performance appraisal.

The respondents gave the following as very important criteria in selecting a candidate for the post of the ward nurse: seniority (9 respondents), the best impression during the interview (8 respondents), other considerations not pertaining to the subject matter (2 respondents). Moreover, during accompanying discussions, the respondents often pointed to a candidate's age, linking this variable with a candidate's professional experience. Among other variables were: education, professional development in a form of external courses and a marital status. In order to find out if there is an important correlation between the above mentioned variables and a winning score in the studied group, the gathered data was put to statistical analysis with the application of chi-square test (χ^2). The findings of a statistical analysis are presented in the table 19.

Table 19. Findings of statistical analysis conducted by means of chi-square (χ^2)

Variables	Value (χ^2)	Value (p)
Age/winning/losing	1,483.49	0.583
Seniority/winning/losing	2,831.755	0.418
Education/winning/losing	3,255.458	0.354
Professional development/winning/losing	2,087.036	0.720
Experience on the posts of a nurse: surgical, coordinating, ward/winning/losing	8,500.198	**0.014**
Earlier participation in a competition/winning/losing	8,386	**0.004**
Social status/winning/losing	0.803	0.370

Further on in the study the respondents were asked about the motives behind their decision to participate in the competition procedure. A prevailing answer was that of a need to self-actualize (27 respondents). Besides, having a possibility to tick off several answers in this question, the respondents pointed to: willingness to gain new experience and skills (15 respondents), willingness to get to know applicable procedures in competition proceedings (7 respondents), promotion (4 respondents), job change (3 respondents), willingness to help a friend currently in charge (2 respondents). These answers, but most of all, informal conversations and analyzing candidates' reactions enabled the author to conclude that only 6 competitions were genuine. The remaining 14, to a greater or lesser extent, turned out to be a farce. Expiration of tenure was a prevailing reason among organizers included in the study of competition procedures. In 11 cases, the ward nurses remained in charge, 3 persons out of 11 did not have rival candidates and had their tenure prolonged by another 3 years. In one case, competition proceedings were initiated owing to a resignation from a post of the ward nurse (4 persons joined competition). In another 7 cases, a competition was organized due to current employees retiring from their jobs. However, having an opportunity to examine the atmosphere during interviews and holding informal talks with candidates, the author concludes that she dealt with only 5 genuine competitions. It is worth mentioning in this place, that out of 40 participants only 17 gave a positive answer to a question: 'Will you ever enter a competition for a similar post again?'. 8 respondents out of this group won a competition.

3.1.3.5. DISCUSSION

This study makes an attempt to evaluate ethical aspects, which accompany competition procedures for managerial positions, run in public health care units. Competitions for the post of ward nurses, which were organized in 5 hospitals in Szczecin in 2009, were taken as a model. These aspects are discussed from a point of view of legislation, which govern them. Opponents argue that in a context of a real competition, a candidate's direct superior has only a limited influence on the candidate's employment situation as he/she constitutes a single voice in the committee's make--up.[290] What it means in reality is that a chance of selecting the best candidate is slim. Besides, a sheer fact of a competition procedure taking place creates favorable conditions for a candidate, who is currently in charge. This is happening because the existing legislation does not provide for conditions (employee's poor performance), which would cause a tenure to expire ahead of time. A lack of certain measures, such as an employee's periodic performance appraisal, for instance, which would definitely be of great help during recruitment and selection, creates the impression of artificiality when it comes to selecting the best candidate. Guidelines on specific rules, which govern the employment policy in the case of managerial post (including ward nurses) and introduce a 'competition' as an obligatory form of selecting a candidate[291] lead, in consequence, to a range of situations, which from an ethical point of view are debatable. Although, there has been an ongoing debate on necessary changes to health care sector, no firm steps have been taken. As a result, it is still perceived as a museum of old centralistic organizations and old red tape system of management.[292] It is, therefore, a real challenge for a health care management to work out a flexible model, based on human potential providing employees with conditions, which would promote professional growth and boost commitment.[293] It requires a strategic approach to employees, which would bring out their potential and make them aware of how important an efficient management is. It is in the best interest of each health care unit, all senior managers, decision-makers and legislators to create a system, which will attract highly competent candidates, especially for managerial posts.[294] All this in accordance with a principle that the appreciated employee is bound to feel a need to be a co-founder of an institution, identifies with it, shapes its image and takes up initiative with a view to strengthening his institution's position on the market. Success of his organization becomes his own and reversely.[295] After all, even the best, well-equipped and well-subsidized organization means nothing without people. To have an effective management means creating optimal conditions to all employees and managing well relations among them.[296] A proper selec-

---

[290] M. Kautsch (2010), *Specyfika zarządzania zakładem opieki zdrowotnej* [in:] M. Kautsch (ed.), *Zarządzanie w opiece zdrowotnej. Nowe wyzwania*, Wolters Kluwer Business, Warszawa, p. 80–81.

[291] V. Kijowska (2010), *Zarządzanie zasobami ludzkimi* [in:] M. Kautsch (ed.), *op. cit.*, p. 236.

[292] M. Durlik (2008), *Zarządzanie w służbie zdrowia. Organizacja procesowa i zarządzanie wiedzą*, Wyd. Placet, Warszawa, p. 99.

[293] A. Woźniakowski (2005), *Globalizacja – różnorodność – zarządzanie talentami* [in:] S. Borkowska (ed.), *Zarządzanie talentami*, Wyd. IPiSS, Warszawa, p. 43.

[294] V. Kijowska (2010), *op. cit.*, p. 266–267.

[295] S. Ostrowska (2009), *Koncentracja na wewnętrznym otoczeniu jednostki* [in:] A. Frączkiewicz-Wronka, A. Austin-Tynda (ed.), *Przywództwo w ochronie zdrowia. Idee i instrumenty*, Wolters Kluwer Business, Warszawa, p. 124.

[296] K. Opolski, G. Dykowska, M. Możdżonek (2009), *Zarządzanie przez jakość w usługach zdrowotnych. Teoria i praktyka*, Wyd. CeDeWu, Warszawa, p. 66–70.

tion of managers, including ward nurses is a key to initiate such changes. Working on a modification of recruitment procedures, one should keep in mind the ongoing transformation of our health care system, which triggers a need for an intensive vocational training of medical staff, particularly those, who actively participate in a management process. These people are expected to execute their tasks in an innovative and dynamic way and to coordinate work in teams they lead.[297] In accordance with a principle that a team development is connected with a development of its leader[298] – a ward nurse, in this case. To participate in a management process, she needs to perform the roles of:

– Creator of knowledge
– Transmitter of knowledge
– A person, who favours changes
– A coach for subordinates
– A paragon of good practice and values.[299]

In last years we have been dealing with a diminishing number of competitions for managerial posts (including ward nurses) in public health care units. Article 44a of public health care units Act puts an obligation to hold such competitions. This arbitrary attitude of assigning tasks without recourse to competition procedures constitutes a breach against the standards of good practice,[300] especially if its sole intention is to get round the existing legislation with a view to allowing incompetent employees to execute their duties. These bad habits as well as management's rather conservative approach give rise to a range of adverse phenomena, which accompany the process of human resource management in public health sector. It may discourage employees or worse still, trigger a staff turnover and escape from a place, which promotes nepotism.

We have been observing changes for some time now, occurring in public institutions, including Health Care Administration Office. We are witnessing an organizational shift towards a new quality. The shift from a traditional model of management, understood as a way of managing employees, to an integrated model, in which a line management (including ward nurses), in collaboration with a human resource department create and implement a personnel policy,[301] taking into account a complexity of the whole process and not focusing on particular elements. It changed from a hierarchical, bond-dependent, reluctant to accept changes and

---

[297] I. Kraśniak, J. Kraśniak (2009), *Kompetencje zarządcze pielęgniarki oddziałowej w świetle wyników badań* [in:] R. Lewandowski, R. Walkowiak, M. Kautsch (ed.), *Współczesne wyzwania menadżerskie w ochronie zdrowia*, Wyd. OWSIiZ, Olsztyn, p. 143.

[298] H. Mruk (2010), *Przywództwo w zakładach opieki zdrowotnej*, Wolters Kluwer Business, Warszawa, p. 25.

[299] B. Buchelt-Nawara, *Podmioty zarządzające zasobami ludzkimi w zakładach opieki zdrowotnej*, [dostęp online: 11.04.2010 r.] http://gollum.uek.krakow.pl/bibl_ae_zasoby/zeszyty/pdf/122879827.pdf.

[300] Stanowisko NRPiP z dn. 12 marca 2008 r. w sprawie nieuzasadnionej likwidacji kierowniczych stanowisk pielęgniarskich/położniczych w zakładach opieki zdrowotnej, [dostęp online: 11.04.2010 r.] http://www.izbapiel.org.pl/uploadf/uchwalystanowiska/marzec2008/Stanowisko2.doc.

[301] V. Kijowska (2010), *op. cit.*, p. 267.

take risks, to performance and customers orientated, promoting risk, innovation and entrepreneurship,[302] without failing to recognize a specificity of public health sector, connected with human dimension, both with respect to a patient and employee. After all, it is possible to meet demands made on employees to treat patients like partners, only if employees treat themselves like partners, too.[303] Therefore, it should be highlighted, that in the long run, those, who will recognize this correlation and a necessity to work out tools, which help to implement changes, will reap benefits. In doing so, one should bear in mind the basic principles of effective human resource management, such as: treating people like an investment, not a cost, integrating organization with a complex personnel policy, creating a uniform system of motivation, ensuring development and vocational training but most of all orientation for a future.[304] All this runs counter to holding a competition for the sake of a formal requirement. As a result, critics of competition procedures propose to scrap them. One should give it a second thought, though. Is it really a right direction? Will it pay to abandon them? Should one rather not think about amending the existing provisions, bearing in mind that there exist a range of considerations speaking in favor of competition procedures, which are only in need of tying up the loopholes with respect to their course. One should ask a range of questions: when? where? one should organize them and who should participate in them in order to get rid of irregularities or doubts of ethical nature.

It is worth commencing a debate on legal provisions, which govern these issues, in order to improve them; bearing in mind the most frequently reported imperfections. Is it legitimate to initiate competition proceedings in a situation when its outcome becomes an open secret right from the start? Would it not be fairer to create provisions, which would prolong tenure of a previous manager? To this end, perhaps one should consider implementing the system of employee's performance appraisal. With respect to the course of a competition procedure, however, it is worth disambiguating legal provisions where it comes to criteria of the best candidate selection. Following the Drücker's words that '*Knowledge and skills brought by an employee are of no value to an organization until they are put into practice.*'[305] A candidate, who scores most points, wins a competition. In order to avoid imperfections from previous proceedings, one should work out a procedure of the course of an interview with a view to getting rid of mistakes relating to a lack of objectivism on the part of members (acquaintances). It is worth, too, thinking about costs incurred by organizers of a competition. Necessity to carry out an economic evaluation of this kind of investment would force organizers to handle human resources in thriftier manner. Perhaps, economic dimension would turn out more stimulating to implement necessary changes. However, in every democratic society the biggest obstacle is to come to

---

[302] A. Frąckiewicz-Wronka (2009), *Zarządzanie publiczne w teorii i praktyce ochrony zdrowia*, Wolters Kluwer Business, Warszawa, p. 157.

[303] K. Krot (2009), *Jakość i marketing usług medycznych*, Wolters Kluwer Business, Warszawa, p. 247.

[304] V. Kijowska (2010), *op. cit.*, p. 267.

[305] W. Kozłowski (2010), *Zarządzanie motywacją pracowników*, Wydawnictwo CeDeWu, Warszawa, p. 113.

mutual conclusions, because irrespective of issues raised, a multitude of opinion, not infrequently, is not caused by holding different views, but boils down to determining whose voice weighs more in a discussion and not the one pointing to better solutions. Hopefully, these obstacles will not be too big and the farce will make room for a real competition. Due to a relatively small sample of respondents, it is to be assumed that this study will contribute to further debates or research. More general reflection with a look ahead, determining the course of action to be taken, would be of certain significance. It is difficult to talk about a long-term planning in the case of hospitals, though. There is a risk, however, of relapsing into bad practice, as a passage of time tends to render, even the most accurate solutions, obsolete. As Heraclites said: *'Everything is subject to never-ending changes'* that is why they seem to be inevitable in this discipline, as well. Therefore, the most important thing is to work out a systemic approach to Human Resource Management, the essence of which is: improvement of recruitment procedures with a view to providing a more open and fairer rivalry for posts, selection of candidates based on a real competition not nomination, recommendation, liking or connections. These pathologies result in posts being occupied by unauthorized persons, deprived of certain characteristics essential to management. The last but not least, competition procedures should be based on a system of performance appraisal, which in the case of current employees should be closely connected[306] with a system of incentives, career paths or promotion.

3.1.3.6. CONCLUSIONS

Upon analysis of this material it should be conclude that.

In spite of complying with formal requirements, a majority of competitions were farce, which testifies about the size of the problem, bearing in mind that the professional group in question is the most numerous one among medical professions. The scale of the problem can testify about a poor quality of management. Steps should be taken as soon as possible to implement changes.

---

[306] J. Jończyk (2008), *Zarządzanie zasobami ludzkimi w zakładach opieki zdrowotnej*, Difin, Warszawa, p. 136–137, 143–145.

3.2. PATIENTS' RIGHTS WHILE QUALITY OF MEDICAL SERVICES

3.2.1. QUALITY OF MEDICAL SERVICES FROM A POINT OF VIEW OF PATIENTS' RIGHTS

In order to ensure quality of medical services, it seems legitimate to recognize the main areas of patient's expectations. A. Lawthers gives the most important areas of patient's expectations:[307]
  – 'Availability,
  – good communication, conveying information in an intelligible way (with respect to a patient's condition, type of treatment etc.),
  – respecting patient's rights as well as preferences with respect to type of treatment, continuity and coordination of the whole of therapeutic process (consultations with other doctors, coordination of a process when given stages of treatment take place in different health care units etc.).
  – mental comfort – during examination and treatment,
  – adapting care to individual expectations and needs.'
  Here is a list of patient's most important needs:[308]
  – of information – a patient wants to be informed about what is going on: what condition he is in, how a given treatment is going to affect him. Satisfying this need usually results in lesser anxiety. A range of psychological research indicates, that realization of what is about to happen allows to decrease stress,
  – of control of a situation – a patient's better sense of control can be enhanced through: giving full information, asking about his/her opinion, consent, leaving room for manoeuvre,
  – of security – it should be born in mind that a patient comes to a health care unit with what he/she has the most valuable – his/her life and health. That is why ensuring security is so important. This need can be satisfied through informing a patient about his condition, expected effects of a therapy and doctor's experience. It is equally important to build and maintain patient's trust in a doctor of a given health care unit. An important trust building factor is cleanness, sterility of a care unit, and even atmosphere among employees,
  – of interest and emotional support – it is an urgent need to pay greater attention to a patient. This does not need to be tantamount to sacrificing more time, but mere active listening, smiling, showing interest in a patient,
  – of respect and acceptation – not infrequently, a patient is compelled to strip off, exposing his weaknesses. It is important, therefore, to show respect with a view to helping a patient maintain his/her right own 'self,'

---

[307] A. Mykowska (2002), *Satysfakcja pacjenta a jakość obsługi medycznej*, "Zdrowie i Zarządzanie", Tom IV, No. 6, p. 70–71.
[308] *Ibidem*, p. 71–73.

– of intimacy and confidentiality – stripping off and confession often causes embarrassment. Failure to provide intimacy and a sense of confidentiality can hinder the treatment process or worse still leave trauma in a patient. Having these aspects in mind helps build trust in a medical personnel and a health care unit,

– of friendly atmosphere – a patient, who is a customer, expects a nice and friendly service and should not be at a mercy of personnel's moods.

The author carried out the study, in which patients were asked if their rights were observed and if they were informed about them. Here are the findings. 'Were you informed about patient's rights?'. Unfortunately, as many as 44.94% of respondents gave a negative answer, 52.07% were positive, 2.99% did not answer.

'Were you informed about patient's right?' Yes – 52.07%, No – 44.94%, No answer – 2.99%

Chart 1. Informing a patient about his rights during an appointment[309]
Were you informed about patient's rights?

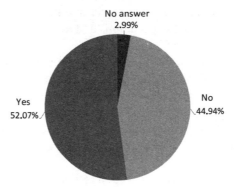

Source: Own study based on survey

---

[309] A. Krukowska-Miler (2010), *Marketing wartości w zarządzaniu niepublicznymi zakładami opieki zdrowotnej w województwie śląskim*, rozprawa doktorska, Politechnika Częstochowska, Wydział Zarządzania.

'Were you informed about your right to refuse or give your consent to perform a given medical service?' Yes – 65.29%, No – 31.03%, No answer – 3.68%

Chart 2. Informing patients about their right to refuse or agree to perform a given medical service[310]

Were you informed about your right to refuse or…

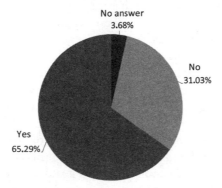

Source: Own study based on survey

'Were you informed about the effects of the treatment?' Yes – 75.86%, No – 20.00%, No answer – 4.14%

Chart 3. Informing patients about the effects of the treatment[311]

Were you informed about effects of the treatment?

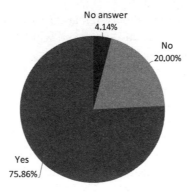

Source: Own study based on survey

Patient's needs can be looked upon through his decision to buy a medical service. From a point of view of medical service, what a patient needs is that his suffering be relieved. He needs a full recovery, which means improving quality of his life. Apart from this basic need, a patient expects a kind and competent approach from medical

---

[310] *Ibidem.*
[311] *Ibidem.*

personnel, clear information about his own condition, undertaken treatment, a well-
-equipped surgery with necessary tools, skilled personnel, intimacy, a spacious and
clean waiting room, clear appointment rules, flexibility of procedures adjusting to
a patient's current situation and the last but not least the surgery's convenient location.

Patient's needs change when it comes to a pre-sale service. A patient needs
a precise information about a health care unit with respect to working hours of
a given doctor, medical disciplines available, appointment rules, required documents,
how to reach a surgery and costs.

In the case of an after-sale service, a patient needs precise information about the
follow-up appointment, if-need-be monitoring, confirmation of the obtained information, which should be clear for a patient, a possibility of submitting a complaint if
a tooth filling falls out, for instance, a possibility of sharing opinion and conclusions
with personnel.

It would be advisable to make a good practice out of observing patients and personnel's behaviour, which may help find out what their needs are and how to satisfy them:[312]
1. 'What does a patient do upon entering a health centre, in what sequence?
2. How long does he wait for his appointment?
3. What does he say, if at all?
4. What does he look like upon leaving?
5. Does he seem satisfied, frustrated, indifferent?
6. Is there anything to his behaviour?
7. Does he report any doubts? Is he resentful? Does he show satisfaction?
8. Whom does he approach when doing so?
9. What are his most frequent questions?
10. Does he receive support?
11. Does personnel react to patients' remarks? How? How quickly?
12. Does it happen that a patient is surprised with something in a positive way?
13. What does he look at most often?
14. Does he often look at his watch?
15. Is he bored while waiting?
16. Do patients talk to one another while waiting?
17. What do they talk about most often?
18. Are they seated or they stand or walk?
19. Would there be enough chairs for everyone to sit on if everyone wanted to?
20. Are there tables? Is it possible to have a drink?
21. Is it possible to have a snack?
22. Is there a sandwich bar or a buffet?
23. Is there a pay phone?
24. Are there leaflets and brochures informing about a full offer of services ren
   dered by a health care unit?
25. Does a patient read them or take them home?

---

[312] A.K. Kapliński, M.R. Łysiak, T.S. Pięcińska (ed.) (2001), *Zakład opieki zdrowotnej w praktyce*, Wydawnictwo Verlag Dashofer Sp. z o.o., Warszawa, p. 10–11.

It is right for such an observation to be carried out by independent, well-trained persons. A next step should be to confront these persons' observations with one another. Drawing conclusions from such observation, one can find new ways of satisfying patients' needs.

Providing a high quality of services being offered is an important factor, which helps attract new customers, but requires from a medical firm to make a significant organizational and financial effort.[313] Those firms, which strive after efficiency with respect to quality, should aim at drawing benefit from values they give to their customers. Customers' fidelity and loyalty towards a firm constitutes an important source of benefit a firm can gain thanks to the values it offers.

Table 20. Quality elements of health care products in private surgeries

Health care product	– Application of modern medical tools and methods of treatment – A sufficient time dedicated to a patient – A doctor's conversations with a patient about his/her health problems, advice concerning preventive treatment – A medical consultations with a patient about applied methods of treatment and their features – A possibility to purchase accessories offered by a doctor – Employing doctor's assistants (nurses, anaesthesiologist) – A doctor's university degree – A doctor's experience – Employing a doctor in a health care unit or hospital
Distribution	– Surgery's working hours – A possibility to make an appointment at a patient's best convenience – Surgery's location – Offering home visits after service – A possibility to make an immediate appointment (availability) – A possibility to make an appointment on the phone – Appointments are always on time – Safe parking space
Contact with the market	– advertising surgery in press, radio and TV – treating famous personalities – doctors' participation in public life – carrying out complicated procedures – doctors' employment by scientific centres (universities, institutions)
Medical fees	– possibility to look at a price list of medical services – receiving a detailed bill with a price for a given service – possibility to pay doctor's assistants for a service – informing a patient about a price before a service – offering cheaper and more expensive alternatives – offering price discounts for regular customers – offering price discounts for frequent customers

---

[313] B.I. Nogalski, J. Rybicki (ed.) (2002), *Nowoczesne zarządzanie zakładem opieki zdrowotnej*, Wydawnictwo Dom Organizatora, Toruń, p. 132–133.

Material aspects	– appearance of surgery
	– outward appearance of a doctor
	– fine service before appointment (waiting room, drinks)
	– having well-displayed diplomas, certificates

A proper communication, both verbal and non-verbal is an important but often underestimated element in a sphere of medical services. Due to a direct contact with a patient, doctors, nurses and other personnel should be familiar with general recommendations concerning such communication. It should be born in mind that in order for doctors' competence to be recognized and appreciated by patients, the following, necessary conditions must be met.

Medical personnel must be:

– available (present)

– approachable (kind)

– safe (faultless, credible).[314]

Here is a list of general principles of verbal communication:[315]

1. Don't apologize – apologizing is tantamount to recognizing one's mistakes, even if they were not committed and diminish interlocutor's prestige.

2. Don't ask – it is better to express one's wish in a firm way.

3. Don't comfort, it is better to support.

4. Don't give advice if you were not a part of a given experience.

5. Don't express conclusive opinion such as ALWAYS, NEVER.

6. Don't ask 'why' questions, but 'how' and 'in what way.'

7. Listen and hear, that is pay attention to what a patient is saying.

8. See and look straight in patient's eyes.

9. If you are to criticize, do it only in a constructive way.

10. Always thank for choosing us.

11. Use a language comprehensible to a patient.

Besides a verbal communication in a doctor's surgery, there exists an equally important non-verbal communication. It includes:[316]

1. Professional image (unfortunately considerably weakened owing to various scandals with doctors and nurses in a forefront, mistreating patients by low-rank employees and bad attitude towards a patient and one's own duties),

2. Private image – your reputation and opinion held by leaders,

3. Impression of professionalism, that is a competence of one's statements and actions, practical skills, knowledge of conventions, that is principles and habits typical of a given occupation, confidence and providing a sense of security, self-control, assertiveness,

4. An image of 'expert,'

5. Thieves of an image – that is an exaggerated modesty, making mistakes, depreciating one's skills, merits, contribution to work, effort, people hampering creativ-

---

[314] A.K. Kapliński, M.R. Łysiak, T.S. Pięcińska (ed.) (2001), *op. cit.*, p. 5.

[315] *Ibidem.*

[316] *Ibidem*, p. 3–6.

ity, lack of necessary knowledge, avoiding answers, excessive apologizing indicating a sense of guilt, low status, using hedge words such as 'but', 'maybe,' which put in question credibility of one's statements, coming late, bad organization, distancing oneself from one's workmates, bad manners, showing bad mood, oversensitivity to criticism, hesitation, excessive perfectionism, excessive fear of discredit, lack of reflectivity, going back on one's promises, insubordination, irresponsibility, disloyalty, unpunctuality, unreliability, instability, inconsistency, sloppiness or bad habits, sloppy clothing – a smock too small, or full of holes etc.,

6. Clothes language and body language – wearing a proper uniform – clean and neat,

7. Ability to listen and see,

8. Ability to conciliate one's environment – to a certain extent, this feature can be worked out, but it is determined by one's personality and temperament,

9. Knowing how to ask accurate questions – a training on a medical case history obtained through a conversation of a doctor with a patient,

10. Comprehension and effective communication,

11. Empathy and affinity,

12. Customs and moral standards,

13. Charisma, style or lack of it,

14. Opinion, reputation.

Apart from a 'human' factor, it is important to bear in mind a place, where a service is performed. Patients pay a particular attention to cleanness and how a surgery is equipped. These should be accurately sized – not too small, not to big, well-lit with natural or artificial light, equipped with necessary devices to perform a service. These devices should have valid safety certificates and be under constant, technical supervision to ensure safety. All compartments should have an accurate temperature allowing a smooth performance of an examination. The disabled people should have access to any facilities, which reduce inconvenience. It is very important to ensure discretion and intimacy in surgeries, which should be equipped with screens and sound-proof front door.

To sum up, value through quality, in a health care sector, can be obtained through a careful listening to patient's needs, designing standards of a given service, a monitoring, a smooth performing of a service and a conformity of this performance with made promises.[317] Moreover, a smoothly conducted internal marketing allows to provide employees with necessary tools to perform a medical service and the application of accurate quality standards and monitoring them enables to maintain a base of satisfied and loyal customers. The last but not least, one should not neglect technical parameters of surgeries, as they, too, play a crucial role in a way patients look upon the performance of medical services.

After going through the whole stage a customer evaluates a given service. He compares the expectations of a desired service (it reflects what a customer thinks can be obtained and should be obtained) with the expectations of an anticipated service

[317] M. Sullivan, D. Adcock (2003), *Marketing w handlu detalicznym*, Oficyna Ekonomiczna, Kraków, p. 326.

(it reflects a quality level of a service anticipated by a customer, which is to take place in accordance with his belief).[318] A customer's satisfaction is calculated through a comparison of the anticipated and perceived service. Thus, a rivalry among service providers is about a maximum adjustment of their offer to the expectations of service takers. It is becoming crucially important to get to know customer's all expectations with respect to the whole of the service provision process.

Unsatisfied customer may not only decide against buying services in a given health care unit, but also undertake firm steps directed against a service provider. They can be divided into two types:[319]

– public action – seeking redress directly in a health care unit, undertaking legal steps in order to obtain redress, lodging a complaint with Physician's Chamber or other type of institution,

– private action – giving up buying services in a given health care unit, warning friends against a unit or a service provider.

– In a pre- and after-sale process, the following factors[320]affect customer's behaviour:

– cultural factors: culture, subculture and a social class,

– social factors: groups of reference, a family, a role in a community and a status,

– personal factors: age, a stage in life, occupation, financial standing, style of life, personality and self-esteem,

– psychological factors: motivation, perception, knowledge, beliefs and attitudes.

Regardless of any economic aspects pertaining to management of a health care unit, it should control its actions with respect to ethics and a social responsibility. The following laws[321] have a direct influence on health care units: The Declaration of Human Rights (1948), which says that every human has a right to live in conditions ensuring a well-being and good health for him and his family. The Declaration of Children Rights (1959), Convention and Declaration of Women Rights (1979, 1993, 1995,1997); International Convention on Economic, Social and Cultural Rights (1996); Convention of Human Rights and Biomedicine (1997). In accordance with the constitution of the World Health Organization: 'attainment of possibly the highest standard of health is every human's one of the basic rights irrespective of race, religion, political beliefs, financial and social standing.' It is bioethics, which deals with these aspects. It contains the most important rights of ethics and deontology, belonging to norms of behaviour between medical personnel and a patient. Certain recommendations of European and international organizations are more deontological than ethical in nature. 'An ill person may have many rights (…), but what is important is that he/she expects an immediate, medical help, which will be up to the mark. Medical ethic constitutes a kind of guarantee that a doctor will always bear in mind a patient's interest and his wishes. Ethics and human rights are interlaced with each other. It is respect for a patient's free and conscious decision, but also respect for

---

[318] A. Styś, *Marketing usług*, PWE, Warszawa, p. 43–47.

[319] *Ibidem*, p. 43–47.

[320] *Ibidem*, p. 53.

[321] J.B. Karski (2003), *Praktyka i teoria – promocja zdrowia. Wybrane zagadnienia*, Wydawnictwo CeDeWu, Warszawa, p. 25–27.

a doctor's decision to choose a type of treatment, which gives sense to an informed consent, respect for life, human dignity, private life and doctor-patient privilege.'[322] It should be remembered that it is the state, which steps in, when it comes to a free access to health care. It does so through undertaking certain measures, thus, becoming a participator in a medical dialogue.

'Scientific progress gives rise, every day, to new ethical problems; genetic manipulations, in vitro fertilization, research into embryos give hope but carry danger, too; a doctor must look for a narrow path between huge benefits and possible abuse and departure from principles.'[323] Medical ethic is restricted by patient's rights as well as the existing limitations of medical help. Bioethical principles of medical personnel are affected by norms and principles applicable in a given society. At the meeting point of these principles and bioethics there may be conflicts. In Poland, medical ethic, to a greater extent, is influenced by doctrines of catholic church. 'Medical moral standards of the church complies with norms of Hippocrates' ethics, enriching them with a notion of sacredness of human life as a God's gift and regarding a sick person to be his son, personifying him with Christ himself. (…) In any case, out of respect for God as well as immortality of human soul, Christian morality cannot be reconciled either with utilitarian or extremely liberal, biological or sociological attitude towards ethics. (…) Human life is regarded as a fundamental value with relation to other values (…) and that is why the church does not approve abortion and euthanasia. The principle of therapy referred to as the principle of entirety occupies a central place in medical ethics. It is in accordance with this principle that a medical intervention is permissible in cases, where it becomes necessary to save human life or restore health in human as entirety. Medical intervention should be based on the principle of freedom and responsibility.'[324]

Doctors' morality and their duties towards a patient are governed by the Code of Medical Ethics.[325] In Poland during the interwar period the Code of Medical Ethics did not exist. It was Hippocratic oath, which served as a basis of ethic action (…) In 1977 Polish Doctors' Association issued a 'Collection of ethic-deontological principles of polish doctor.' It was effective until 1993, when it was adopted as a constitution[326] during the National Doctors' Convention held on 12–14.12.1993.

The Code of Medical Ethic sets forth what constitutes a violation of ethics when exercising a medical profession. In many situations violation of ethical principles is tantamount to violation of law. In such situations, apart from the Code of Medical Ethic, it is doctor's profession law from 28 October 1950 and the Ministry of Health's resolution on doctor's professional liability from 26 September 1990 that is applicable. There are situations when a violation of law does not entail violation of norms set forth by the Code of Medical Ethic and not every violation of ethic results in legal liability.[327]

---

[322] *Ibidem*, p. 27.

[323] *Ibidem*, p. 27.

[324] *Ibidem*, p. 28–29.

[325] A.K. Kapliński, M.R. Łysiak, T.S. Pięcińska (ed.) (2001), *op. cit.*, cz. 12, rozdz. 4, podrozdz. 1, p. 1.

[326] *Ibidem*.

[327] *Ibidem*, p. 2.

'In case of illegal acts , a doctor is liable to civil proceedings in Doctor's Court, and if these acts involve criminal responsibility, he is liable to criminal proceedings in a Criminal Court.'[328]

Ethical aspects of doctors' behaviour should be highlighted and subject to control all the time, as this is human health and life that is entrusted to them. One must not lose from sight this crucial element. All undertakings directed at creation of medical services, their promotion, distribution and price should be subordinated to these ethical issues.

Conclusions. On the basis of this study it appears that people related to health care, should pay greater attention to patient's needs. They are often articulated but not all of them. Needs should always be recognized and monitored by people trained for this purpose. It is important as well to provide optimal environment, in which medical services are performed – availability, convenient appointment rules, well equipped surgeries, trainings and upgrading skills for medical personnel. Medical personnel should also be characterized by excellent manners and ability to establish interpersonal relations. During a process of rendering medical services, one should not forget about patients' rights and adhering to principles of medical ethics. Most of all, a greater emphasis should be put on informing patients about their rights and possibility of their enforcement. It seems that these elements can help enhance the quality of medical services and contribute to a better competitiveness of a given health care unit.

3.2.2. PATIENTS' SATISFACTION IN THE MEDICAL SERVICES QUALITY MANAGEMENT – RESEARCH PROBLEMS

3.2.2.1. INTRODUCTION

The problem of the satisfaction of customers is one of the prevailing ones in the area of quality management. All organizations which have normalized quality management systems examine customer's satisfaction and the results of the research are discussed during management reviews. The customer's satisfaction plays a significant role in excellence models. The customer's satisfaction is quite easy to be surveyed in branches other than medical, but in case of medical services a number of specific factors should be taken into account including: lack of guarantee for all kinds of services, social character of activity, direct influence on the quality of life, interaction (including: lack of medical knowledge and possibility of quality assessment by patients), dependence (not only in the area of biological organisms but also at the place of providing the services), complexity (concerning the realization procedures as well as the result of the treatment), lack of correlation between the price and demand.

---

[328] *Ibidem.*

In the sector of health care evaluation is the derivative of many variables. Hence, in medical services perceptible satisfaction is not directly linked with loyalty, but there is a correlation between the perceptible level of satisfaction and the state of health.

3.2.2.2. FACTORS AFFECTING SATISFACTION

Generally, it is approved that satisfaction from the performed services in medical organizations is mainly dependent on the quality of doctor-patient interaction. In some cases medical skills are low, but the patients still are prone to ascribe favorable opinions to doctor's work. It happens when doctors have a high level of interpersonal skills. The quality of such interactions is affected by the possibility of giving detailed information by patients (the possibility of "talking oneself out"), the doctor's ability to present the problem in a concrete manner (comprehensibility of the message), waiting time for an appointment, and the amount of information given. However, it should be stressed that quality of the provided medical advice is more important.

Yet, such understanding of the patients' satisfaction is much restricted and the construction of research tools accounting only for the conception of features is a considerable misunderstanding. For it is generally known that the patient's satisfaction is influenced by a number of other factors (e.g. its surroundings, their experience, groups of reference etc.).

Interactions between doctors and their patients are characterized by insecurity and asymmetry of knowledge.[329,330]

The smaller patients' insecurity is, the bigger satisfaction they feel. Yet the problem is the uneven allocation of knowledge. On the one hand, patients who are given to understand that their awareness has no influence on the way the service is provided may feel insufficiency. On the other hand, the doctor must articulate the knowledge, since it is the attribute of power/authority and determines the jurisdiction trust.

The problem is the delivery of genuine information by patients. According to Jill Thistelthwaite (2005), doctors are aware of the fact that patients lie and, what is more, accept minor lies (white lies in their opinion). Patients know that doctors not always tell them everything- they hide secret information. Yet, sometimes for various reasons patients want to live a lie. Even obvious facts are kept secret. An extra factor lowering the quality of interactions is a collection of various situations beyond doctor's control. Doctors do not know how a disease will develop. The period of treatment sometimes cannot be conscientiously determined. Robert Langreth (2009) describes a few cases of patients who recovered despite being terminally ill (the last stadium of cancer). In each case patients were informed that they have a few months of life left.

---

[329] L.E.M. Choongsup (1999), *Optimal medical treatment under asymmetric information*, "Journal of Heath Economics", Vol. 14 (4).

[330] C. Herrera-Espiñeira, M. Rodríguez del Aguila, M. Rodríguez del Castillo, A.F. Valdivia, I.R. Sánchez (2009), *Relationship between anxiety level of patients and their satisfaction with different aspects of healthcare*, "Health Policy", Vol. 89, Issue 1.

Many surveys indicate that patients want to be treated individually, but also pay attentions to how other patients are treated. According to some hospitals, patients have a right to get full information about the way the service is provided. Doctors apologize to patients for minor mistakes, give them flowers in order to fully apologize for the delays, inconveniences etc. Not only the asymmetry of knowledge, but also other theories may be useful for the analysis of the patient-doctor interaction. One of them is the social comparisons theory. Patients judge their relations, but also the way other patients are treated. If they were provided the perfect service and others' was not the best one, then their satisfaction decreases.

The architecture, the layout of the building and all the rooms, attention to infrastructure and service environment have a big influence on the level of patients' satisfaction.[331] These factors come a little below medical care in the 'ranking' of factors favourable to patients' satisfaction.

Patients' satisfaction depends not only on medical care. Additional services have great influence on the general level of satisfaction. That is why big hospitals conduct surveys aiming to measure patients' satisfaction with meals and medical care. Apart from food quality, also the way meals are served is of great importance. Patients judge not only the quality of a meal but also if the food is appropriately portioned and whether it is wasted. Some hospitals introduced self-service or a system of portioning. It turns out that proper quality distribution may reduce costs (including 'defects' costs) and increase the level o patients' satisfaction.[332]

Quality perception surveys indicate that there are differences between categories and types of insurance. For example Priporas, Laspa and Kamenidou showed that men and younger patients tend to judge the level of satisfaction a little higher than women and elderly people.

However, in this case, to draw any general conclusions, one would have to take into account cultural, environmental and economic differences. Behavior of the medium-level medical personnel has a very positive influence on the satisfaction. It has been proven that nurses who regularly tend patients significantly improve the level of satisfaction.[333]

Some researches attempt to combine various approaches and apply a system concept. This results from the fact that patients' satisfaction is influenced by factors that belong to different subsystems. Medical support system has also a significant influence. Perception of this support influences subsequent expectations of patients and the reputation of a hospital or a clinic.

What hinders research interpretation and influences the level of satisfaction are key factors. Like in every process, they have the greatest influence on service quality.

---

[331] P.B. Harris, Ch. Ross, G. McBride, L. Curtis (2002), *A Place to Heal: Environmental Sources of Satisfaction Among Hospital Patients,* "Journal of Applied Social Psychology", Vol. 32, Issue 6.

[332] K. Kuperberg, A. Caruso, S. Dello, D. Mager (2008), *How will a room service delivery system affect dietary intake, food costs, food waste and patient satisfaction in a paediatric hospital? A pilot study,* "Journal of Foodservice", Vol. 19, Issue 5.

[333] T. Sobaski, M. Abraham, R. Fillmore, D.E. McFall, R. Davidhizar (2008), *The Effect of Routine Rounding by Nursing Staff on Patient Satisfaction on a Cardiac Telemetry Unit,* "Health Care Manager", Vol. 27, Issue 4.

Such key factors are some crucial stages of providing service (e.g. admission after an accident). One should also remember about the influence of cultural traits on the level of satisfaction. For example, patients in Japan are sensitive about the sense of harmony and high empathic skills of doctors.

Patients' satisfaction depends on the satisfaction of medical staff but a satisfied doctor does not have to take care of their patients' needs to a larger extent. These interrelations have been affirmed a long time ago. In health-care institutions, satisfaction of employees is a prerequisite to satisfaction of patients. The source of satisfaction for employees is well performed work. However, if the employees' satisfaction is low – and such is the situation in most hospitals today – the problem of patients' satisfaction becomes a basic one. Contrary to popular belief, the key to high satisfaction of employees is not only a higher salary but also professional stabilization. Wherever a long lasting and volatile health care reform takes place, achieving professional satisfaction is very difficult.

The external opinion spread and repeated by the media affects the level of satisfaction. Health care system is usually spoken of negatively. When patients receive a service of different quality than they expected, they experience a positive "disappointment". Satisfaction increases but does not last for long. This negative image increases the number of negative opinions, prejudices and distortions.

An underestimated factor which influences satisfaction is the organizational structure. According to theory of organization, organization influences employees' behavior, but it is not the most important factor in this case. One should assume that the structure directly affects clients' satisfaction. For example, in Japan, there are small wards which offer specialized services. Patients have very good care and at the same time, thanks to the structure of these wards, the doctors do not have to take part in numerous procedures. Therefore, a question arises as to the possibilities of medical competence and their influence on the level of satisfaction.

More recent research suggestions relate to indirect measurements of patients' satisfaction. The subjects of these researches are the tendency to follow medical advice and the tendency to return the same clinic or hospital.

3.2.2.3. SERVICE PROCEDURES

System procedures play a significant role in quality management. Some of them are compulsory (i.e. records and documents supervision, undertaking preventive actions). When we include recommendation regarding creating quality systems and two theories, that is justice and trust, we can consider creating patient service procedures. However, we have to remember about restrictions. Normative trust is easily created in contrast to competence, interpersonal trust. During formation of the procedure we can use common knowledge of safe service. For example, no-one during the procedure can disturb the medical staff. All documents have to be filled out in a secluded room, patients have to have access to press, television, they can use coffee express, etc. Every service can be assessed by patients. However, most important for them is access to information about the course of treatment. Some hospitals tend to finalize the procedure in one day. It means that if an x-ray shows that further examination is needed, it is realized in the same day. In our country this is very often impossible. Sometimes the patient has to wait several months for another visit. Another barrier is the financing method of medical services. As a consequence, not only the patient, but the entire health service suffers.

Communication procedures may play a positive role in quality system. Many errors in medical service are made because of improper communication (according to American Medical Association most of errors). It was noticed that communication methods may be important for patients' satisfaction. That is why it is recommended to structuralize the service process. For example, it is advised that the entire communication procedure should be divided into several unambiguous stages. Actions preceding registration should consist of giving detailed information (when patients have to apply, what time, what documents to bring, what to expect etc.). At this stage the health centers send all the necessary documents via email. The second stage is patient education (before accepting, e.g. to the hospital). Patients are informed about what to eat, how to deal with the sickness, how to take care of themselves etc. This information is very important, especially when patients are waiting for the procedure. Sometimes, when patient is waiting for the procedure, we measure his level of satisfaction. Another stage is delivering information booklet with information about health center, hospital and procedures we realize. Before the procedure the patient has to be informed about the procedure and about possible complications which is one of the hardest tasks. Communication with patients takes place also after the procedure – they are informed, on a daily basis what to do. This communication has also another point – promotional. It underlines that direct communication is necessary for satisfaction.

The creation of procedures, for example patient service is meaningful in the first stages of incorporating quality systems; however, we have to remember that procedures create standards. That is why in several reports from studies, one of the factors responsible for decreasing of satisfaction are non-procedural actions. Using patient empowerment we can avert this; however, due to information asymmetry we can do it only to a small degree.

3.2.2.4. SATISFACTION MEASUREMENT

Satisfaction measurement in clients has become widely known thanks to the normalized systems of quality management and because of the excellence models (e.g. EFQM). Many hospitals in the USA and Western Europe have reached for the recommendations resulting from the TQM conception.

The patients' satisfaction is studied through the use of the two basic approaches:
– the process approach – in which the whole process of supply and realization of services is studied – from the input through the output, with taking into consideration the interactions (not only in the doctor-patient interaction),

– the "physical attributes" approach – in which the appearance of the room is studied (the evaluation concerns the appearance and the state of the room, cleanliness,[334] alarm system, comfort, temperature).

Because of the economic and demographic conditions, the organizations that provide medical services are becoming in a larger scale open systems. Many services will be provided in the patient's house or in health centers, and this is why the process approach seems to be fully justified.

In most cases the patient's satisfaction is analyzed on the basis of the specially prepared survey or interview forms. The forms vary in structure, but we may talk about some key factors of satisfaction, that are very frequently taken into consideration in their creation. These factors include the quality of the information obtained, respect of privacy, professionalism of the services, friendly environment. Of course, when the patients evaluate the professionalism, in fact they evaluate the organizational behaviors of the doctors (their interpersonal skills). The following items are subject to the study: general level of satisfaction, just and fair treatment, patients expectations, the scale of satisfaction.

The study of satisfaction is carried out with the worn-out SERVQUEL scale, which was created on the basis of the feature conception. The form that is worth recommending is the form by Swan, Sawyer and Van Matre, whose structure has three basic elements: the level of the general satisfaction (the evaluation of the infrastructure and the medical care), the level of the satisfaction of expectations (the difference between the expectations and the actual service provided), equality and honesty (the services in relation to the means used, the level of pain experienced etc.). The study may be carried out during any month because the data obtained are reliable (the group of patients varies, there is no need to add a particular research sample – the study is carried out in all patients).

The best hospitals face some other problem – how to evaluate and create the client's satisfaction when all the prior study results were exceptionally high? Additional obstacles in the satisfaction measurement are met by the private health centers, the hospitals, where patients pay for the medical services (the bills are not regulated by the Ministry of Health). The fees, especially the high ones, cause the increase of expectations. The higher these expectations are, the higher the standard of the services supposed to be. Unfortunately, sometimes these expectations are unrealistic. There is a clash between the means used and the quality level. However, the financial engagement itself increases the level of faith in the positive outcome of the treatment.

3.2.2.5. OTHER ORGANIZATIONAL VALUES

The satisfaction study itself, with taking into consideration only situational, environmental and psycho-social factors, is a good step on the path to creation of a pro-

---

[334] Cleanliness in some researches has position No. 3. Patients consider cleanliness as a standard and that is why to assess such a factor is very difficult and minor.

qualitative organization. However, the next step has to be the study of either different organizational values, or satisfaction, that is fully determined by these values. Numerous studies indicate the existence of a certain system of organizational values in which satisfaction plays a secondary role. The original values are, for instance, trust and justice (procedural justice is achieved, among other things, via procedures of patient service). A key value in managing medical organizations is trust, mainly due to the situation of uncertainty and risk. In managing hospitals and other organizations, the phenomenon of trust is mentioned.[335] The importance of trust will increase. Many medical services are already provided online. Beside interpersonal trust, technological trust will gain significance as well.

Therefore, the newest studies analyze not only the influence of satisfaction, but also, in accordance with the theory of values, the influence of trust, satisfaction and commitment.[336] Many interesting relations take place between particular kinds of trust, as well as between other values. The patients' trust cannot be built without trust in doctors and middle-level medical staff, trust concerning competence, as well as procedural and institutional trust. It is beyond doubt that the most important trust is the trust in doctors. Studies that pertained to service organizations allow one to even draw a conclusion that this trust can last despite the lack of trust in the organizations. Studies conducted in the medical sector so far result in an unequivocal conclusion that the patients' trust and satisfaction depend on the doctors' reputation.[337]

Formation of organizational values by organizations providing medical services is a difficult and limited task. For instance, implementing two different models of patient service, where one group of patients is better because they have additional insurance and the other group is worse, will cause destruction of trust and satisfaction and thus will reduce the number of patients. This remark pertains to centers that will provide services for differentiated groups of patients. Moreover, according to the theory of justice, the decrease of trust and satisfaction will be observed both in the group that pays additional money and in the group that makes use of the traditional social insurance system. The comparison of service methods is not favorable to satisfaction of patients who can afford additional services.

Trust formation is not easy, but one can make use of rich knowledge of private organizations, whose programs of maintaining consumer trust are carried out on an everyday basis. The examples of activities include: education of patients, improvement of service provision processes, service personalization, self-presentation and trust articulation.

---

[335] P.R. Brown (2009), *The phenomenology of trust: A Schutzian analysis of the social construction of knowledge by gynae-oncology patients*, "Health, Risk & Society", Vol. 11, Issue 5, p. 391–407.

[336] D.F. Spake, J.S. Bishop Jr. (2009), *The Impact of Perceived Closeness on the Differing Roles of Satisfaction, Trust, Commitment, and Comfort on Intention to Remain with a Physician*, "Health Marketing Quarterly", Vol. 26, Issue 1, p. 1–15.

[337] E. Torres, A.Z. Vasques-Parraga, C. Barra (2009), *The Path of Patient Loyalty and the Role of Doctor Reputation*, "Health Marketing Quarterly", Vol. 26, Issue 3, p. 183–197.

3.2.2.6. CONCLUSION

Usefulness of studies conducted today in hospitals and clinics is little. They are carried out negligently, often only to fulfill requirements of the ISO 9001:2008 norm. One can observe the lack of professional methods of sample selection, specification of key factors (for further analyses and programs) etc. Taking into account the enormous significance of satisfaction and other values in the processes of patient treatment and prevention, conducting those studies professionally should be the aim. One of the basic problems is significance of the quality management systems themselves. The basic condition of changes is abandoning the conviction that quality systems are implemented solely to obtain a certificate and additional points during making contracts. Paying for quality reduces motivation and subjects responsible for health promotion should bear this rule in mind.

3.2.3. PERSPECTIVE OF PATIENT IN MANAGING QUALITY OF MEDICAL SERVICES

3.2.3.1. INTRODUCTION

Dynamic changes in Polish health care sector- an after-effect of social and economic transformations, resulted in a search for optimal solutions, the aim of which is to improve a quality of medical services. It was observed that there exists an essential correlation between a successful health care unit and a quality of services it renders. An effective rivalry and providing patients with anticipated 'value,' forced managers to devise a range of performance-measuring yardsticks, which go far beyond an economic sphere.

The realization of having to optimize the quality costs seems to have permeated the sphere of health care unit management. In accordance with this realization, a well-balanced functioning entails obtaining right proportions between the quality of services and the cost they generate; In management terms such philosophy is referred to as 'quality at a reasonable price.' In market-oriented health care units, a customer and his needs should serve as a starting point for any decision making. Getting to know the customers' needs and preferences is essential to design medical services, evaluate how they are perceived and a constant improvement; It is impossible to overestimate the customers' feedback for health care managers.

In this paper, the authors made an attempt to highlight a problem of quality from a patients' point of view, laying emphasis on specificity of this quality and a customers' potential influence on quality-promoting actions of health care units.

3.2.3.2. SPECIFICITY OF MEDICAL SERVICE QUALITY

Majority of undertakings in a health care system are processes, which aim at generating a medical service, being an end product of these processes. Such an approach requires that there be a supplier of a service and a customer (a patient) – a service receiver. Medical services rendered to a patient are a set of medical and non-medical services, the aim of which is to restore, maintain and improve patient's health.

Medical and non-medical processes, performed by a service supplier strictly depend on resources he has at his disposal. These include not only infrastructure but also applied systems and methods of management, which all constitute essential conditions, which a functioning of this specific service provider hinges upon. A quality of medical services happens to be assessed through a prism of such conditions.[338]

Defining the quality of medical services is not an easy thing as one needs to take into account their specific features, not to be compared with others: a social dimension, disjoining a service receiver from a payer: a patient being forced by his ailments to receive a service and a difficulty to measure efficiency of the applied treatment. Moreover, health care, apart from a range of universal features, typical of service industry, such as: immateriality, indivisibility, impermanence, changeability, is characterized by:

– uncertainty and risk – a patient's condition, injury, ailment is often unpredictable, difficult to control and happens to be changeable, this depending on complexity of a patient's illness, effects of treatment,

– highly-skilled personnel – medical employees are subject to stringent legislation, which sets forth their minimal qualifications and duties towards patients,

– patient's limitation on choice of technology and a range of service – a patient, who undergoes treatment, delegates his decision making to a doctor, limiting his/her sovereignty; a doctor, on the other hand, has a right to exercise his profession, which authorizes him to make independent decisions with respect to a course of treatment,

– complexity of a process of satisfying health needs – it means supplying various services and it pertains to a complexity of both personnel's skills as well as procedures,

– interrelation between effects of treatment and a service receiver's given attitude – a choice of optimal type of treatment does not guarantee a positive effect, if it is not approved by a patient (for example, taking drugs as prescribed, giving up addiction, following recommended diets, preventive treatment).

In the case of medical services, what is characteristic is a shortage of information, which stems from a high specialization of these services. Patients, as non-professionals, do not have sufficient knowledge to formulate credible judgments, which results in limitation on making an informed, consumer decision. Furthermore, non-market-economy nature of these decisions and NHS' and rival health care units' simultaneous attempts to impose market-economy attitudes constitutes a considerable dilemma

---

[338] A. Maciąg, K. Kuszewski, K. Topczewska-Tylińska, J. Michalak (2007), *Rola procesów, standardów i procedur w kształtowaniu jakości świadczeń zdrowotnych*, Wyd. Alfamedica, Bielsko-Biała.

for health care. Market-economy mechanisms are particularly visible in a process of service contracting, complying with legal requirements, adopting a marketing orientation by health care units.

Medical services are processual – a psychotherapy, for example, or can be emergencies – an appendix removal, and they are performed within a given time limit. These services are characterized by a high level of laboriousness and require highly skilled personnel. They are diverse, both with respect to quantity and quality and their form, purpose and construction must meet external customers' needs, including patients and their families.[339]

The above-mentioned specific features of medical services make it difficult to work out an unambiguous definition of their quality. One can find diverse definitions of quality in literature. The most important thing for a patient is a compatibility of a medical service with his subjective expectations. Health care management must not lose sight of quality as a technical aspect, as well as end processes, which take into account economic criteria.

It is difficult to talk about measuring a quality, in a situation when one cannot determine it. Unfortunately, marketing, management and medical science do not know one, universal definition of quality, which one could refer to and adapt in order to determine what a quality of medical service is. A lack of a uniform definition of quality is not indifferent to service rendering processes and exerts an important influence on a type of information passed to patients and service providers. In consequence, consumers come up against obstacles, when it comes to measure a quality. Their perception of given elements of medical services becomes disrupted. The differences with respect to defining a quality also result in a lack of comparability of quality measuring results in rival health care units.

Contemporary technology in the domain of quality is extremely dynamic. Its development started during the World War II, when a methodological study into a quality was initiated. Generally, an approach to quality can be identified with the following suggestions.[340]

– quality as a feature – a product's compatibility with specified requirements,
– quality as a relation – a customer's level of satisfaction,
– quality as a set of features affecting a relation – an anticipated level of uniformity and reliability, combined with low costs and adjustment to market demands.

---

[339] See M. Kautsch, M. Whitfield, J. Klich (ed.) (2001), *Zarządzanie w opiece zdrowotnej*, Wydawnictwo Uniwersytetu Jagiellońskiego, Kraków.

[340] M. Dobska, P. Dobski (2004), *TQM zarządzanie przez jakość w zakładach opieki zdrowotnej*, Wyd. Mars Graf, Poznań.

Picture 7. Service quality model

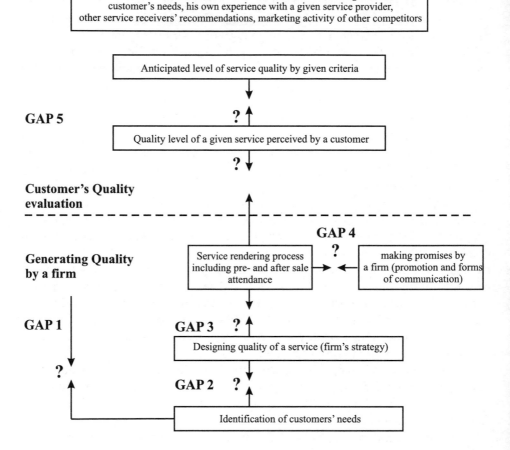

Source: J. Mazur, *Service Marketing Management*, Difin, Warszawa, p. 93.

Quality of services is much more complicated to define than a quality of goods. As a rule, a customer actively participates in a process of generating a service and his attitudes and feelings have an influence on a final effect. It is a service receiver, who evaluates quality of a given service. This evaluation can concern both, the effects of the service and its course. The quality of services as a complex term, has many dimensions, which is reflected in the existence of numerous models, which conceptualize them. One of a more popular models of service quality is the model of gaps, exposing elements (gaps), which disrupt a process of service provision to a service receiver. The model of service quality, taking into account the above-mentioned gaps were presented on picture 7.

These include:

– gap 1 – a difference between customers' expectations and how these expectations are perceived,

– gap 2 – a difference between how customers' expectations are perceived by managing personnel and specificities of a service quality,

– gap 3 – a difference between specificities of service quality and a quality of service rendering,

– gap 4 – determines a dispersion between a quality of service rendering and information, which a customer obtained about it,

– gap 5 – expresses a difference between extent to which expectations are satisfied and how a service is perceived by a customer.[341]

One should also take a note of a certain delay in scientific research into a service quality: the research into the quality of goods were conducted much earlier. R. Kolman and T. Tkaczyk, in their paper from 1996,[342] set forth the most essential elements determining quality deficiencies in services. According to them, these include:

– lack of convincing and consistent promotion of quality in media,

– failure to recognize a quality by businessmen,

– poor knowledge of quality by businessmen,

– lack of experience or little experience in reaping benefits from quality promoting actions,

– poor awareness of benefits coupled with conscious actions, which promote quality,

– lack of popular and dedicated literature on a service quality,

– shortage of skilled personnel in service industry,

– shortage of specialists in medical service quality.

Looking back on the last decade, it would be interesting to conduct an empirical verification of validity of the above-mentioned statements; the authors of this paper believe that a majority of them is still valid.

Moving on to the ground of Polish health care system, it is worth taking a note that there has been recently a significant evolution with respect to our approach to the quality of medical services. The implementation of quality management systems complying with ISO 9000 norm, in many health care units, serves as evidence of this phenomenon. The idea standing behind these systems is to streamline processes, which affect health care units functioning and to improve their image and credibility in the environment. There are many levels on which to study effects of the implementation of these systems but it is a customers' feedback, which seems to be the most important. After all, it is patients, who should be chief beneficiaries of quality management systems, through receiving better care and service. A high quality is a prerequisite for the existence of the patient's subjective satisfaction and his objective benefits.

---

[341] R. Karaszewski (2003), *Systemy zarządzania jakością największych korporacji świata i ich dyfuzja*, Wyd. Uniwersytetu im. M. Kopernika, Toruń.

[342] R. Kolman, T. Tkaczyk (1996), *Jakość usług. Poradnik*, Wyd. Ośrodek Postępu Organizacyjnego, Bydgoszcz.

3.2.3.3. Patients' influence on quality promoting actions in health care units

The context, in which quality management systems in health care units are functioning, leaves ample space for analysis of any parties involved in the functioning of these units. These include:[343]
  – patients, as direct customers, external ones,
  – personnel as indirect customers, internal ones,
  – managing personnel of health care units,
  – experts on quality,
  – politicians, lobbies, media,
  – the state, self-government,
  – NHS
  – suppliers, strategic partners
  – competition in a form of public and private health care units,
  – public institutions: banks, courts, supervisory bodies,
  Without any doubts, the importance of service quality translates itself also through a subjective perception of organization by various interested parties. Potential customers of health care units do not necessarily need to apply the same lens to the quality rendered by them. For example, patients and their families focus their attention on effects of treatment as well as material and immaterial aspects of services. Meanwhile, health care employees associate quality, mainly with reliable execution of entrusted tasks, performing a service in accordance with possessed expertise. Two main aspects of health care quality dominate in dedicated literature. One concerns a clinical quality, the other reflects the extent, to which consumers' expectations are satisfied or patients' experience. A difference between an anticipated service and the actual one is an individual and subjective matter from a receiver's point of view. Moreover, a difficulty in identification of patients' preferences, stem, among other things, from a fact that a financing institution and the actual receiver of a service are two different entities. Getting to know expectations of service receivers gains special significance, given that patients' attitudes keep changing. They become more aware, define more precisely their expectations, pose questions, report doubts.

Under the national health insurance scheme, a patient has a right to an equal access to medical services, financed by the state budget. In this area, we can differentiate clinical services, irrespective of the ill person's financial standing. Health care services financed by the state budget include a right to: medical services, material services and concomitant services. Medical services are actions oriented at preventive treatment, maintaining, rescuing, restoring or improving health, as well as other action undertaken by medical personnel. Material services include medications, medical products, orthopedic equipment and accessories. Concomitant services include accommodation, food and ambulance transportation.

---

[343] K. Opolski, G. Dykowska, M. Możdżonek (2005), *Zarządzanie przez jakość w usługach zdrowotnych. Teoria i praktyka*, Wyd. CeDeWu, Warszawa.

In a majority of European countries, there has been recently a significant increase in importance as well as patients' active participation in a health care system. Although, patients and their families have always been an integral part of the health care process, far too often, their voices in a public debate on improvement, were missing. It still happens, unfortunately, that consumers' opinion is ignored, and their attempt to define expectations, futile. On the one hand, it stems from patients' unawareness of health care system's internal regulations, on the other one, however, from a permission of medical environment to approve of attitudes formed in the previous era.[344]

Patients' needs and their satisfaction are considered to be a multi dimensional aspect, based on a correlation between their experience and expectations. Patients are most anxious to obtain an effective, smooth and safe treatment and care. The quality so perceived, depends, among other things, on skills of medical personnel and conditions, in which services are rendered, but also on procedures and organizational climate, in which they are to be performed. The last but not least, it depends on a patient's speedy recovery, once he leaves a hospital. Examining the quality of medical services from a customer's point of view, one should take into account certain elements, which include: personnel's professionalism, patient's safety, a quick access to proper counseling, effective treatment performed by trustworthy specialists, access to clear and intelligible information, participation in a decision making with respect to a treatment and care, respect and intimacy during diagnosis and treatment. A patient bases his appraisal of quality on effects of treatment, but does not ignore material elements, previous experiences and attitudes of medical personnel. One should bear in mine, however, that the above-mentioned factors will gain significance, if a technical quality is low.

3.2.3.4. PATIENT'S RIGHTS

Patients' satisfaction with non-medical aspects of care, often correlates with an accurate understanding of obtained feedback and better observance of doctor's instructions, which has a substantial influence on successful treatment. The latest recommendations of World Health Organization point to sensitivity to patients' needs. In Polish legislation, this issue is thoroughly addressed in the Bill referred to as the Bill of patient's rights.[345] Patient's rights were set forth in order to, through enforcing them, boost quality of medical services and establish, unambiguously, a patient's position as an equal participator of a treatment process. At the same time, patient's rights normalize relations between a health care unit and a patient. The bill of patient's rights identifies several main components, determining a quality. These include:

A right to dignity and intimacy, including a right to be treated with respect, kindness, patients; a closed-circle atmosphere of medical examination, pertaining to

---

[344] P. Gruca-Wójtowicz (2009), *Jakość usług medycznych w kontekście zróżnicowanych oczekiwań stron zainteresowanych*, "Problemy Jakości", No. 3, p. 22–26.

[345] Ustawa z dnia 6 listopada 2008 r. o Prawach Pacjenta i Rzeczniku Praw Pacjenta (Dz. U. z dnia 31 marca 2009 r.).

a presence of only indispensable staff; preventing unauthorized persons from entering a surgery; medical examination and a procedure performed in a place, which
rules out a likelihood of a patient being looked at or eavesdropped; discretion when
asking questions in a presence of third parties; encouraging to ask questions; a right
to inform about a patient's condition and alternative methods of treatment; a right
to discus patients' preferences and expectations; a patient has a right to know, even
if prognosis is unfavourable, he has also a right to refuse to make any comment on
that; a right to die in dignity, including a right to relieve pain and suffering; a right to
pastoral service.

A right to information, including: intelligible explanation of a patient's condition, determining a planned method of treatment, including a right to express one's
autonomous, independent consent; giving unambiguous information as to where,
when, and who will inform a patient about progress; describing a course of a medical
procedure, diagnosis examination, taking into account all, potential complications
and a possibility of applying alternative methods of treatment; it is up to a patient to
give access to medical data to persons he points to.; in case of doubts as to doctor's
diagnosis, a patient is entitled to have an extra consultation, he can also abandon his
right to be informed; upon termination of his hospitalization, a patient is entitled to
receive a patient's case history, which contains: diagnosis, test results, applied treatment, further indications.

A right to confidentiality, which includes strict observance of doctor-patient privilege, a full protection of personal data, contained in medical documentation; apart
a medical personnel, only persons authorized by a patient, have access to patient's
documentation.

A right to have access to benefits, including: a patient insured under NHS scheme,
has a right to profit from all benefits, contained in the so called positive benefit basket
and governed by the NHS and Ministry of health's resolution; a right to obtain an immediate medical assistance in emergencies; in the case of medical procedures, consultations, outpatient counselling, a patient can count to get an appointment within
a reasonable time limit; a patient has a right to choose a service provider, a doctor,
a nurse or a midwife.

– A right to use currently applied medical technologies, including: a doctor is
free to choose from among available methods of treatment, which he deems the most
effective, he must not, however, use methods, considered to be obsolete or have
a negative opinion.

– A right to have a contact with one's relatives, including: a patient has a right to
be accompanied by his relative during a visit; access to social and psychological support; he also has a right to refuse to contact anyone.

Patient will be satisfied only if the existing standards are up to his wishes or
if these standards exceed his expectations; these, in turn, need recognizing on
a regular basis. Patients are most anxious to know professional qualifications and
skills of medical personnel, including nurses and analysts. They expect to receive
a suitable analysis of symptoms of their condition, diagnosis of a problem as well
as accurate treatment. Failure to inform a patient about a legitimacy and a course
of examination and the sustained feeling of a patient's lack of trust in a person

performing the examination, cause a patient to believe that his health and life are in danger. In such a case, a patient becomes anxious, aggressive and makes the examination difficult or even impossible, which, not infrequently, results in complications.

Health care sector functioning, based on economy model, contributes more and more to a change in relations between a patient and a doctor. Interpersonal relation between a person being treated and the one performing a treatment, constitutes an essential element shaping a functional quality of the service, because it is this relation that a course of a service process depends on. Those, who represent service providers should, then, regard their patients not as a 'case of pathology to be treated' but as customers with unsatisfied needs and certain preferences. An attitude and personality of a person performing a treatment, contribute to better effectiveness of medical process. It is also very important to involve a patient in the process of service generation: in management terms, such an attitude is referred to as 'presumption.' For example, even the best balanced diet will not be effective with an ill person failing to follow it in a systematic and reasonable way.[346] In the case of interpersonal relations between a customer and a service provider, the following characteristics of the latter are particularly valued: kindness, modesty, discretion, openness. Patients like to be treated as equal interlocutors, not as impersonal petitioners.

Patients appreciate as well, various conveniences in a form of a well-functioning infrastructure, access to necessary accessories and proper equipment. As a rule, patients are quick to spot the following features:
– a neat-looking building – ramps, facilities for the disabled, signs,
– running water and electricity to be used without limits,
– cleanness and availability of lavatories,
– privacy and comfort of medical examination – screens, partition walls, ample sitting place, private rooms.

Moreover, the following criteria may be of certain significance in the evaluation of medical service quality:[347]
– smooth and customer-friendly organization in an emergency room,
– time spent for an appointment, diagnosis or admission to hospital,
– calm, haste-less conversation with a doctor or a nurse,
– a range and a form of information obtained at a reception desk,
– chatting medical personnel, who at different stages of exercising care over a patient, talks about success and failure, as well as about difficulties, suggesting how to overcome them,
– a number of involved personnel,
– wake-up time for meals for hospitalized patients,
– suggested forms of spending one's free time – trainings and health promoting meetings.

---

[346] I. Rudawska (2005), *Jakość relacji pacjent–profesjonalista w sektorze usług medycznych*, "Problemy Jakości", No. 3, p. 12–15.

[347] A. Palczewska (2008), *Jakość usług medycznych w opiece paliatywnej*, "Problemy Pielęgniarstwa", No. 16, p. 186–191.

– well-kept lavatories,
– cleanness of premises,
– equipping premises with items, which help reduce waiting time,
– listening to and following up patients' complaints, which serves as a feedback for a health care,
– fixing a confidentiality box, whose anonymity guarantees sincerity of statements herein contained,
– conducting anonymous questionnaires with well-devised questions,
– meeting with a health-promoting person, a possibility to ask questions and to clear up doubts pertaining to one's health.

3.2.3.5. CONCLUSION

This paper touched upon issues pertaining to patients' role in shaping quality of contemporary medical services. Patients were treated as one of key parties interested in health care units functioning; a party, whose expectations pertaining to medical services quality, are characterized by high 'level of aspirations.' The authors made an attempt to prove a thesis of non-neutrality of expectations and patient's rights against quality of medical services performed for them. Hence illustration of the existing evidence and postulated arguments, suggesting that feedback coming from patients is a key element in the process of service provision, service evaluation and service improvement.

3.2.4. QUALITY IMPROVEMENT IN HOSPITAL USING THE QFD METHOD

3.2.4.1. INTRODUCTION

In recent years the methods and tools of quality management traditionally used in industry been also applied in medical services. Nowadays, after the health care system reform of 1999, medical care centres operate in a system similar to the competition system though still maintaining the typical features of medical services. Among other things, attitude to the patient has changed and now more and more often they are treated like a customer by using methods and tools which so far have been used only for typically commercial services. In modern organisations quality constitutes an important factor which has an influence on the market success of the organisation or, in many cases, even its survival on the competitive market. In such circumstances medical organisations more and more often turn to various pro-quality solutions. Usually those solutions consist in using ISO norms of series 9000 but less frequently make use of various methods and tools of measuring and improving quality of the performed services. This publication presents an example of applying one of the quality management methods, the QFD[348] method, in medical services.

---

[348] The acronym QFD stands for Quality Function Deployment.

3.2.4.2. QUALITY ISSUE IN MEDICAL SERVICES

Quality of life to a large extent is determined by quality of services delivered by different institutions, companies and other entities. The currently legally binding Polish Classification of Products and Services specifies various activities which constitute performable services e.g. personnel consultancy, accounting and bookkeeping services, personnel selection and recruitment, tax counselling, medical services, internet services, transport services, consulting services etc. At present the importance of the services sector seems to be growing and the number of people employed in the services area is increasing as well.

In the case of medical services, the question of quality is extremely important as it influences not only satisfaction of the customer but also their health or even life. Hospital is a specific organisational unit whose goal is to undertake actions aimed at improving the health condition of its customers/patients. If medical care centres seek to improve the quality of the delivered services, they ought to provide their patients with high level doctor and nurse assistance, appropriate medical examination, and safety while performing medical services. Currently in Poland the issue of quality in medical services is attracting more and more interest, which is also a result of the growing competition between public and private medical centres. Patients are also becoming more aware of their rights and they can clearly define their expectations and requirements. In order to fulfil them, medical centres ought to aim at raising the quality of the medical services they provide.

Medical services performed at medical care centres are very specific professional services the quality of which plays a very important role as it influences not only customer satisfaction but also the most vital values of human life i.e. health or even life of the patient. The level of the performed medical services determines people's health condition. Nowadays, the notion of quality in health care is gaining more importance both for those managing the hospitals and the patients. Customers are increasing their awareness of the rights they can claim and can define their expectations. It is the medical centres managers who should give the utmost care to improve the quality of their medical services as it allows them to enhance their competitiveness. Medical care centres are increasingly interested in implementing quality management systems which improve the quality level of their services, facilitate better operation of the hospitals, and also reduce the running costs.

According to WHO (World Health Organisation) a patient is any person receiving medical treatment or health care irrespective of whether they are ill or healthy. Patient is a customer of institutions providing medical services.[349]

Health care services in turn can be defined as any actions aimed at preserving, saving, restoring and improving health and other medical actions related to the process of curing treatment or based on other legal regulations stipulating the conditions of performing thereof particularly those connected with medical examination and counselling, medical treatment, psychological examination and therapy, medical re-

---

[349] K. Opolski, G. Dykowska, M. Możdżonek (2009), *Zarządzanie przez jakość w usługach zdrowotnych*, Wyd. CeDeWu, Warszawa, p. 58.

habilitation, diagnostic check-up including medical analytics, nursing of the ill, pal-liative and hospice care, health condition adjudication and opinions, prevention of injuries and diseases by prophylactic measures and preventive vaccinations, techni-cal activities in prosthodontics and orthodontics, activities related to supply of ortho-paedic objects and auxiliary materials.[350]

While looking at medical services one should take into account a few issues which are specific for this area. The medical services market can be defined as the relation-ships occurring between suppliers of services in prophylaxis and health care at a given price and the purchasers in demand of such services and which are covered by their buying funds or funds of the medical insurance institutions. Factors influencing the relations between the service recipient (patient) and service provider are connected with the specificity of medical services which is shaped by the following features:[351]

– delivering this kind of service is largely a psychological process carried out in the patient's presence,

– medical service entails initiation of a social relationship between the doctor (or nurse) and the patient, therefore the level of communication and empathy skills of the former influences the patient's satisfaction from the meeting,

– patient is always burdened with stress as they are personally involved in the result of the meeting,

– doctor or nurse are not able to meet the patient's expectations in every single case,

– bearing in mind the terminology specificity and specialist medical knowledge, the doctor should try to establish a rapport with the patient and be communicative, which, as a result, might contribute to the patient's increased trust towards the doctor,

– the level of trust is also influenced by the service offer as the quality and versa-tility of the service offer boosts the credibility of the service provider.

As it is the case with other services, in medical services area one ought to assess expectations and perception of those expectations by the patients. Patient's satisfac-tion can be defined as the extent to which medical care is acceptable by the patient in meeting their needs and expectations.[352]

Due to the fact that quality has a different meaning to different sides involved in the service, there are some difficulties with an objective assessment of quality in health care service. Only a very comprehensive approach to the issue of quality assessment could make the level evaluation bring some reliable findings. The quality of the medi-cal service can be assessed from two different points of view. From the standpoint of the medical centre, it means compliance with the standards, norms and other specified conditions. If looked at from the outside, the base of the quality measurement would be a subjective assessment of the service made by the patient/customer.[353]

---

[350] *Ibidem.*

[351] A. Rodzewicz (2008), *Jakość usług medycznych (prywatne czy publiczne)*, "Problemy Jakości", No. 3, p. 39–40.

[352] B. Skotnicka-Zasadzień, D. Glenc (2006), *Rola pacjenta w ocenie jakości usług medycznych*, "Problemy Jakości", No. 6, p. 38.

[353] A. Bukowska-Piestrzyńska, A. Fijałkowska (2007), *Znaczenie jakości w budowaniu pozytyw-nego wizerunku placówki zdrowotnej*, "Problemy Jakości", No. 6, p. 32.

Medical treatment results are an area where it is really hard to get the patient's objective opinions as they do not possess the necessary medical knowledge and, while making assessments, they rely on their own feelings and emotions. The most crucial aspect of the assessment is the relationship with the health service personnel. It is them who the patients have a constant and direct contact with. They take into consideration not only the personnel's attire and tidiness but, most of all, their over-all relationship with the patients. Patients objectively assess material substrates. The elements which they pay attention to are connected with the room appearance, easy access, and hygiene. What has to be taken into consideration, however, is the fact that illness is a state which is accompanied by stress, pain and suffering. More often than not, patients make negative judgements about operation of a given medical facility while being affected by their annoyance or based on unfavourable opinions spread by other patients. Customers often judge the quality of medical services as a whole e.g. normally they do not know anything about functioning of the laundry unless they get dirty bedding; simultaneously they will express a negative opinion not only about the laundry but also about the nurse who made their bed.

The research shows that creating quality in medical health service is a much more complex task than it is in the case of material goods as during all the process of receiv-ing a medical service, the patient's behaviour and feelings affect the perceived quality of the service they receive. Therefore, medical centres should do research and analyse the quality-related factors among the patients in order to identify and improve those which are ranked the lowest. So as to get the patient's satisfaction it might be also use-ful to identify within the medical care centre any medical service parameters which, if delivered at an appropriate level, could help increase the patient's satisfaction.[354]

3.2.4.3. QFD METHOD – BASIC ISSUES[355]

For the customer to be content with the medical services, they must be provided with a product or service which fulfils their needs. In reality, however, developing a top-

---

[354] Additional information about the issue of quality in medical services can be found in M. Popis (2009), *Systemy zapewnienia jakości w opiece medycznej w Polsce*, „Problemy Jakości", No. 10; W. Kapała (2006), *Pielęgniarstwo a jakość*, "Problemy Jakości", No. 3; M. Wiśniewska, J. Nowoszyńska (2009), *Akredytacja i systemy zarządzania jakością w placówkach opieki zdro-wotnej*, "Problemy Jakości", No. 7.

[355] Due to the restricted article size, the publication does not contain a profound presentation of all the rules concerning application of the QFD method. The issue is widely discussed in the subject literature and additional information can be found for instance in the following works: J.R. Clausing, D. Clausing (1988), *The House of Quality*, "Harvard Business Review", No. 5–6, p. 63–73; A. Ham-rol (2005), *Zarządzanie jakością z przykładami*, PWN, Warszawa; E. Kreier, J. Łuczak (2006), *ISO 9000. Łatwy i skuteczny sposób uzyskania certyfikatu jakości*. Tomy 1–3, FORUM, Poznań; J. Łuczak, A. Matuszak-Flejszman (2007), *Metody i techniki zarządzania jakością. Kompendium wiedzy*, Quality Progress, Poznań; R. Wolniak, B. Skotnicka (2008), *Metody i narzędzia zarządzania jakością. Teoria i praktyka*, Wydawnictwo Politechniki Śląskiej, Gliwice; R. Wolniak (2003), *Koncepcja trzydziestoma-cierzowego rozwinięcia metody QFD*, "Problemy Jakości", No. 9, p. 17–29; R. Wolniak (2006), *Wybrane metody zarządzania jakością w sektorze usług finansowych – teoria i praktyka*, Wyższa Szkoła Bankowości i Finansów, Bielsko-Biała.

of-the-range product or service is usually very costly. It is not always possible to meet all of the customer's requirements. A product which does not meet the customer's expectations, even if perfect from the technical point of view, will not find buyers on the contemporary highly competitive market. Therefore, a precise customer needs analysis should constitute the most important action item in the process of designing new products and services.

The QFD method is used to design new products and services and to modify the existing ones so that they could satisfy the requirements specified by the customers as much as it is only possible. The method was applied for the first time in the Kobe shipyard. It was then used in the Japanese motor industry. At first, the method was applied only in the industry but over the last ten years it has been increasingly used also in services. It is a customer-oriented method of design. It means that when designing the work does not start with determining the product features but rather analysing the customer's requirements and then developing a product or service to fulfil those requirements. For the new product to be successful it has to well-designed in the first place. A good new product or service should bear the following characteristics:[356]

Substantially contributes to making the customer's life easier – it can be achieved through a detailed determination of their needs,

Must provide the customer with a higher value than the competitive products – use of benchmarking is necessary and so are careful planning of the technology portfolio and innovation development in the organisation to ensure being always one step ahead of the competition,

it should be accompanied by a suitable marketing strategy and good preparation and organisation of its launch on the market (customers should be aware of the product and it should be easily available).

It goes without saying that the points mentioned above are fully compliant with what marketing specialists say about product management. Based on the Kotler's concept of five product levels[357] analysis with the QFD method can also include such elements as: basic product, expected product, improved product or potential product. This method is a systematic process of concentrating the company activity on their customer and their needs. A vital prerequisite for an appropriate application of the method is marketing customer needs analysis. This research is supposed to answer the following three questions:[358]

– What do the customers want?

– How important is it for them?

– Is there consistency between their expectations and our products?

Knowledge of the answers to those questions is absolutely necessary and conditions effectiveness of any further analysis.

The QFD method is a very comfortable tool which enables analysing customer needs, converting them into technical parameters and comparing position of the company against the competitors using the identified customer parameters. It is

---

[356] R. Wolniak, *Wybrane metody zarządzania jakością...*, p. 17.

[357] P. Kotler (1994), *Marketing. Analiza, planowanie, wdrożenie i kontrola*, Gebethner i S-ka, Warszawa, p. 400–401.

[358] R. Wolniak, Wybrane *metody zarządzania jakością...*, p. 56.

a fine tool allowing the company to create a product which will successfully meet the customer's needs. Periodic application of the method enables controlling the level of customer satisfaction and constant optimization of the products and services according to the TQM assumptions.

The QFD method can be defined as a system necessary for transmitting the customer's requirements to the suitable company requirements at every stage i.e. research and development, design and production, marketing, sales and distribution. The matrix made using the QFD method and which shows the connections between the customer needs and product or service parameters usually in the subject literature is referred to as "house of house' or "quality house'.

3.2.4.4. SCOPE OF RESEARCH

Analysis presented in this publication is based on the example of the hospital in Czeladź. The research was carried out using a survey questionnaire and direct interview. The questionnaire consisted of three parts: in the first part the patients were asked to rate importance of the patient's attributes in a five-grade scale in three areas of quality in medical service; in the second one they were asked to apply a five-grade scale to rate the extent to which particular attributes were fulfilled at the given hospital ward, and the third part of the survey contained essential details about the respondent. The questionnaires were filled out by the patients (or based on their answers to the questions if they did not feel very well) on one of their last days of hospital stay. The research was realised in nine wards of the Municipal Hospital in Czeladź: internal diseases C, internal diseases D, rehabilitation, surgical, gynaecological, trauma and orthopaedics, laryngological, ophthalmological, and neurological. Due to an inability to communicate with the patients, the research did not incorporate the following wards: juvenile, nursing care and psychiatric. The research encompassed 180 patients in total (20 patients of each analysed ward). As far as gender is concerned, the sample group comprised 50.6% women and 49.4% men. Most of the sample patients were aged between 41 and 60 years (44.4%), above the age of 60 (33.5%), and then those aged between 21 and 40 years (18.2%). The least patients (3.9% of the sample group) were aged under 20. Majority of the patients could boast secondary education (50.6%), then university education (24.4%), basic vocational (17.2%) and the least of them had only elementary education (7.8%).

The hospital in Czeladź was founded by duke Hugo zu Hohenlohe-Oehringen, a German industrialist who, after having made a fortune in Czeladź, heavily invested there. The initial investments such as outpatient clinic with a little hospital and cholera barrack proved insufficient at some point and he was forced to found a proper modern hospital. According to the local parish's chronicle, the hospital construction works started in year 1896. The grand opening took place on 6 April 1899.[359]

---

[359] W. Kwaśniak, A. Horzelska-Matyja (1998), *100 lat szpitala w Czeladzi*, Czeladź, p. 20–26.

The twentieth century brought about many changes in the hospital and they were described in the literature.[360] The latest huge changes took place in year 2004 when out of two hospitals, Będzin hospital and Czeladź hospital, they created one organisation called County Assembly of Health Care Centres (PZZOZ). The founding and supervisory body is Będzin County Council. The hospital were merged as their debts had been growing and their independent existence was endangered. Setting up a new organisation was accompanied by comprehensive restructuring. It was now possible to introduce efficient management of the county's health care human resources and assets which earlier were controlled by two independent organisations. A single and powerful unit with strong personnel team and facilities all united in one assembly could take a much better position while negotiating new contracts with the National Health Fund.

Capacity of the hospital in question is 79,070 m³. The ancillary facilities of the hospital include: kitchen, laundry, storehouses: (food supplies, linen, dispensary, materials), repair workshops and heating facility. In Czeladź hospital there are 12 wards: internal diseases C, internal diseases D, rehabilitation, surgical, gynaecological, trauma and orthopaedics, laryngological, ophthalmological, neurological, juvenile, nursing care and psychiatric.

The purpose of the survey questionnaire was to get to know the patients' opinions of the medical care services performed on the analysed wards. Those opinions were necessary for the QFD method to be applied. The purpose of the QFD analysis was to identify the relationships between the patients' needs and technical aspects of the medical services on given wards and finally to determine the ways and means of improving the services performed by the analysed hospital.

3.2.4.5. APPLICATION OF QFD METHOD IN HOSPITAL

The QFD method was applied to 9 wards of the hospital according to the scheme depicted in the subject literature stipulating how to implement the QFD method.[361] First of all, 19 patient's attributes were defined and then they were divided into 3 groups: material aspect, doctor and nurse care, keeping patients informed. The material aspect referred to the following attributes: cleanness and tidiness on the ward and in the rooms, equipment in the ward rooms, suitable temperature in the rooms, access to telephone/TV/radio, medical equipment in good working order, quality of the meals. The doctor and nurse care included the following attributes: response time after calling a nurse, reducing pain, assuring intimacy, individual approach to the patient, gentleness and consideration while nursing or examining, sufficient amount of time devoted to the patient, friendliness and politeness of the personnel. The keeping patients informed category referred to the following attributes: personnel expressing things in a comprehensible way, informing about the Patients' Rights, informing about any possible complications which might result from examinations, treatments or operations, availability of doctors if needed.

---

[360] *Ibidem.*
[361] Based on an idea depicted in the work: R. Wolniak, B. Skotnicka (2008), *Metody i narzędzia zarządzania jakością. Teoria i praktyka*, Wydawnictwo Politechniki Śląskiej, Gliwice.

As a next step, a questionnaire containing the patient's attributes was compiled and handed out to the patients on the given wards to fill out. Based on the question-naire's results, both significance of particular patient's attributes and their assessment on given wards were identified. This assessment can be used to compare fulfilment of the attributes on the analysed wards.

Later on, 8 parameters of medical services were determined: ward area size, number of nurses, number of doctors, quantity of medical equipment, number of beds, average duration of stay, percentage of occupied beds and death rate. Data gath-ered in the hospital enabled to generate a listing of values of the service parameters on given wards and determine the type of particular parameters (maximal, minimal or nominal).

Another stage was filling out a chart illustrating interrelationships between the patient's attributes and the service parameters by numerical presentation of the de-pendency (9 – strong link, 3 – average link, 1 – weak link). If there was no rela-tionship between a given service parameter and a given attribute, the gap remained empty. The next step was to fill in the 'house of quality' by identifying the correlation between the medical service parameters. Those relationships could be positive '+' (improvement of one parameter causes improvement of another one), negative '–' (improvement of one parameter causes deterioration of another) or there could be a blank which means no correlation. The roof of the house of quality is dominated by neutral values, which means there are still possibilities of improving the medical service parameters without affecting other values of the parameters. However, there are also some positive correlations, which means that in some cases (e.g. the death rate parameter) there are few possibilities of improvement.

The importance of the service's parameters was calculated based on the average weight of the patient's attributes and the defined relationship between the service's parameter and the patient's attribute. A percentage value of the importance of the service's parameter was then established. Based on the parameters importance re-sults, 3 critical features were identified and they were those which got the most points.

Next the parameters of the service quality at the given ward were rated from 1 to 5, with 1 indicating the parameter fulfilled to a very little degree at the ward and 5 for a parameter fulfilled to a very large degree. The collected data was then used to pre-pare a listing of the parameters of the medical service at the analysed wards of the PZZOZ, hospital in Czeladź. Afterwards, the desired values of the service parameters were established – those which would allow to increase the patients' satisfaction by meeting their needs and expectations.

The last phase of the process was marking from 1 to 5 the difficulty in achieving the desired final values of the parameters, 1 meaning very little difficulty in achiev-ing a particular final value and 5 meaning likelihood that there will be a difficulty in achieving a particular final parameter value.

3.2.4.6. INTERNAL WARD[362]

Picture 8 shows a matrix made based on the research and which presents the links between the customer's needs (patient's attributes) and the parameters of the analysed service for the Internal Ward C[363] – house of quality for the Internal Diseased Ward C. For patients at this ward the most significant are the following attributes: medical apparatus in good working order (rate 5 in a 5-point scale), reducing pain (5), appropriate amount of time devoted to the patient (4.8), informing about health condition and treatment process (5), informing about possible complications resulting from examinations, operations, treatments (4.8) and availability of doctors when needed (5).

During assessment of the attributes the patients showed that the attributes of the lowest quality were: equipment of the ward rooms (3.25) and quality of the meals (3.05). Among other things, the patients emphasised the following problems: too few chairs in their rooms, unusable washbasins, draughty windows, and faulty cupboards. Quality of the meals was considered low due to too little food served, serving cold meals and insufficient food diversification. The highest rated requirements were ward markings and informing about health condition and treatment process.

The lowest rated medical service parameters were: ward area size, death rate and number of nurses. With such a large number of beds and their intensive use, the ward area seems to be definitely too small, which results in small ward rooms with many beds inside and discontented patients. The ward is also characterised by a high death rate – second worst in the hospital. The reason for that might be severe internal diseases but also too few staff and the insufficient quality and quantity of suitable medical equipment.

According to the analysis it might be concluded that at this ward some actions should be taken in order to extend its area size and take on more personnel, which might prove quite difficult bearing in mind the current insufficient number of medical care qualified people in some areas ready to work in Polish hospitals. The percentage of bed occupancy is a critical parameter as it achieved the highest number of points according to significance. It interacts with the biggest number of the patient's attributes. Keeping this parameter at an appropriate level will allow to satisfy expectations of the patients and also other entities cooperating with health care system. At this ward this parameter is fulfilled to a large extent as the beds are effectively at 91.1% whereas the desired value is 100%. The other critical features with a huge number of points are the number of nurses and number of doctors.

---

[362] Due to the limited article size, the publication presents the achieved research results only for a few chosen wards.

[363] Due to the limited article size, the publication presents the house of quality only for one sample ward but similarly it is possible to create matrixes for the other analysed wards.

3.2.4.7. REHABILITATION WARD

For the rehabilitation ward patients the attributes of the highest significance are as follows: medical apparatus in good working order (5), ensuring intimacy (5), response time after calling for a nurse (5) and announcing the health condition and course of the treatment (5). During assessment of the attributes the patients showed that the attribute of the lowest quality is ensuring intimacy (2.7). The rooms, where the patients stay are small and there are too beds there. Majority of the patients are bedridden and entirely dependent on other people and therefore ensuring intimacy is so important for them as it is the nurses who make all nursing activities for them. None of the requirements was given the highest rate (5). The highest rated requirements included: announcing possible complications connected with examinations, operations, treatments and availability of doctors if needed. The other requirements on average were rated 3–4.

Parameters of medical service which were rated the lowest were: ward size area, number of beds and percentage of bed occupancy. Generally almost all of the parameters of the service are on the rock bottom. There are many patients staying here; sometimes there is not enough space for them inside the rooms and they have to lie on beds in the corridor. There are too few nurses for such a number of patients, and they must look after patients majority of whom need permanent care. There is also too small quantity of medical equipment for exercise. As a result, the length of hospital stay unnecessarily extends, as they must wait for their turn to do the recommended exercise.

It is necessary to take actions to expand the ward premises size and increase the number of available beds. The following actions are recommended: swapping the rehabilitation ward with the general surgery ward as there is a lot of unused area. The parameter of the percentage of beds occupancy in the ward is a critical parameter, because it got the largest number of points according to importance. In this ward this parameter is fulfilled to a too large degree as beds are being used at 114.23% while the target value is 100%.[364] The other critical features with a high number of points are: number of nurses and number of doctors.

---

[364] It is caused by a situation described earlier – additional beds are put on the corridors.

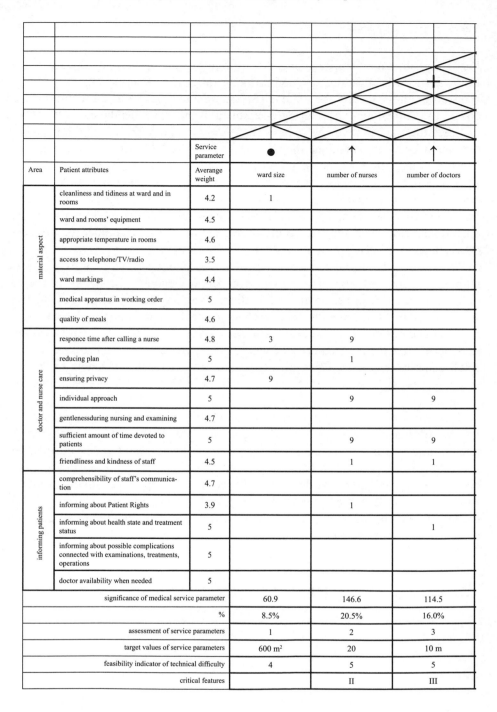

Area	Patient attributes	Service parameter / Average weight	● ward size	↑ number of nurses	↑ number of doctors
material aspect	cleanliness and tidiness at ward and in rooms	4.2	1		
	ward and rooms' equipment	4.5			
	appropriate temperature in rooms	4.6			
	access to telephone/TV/radio	3.5			
	ward markings	4.4			
	medical apparatus in working order	5			
	quality of meals	4.6			
doctor and nurse care	responce time after calling a nurse	4.8	3	9	
	reducing plan	5		1	
	ensuring privacy	4.7	9		
	individual approach	5		9	9
	gentlenessduring nursing and examining	4.7			
	sufficient amount of time devoted to patients	5		9	9
	friendliness and kindness of staff	4.5		1	1
informing patients	comprehensibility of staff's communication	4.7			
	informing about Patient Rights	3.9		1	
	informing about health state and treatment status	5			1
	informing about possible complications connected with examinations, treatments, operations	5			
	doctor availability when needed	5			
	significance of medical service parameter		60.9	146.6	114.5
	%		8.5%	20.5%	16.0%
	assessment of service parameters		1	2	3
	target values of service parameters		600 m²	20	10 m
	feasibility indicator of technical difficulty		4	5	5
	critical features			II	III

Picture 8. Matrix of links between customer needs (patient attributes) and parameters of medical service at the internal diseases ward C

quanity of medical apparatus	number of beds	average stay length	% of bed occupancy	death rate	averange rating of patient attributes
↑	●	●	↑	↓	
1	1		1		4
1	1				2.5
	3		3		4.25
					4.25
					4.75
1		3		9	3.75
					2.75
			9	3	4
1			1		4.25
	9		9		3.5
			3	3	4.25
					4.25
		1	3	3	3.5
					4
					4.25
					3.5
					4.5
					4
			9	3	3.5
18.7	64.8	20	183.5	104.4	
2.6%	9.1%	2.8%	25.7%	14.6%	
3	3	3	4	1	
15 m	45		100%	0	
3	2		2	5	
			1		

3.2.4.8. GENERAL SURGERY WARD

In the case of patients treated on the general surgery ward, the most important attributes were medical apparatus in good working order (5) and reducing pain (5). During assessment of the attributes the patients pointed out that attribute of the lowest quality was access to the phone /TV/radio (1.4). The ward does not even offer access to paid TV, whereas it is available on other wards. None of the requirements was granted the highest rate (5). The highest rated requirements were personnel speaking in a comprehensible way (4.8), announcing possible complications connected with tests, operations, treatments (4.8) and availability of doctors if needed (4.8).

The lowest rated parameters of medical service were size area of the ward and percentage of bed occupancy. On this ward no information about the medical equipment was obtained. The ward has too huge area and too many beds compared to the low percentage of bed occupancy. It is necessary to take actions in order to reduce the area size of the ward and remove any unused beds. It is suggested to swap the general surgery ward with rehabilitation ward as the latter suffers from insufficient size and number of beds. On the ward there are enough doctors and nurses.

The parameter of percentage of bed occupancy on the ward is a critical one as it achieved the largest number of points in terms of importance. This parameter is not fulfilled to a very large degree as only 27.10% of beds are occupied whereas the desired value is 100%. This is the lowest percentage of bed occupancy in the hospital. Other critical features with a high number of points are the number of nurses and the number of doctors.

3.2.4.9. GYNAECOLOGICAL WARD

According to the patients, the most important attributes on the gynaecological ward are medical apparatus in good working order (5), reducing pain (5), ensuring intimacy (5), kindliness and politeness of the staff (5), personnel speaking in a comprehensible way (5), informing about the health state and course of the treatment (5), announcing possible complications connected with tests, operations, treatments (5) and also availability of doctors if needed (5). During evaluation of the attributes the patients demonstrated that the lowest quality attributes were informing about the Patients' Rights (3.55) and quality of the meals (3.6). More often than not, female patients during admission to the ward were not informed about the Patients' Rights, though they were informed about their health condition and course of the treatment. Another highly scoring patient attribute was reducing pain. The other requirements were usually rated over 4. None of the requirements was given the highest rate (5). It is a specific ward where providing intimacy for women is very important and this attribute is well realised by the ward (on average the patients give it a rate of 4.65).

The lowest scoring parameters of medical service were size area of the ward and percentage of bed occupancy. For the given number of beds and percentage of bed occupancy, the size of the ward is too large. It is recommended to make a better use of the unnecessary part and, for instance, convert it into exercises rooms for the

Rehabilitation ward patients which is located just next to the gynaecological ward. The remaining parameters were rated quite high. This ward is one of the two in the hospital where the death rate is zero.

On the basis of the conducted research it is possible to state that the parameter of percentage of bed occupancy on the ward is a critical one as it achieved the highest number of points according to importance. The parameter is fulfilled at a medium level as the bed occupancy is 42.95% whereas the target value is 100%. The other critical features with a high number of points are the number of nurses and the number of doctors. The number of both nurses and doctors on this ward is absolutely sufficient.

3.2.4.10. TRAUMATIC AND ORTHOPAEDIC WARD

The results from the conducted research show that on the traumatic and orthopaedic ward the most important attributes are equipment of the ward rooms (5), medical apparatus in good working order (5), reducing pain (5), ensuring intimacy (5), gentleness during the care and examination activities (5), kindliness and politeness of the staff (5), staff expressing things comprehensibly (5), informing about the Patients' Rights (5), informing about the health condition and course of the treatment (5) and announcing possible complications connected with tests, operations, treatments (5). During the evaluation of the attributes the patients demonstrated that the lowest quality attributes were equipment of the ward rooms (2.9) and ensuring intimacy (3.1).

Majority of the patients staying on the ward suffer from serious injuries and they are often incapable of moving and require constant care. Because of these circumstances the rooms should be appropriately equipped both with facilities helping get out of bed and maintain hygiene. Kindliness and politeness of the staff are the only attribute which was rewarded with the highest number of points. The respondents praised the staff for their concern and interest in each of the patients and also for treating them with respect and understanding. Other highly scoring requirements were informing about the health condition and course of the treatment and understandable language used by the staff.

The lowest rated parameter of medical service was the quantity of medical equipment. On this ward medical equipment is needed in the appropriate amount and of very good quality as it must help the patients both stay on the ward and regain physical fitness. The ward has an appropriate size area and enough staff. Parameter of percentage of bed occupancy on the ward is a critical one as it achieved the highest number of points according to importance. The parameter is fulfilled at a medium level as the bed occupancy is 60.91% whereas the target value is 100%. The other critical features with a high number of points are the number of nurses and the death rate which is quite high on this ward.

3.2.5. Ethical programme of hospitals

3.2.5.1. Introduction

Rapid economic development has substantially contributed to the changes in the functioning of various enterprises. Competition increase, changing environment and constant race for market advantage have become the source of market's interest in new management techniques. These changes concern also non-profit organizations such as hospitals.

One of the modern management techniques, which has become almost the norm, is quality management. According to ISO (International Organization for Standardization) regulations, quality is defined as 'to what extent a collection of inherent properties meets requirements.'[365] By adapting this definition for the use of management, we may say that quality in a modern understanding is a new way of thinking which concerns a constant search for solutions.[366] Quality is an important factor in the management of public institutions such as health service institutions. Owing to the fact that hospitals are state-funded and their actions are concerned with the highest value, namely, human life and health, they are supposed to provide services of the highest quality. It is worth mentioning that the most important thing about such organizations, as opposed to private enterprises, is not profit but customer satisfaction. In professional services such as medical ones, professional knowledge, experience and effectiveness are desired by a patient.[367] The importance of patient satisfaction is described by a well-known in the medical field proverb 'There are three preconditions of success: availability, kindness and knowledge – in this particular order.'[368]

Due to its sole existence, hospital expresses its readiness to provide medical care of the highest possible quality and assures its availability and a fair division of the services. However, how is it possible to meet patient's expectations and recognize the constitutional right to equality in a state of constant financial deficiency? Every day a worker of a health institution confronts this kind of dilemma. On themselves the one hand, proper fulfillment of social needs guarantees patient satisfaction, but on the other hand, financial deficiency to cover treatment expenses forces them to lower the quality of a given service. Individual workers make such decisions themselves which means that the decisions and their quality are utterly dependent on personal honesty, sensitivity and a doctor's diligence. Workers of medical institutions can base their decisions on the medical code of ethics in difficult situations. The sole fact that Hippocrates Oath is one of the oldest collections of professional ethics laws and rules proves the importance of maintaining certain standards in this field. While the carefully phrased rules and laws of medical ethics facilitate doctors' work, en-

---

[365] PN-EN ISO 9000:2001, *Systemy zarządzania jakością*, Terminologia, PKN 2001, p. 23.
[366] E. Skrzypek (2000), *Jakość i efektywność*, Wyd. UMCS, Lublin, p. 26.
[367] D.M. Maister (2006), *Zarządzanie firmą usług profesjonalnych*, Helion, Gliwice, p. 43.
[368] *Ibidem*, p. 105.

hance its prestige and help to solve conflicts,[369] in many situations they appear to be insufficient. What is more, research on American enterprises shows that codes of professional ethics very often do not produce the desired results, or in extreme cases, they are even counter effective.[370] Analogous situations may appear in the medical service. Certainly, it can result in the quality of a given service being lowered which is directly connected with the fact that the majority of Polish patients is dissatisfied with the functioning of the National Health Service.[371] Therefore, how to assist workers of health service in making decisions which involve ethical issues and at the same time to standardize such procedures within an organization?

3.2.5.2. THE ESSENCE OF ETHICAL PROGRAMMES

The solution to the problem can be extensive ethical programmes which are defined as 'extensive undertakings directed at turning business ethics into the highest standard of a strategic meaning'.[372] The fundamental aim of ethical programmes is to turn business ethics into the highest standard of behaviour of workers, organizations on the market and in the community in which it operates.[373] The solution is mainly aimed at enterprises which realize that ethical conduct not only raises the quality of services, but also increases the value of a company. Due to this fact, it may be concluded that if an organization abides by ethical rules, it takes responsibility for its customers. It is worth mentioning that an ethical programme is a tool preventing an organization from losses which may result from lost trust, poor reputation or unethical behaviour of staff (the point being that health service has been perceived for many years as a field most exposed to corruption[374]).

Ethical programmes constitute an extension to codes of professional ethics by complementing it with additional elements and actions. Such an extensive ethical programme should consist of the following elements (at least of some of them):
– establishing an organization's mission,
– establishing ethical and professional standards,
– establishing of the Code of Ethics,
– creating an ethical programme,
– appointing a position (section) for ethics,
– promoting ethical conduct (rewards for ethical conduct and punishments for unethical one),

---

[369] B. Nogalski, J. Śniadecki (2001), *Etyka zarządzania przedsiębiorstwem*, Oficyna Wydawnicza Ośrodka Postępu Organizacyjnego, Bydgoszcz, p. 209.

[370] L. Karczewski (2008), *Etyka biznesu. Kulturowe uwarunkowania*, Wyd. Politechniki Opolskiej, Opole, p. 165.

[371] M. Musielak (2004), *Wybrane etyczne aspekty zarządzania służbą zdrowia w Polsce*, "Nowiny Lekarskie", No. 4, p. 312.

[372] www.odpowiedzialnybiznes.pl, artykuł: W. Gasparski (2008), *Programy etyczne firm*, May. 126. www.opoka.org.pl/biblioteka.

[373] www.emedyk.pl, Programy i kodeksy etyczne, March 2010.

[374] M. Gałuszka (2007), *Korupcja i działania antykorupcyjne w systemie ochrony zdrowia*, "Lekarz Rodzinny", September, p. 906.

– constant checking whether the rules and standards are abode by,

– ethical hotline,

– ethical audit and application of necessary corrections to the Code and the norms.[375]

The first element of an ethical programme, namely, establishing an organization's mission should begin with finding a vision and defining values which are fundamental for a particular enterprise. The vision of an organization, that is, identification of a company's dreams and ambitions, allows to determine an image which an enterprise would like to create and it also 'constitutes the basis according to which all problems and conflicts will be resolved.'[376] Thus, the basis will allow to formulate the mission. While determining the mission, it is important to determine what is responsible for the success of a company (i.e. the quality of a service, the knowledge of employees, customer loyalty), what is most important for it and what it is directed at. It is this short message which should include all the 'values which are perceived as most important by a company and which should be reflected in particular patterns of behaviour of a company's employees.[377] According to Chapell's, the mission of an enterprise should be focused on the following problems:

1. Providing customers with products of high quality.

2. Developing relations with a customer based on a dialogue, which go beyond merely selling a product.

3. Respecting and appreciating all customers.

4. Providing employees with honest, safe work and reasonable salary which influence self-discipline and openness towards others.[378]

Formulated in such a way, the mission becomes the base for further actions directed at the increase of meaning of ethics in an organization's management. However, it is worth remembering that the mission should be not only well-known to every customer, but also it should be comprehensible, so that they are aware of its rightness. It should be also emphasized that an image of an enterprise which is outlined in the mission exerts a significant influence on its reception by the environment. Moreover, described in the mission 'truth about an individual can create a hope for mutual trust and benefits which are not always measurable in business.'[379]

A successive stage of developing an ethical programme is creating professional ethical standards. The standards determine certain norms, rules and procedures of conduct in a particular field. Unfortunately, in the case of Polish National Health Service the realization of this stage is difficult. While the standards of clinical conduct are shaped by national or local consultants (to whom access is hard to gain), there are no national or local experts in ethics.[380] This arises from the fact that the only indicator in the process of creating such standards is a payer, that is, the National Health Service and the anticipated one is insurance companies.

[375] www.odpowiedzialnybiznes.pl, artykuł: W. Gasparski (2008), *Programy etyczne firm*, May. 126. www.opoka.org.pl/biblioteka.

[376] J. Brilman (2002), *Nowoczesne koncepcje i metody zarządzania*, PWE, Warszawa, p. 79.

[377] G. Aniszewska (2007), *Kultura organizacyjna w zarządzaniu*, PWE, Warszawa, p. 44.

[378] T. Chappell (1998), *Dusza biznesu*, Wydawnictwo Studio Emka, Warszawa, p. 76.

[379] L. Berliński (2009), *Modelowanie strategii biznesu*, Wyd. Dom Organizatora, Toruń, p. 156.

[380] G. Luboiński (2008), *Standardy etyczne*, "Standardy Medyczne", No. 5, p. 334.

The code of ethics is a reflection of values in relation to everyday rules of conduct held by members of an organization. Obviously, the fundamental rule of the code is its conformity to the law due to the fact that it is the law which is superior to any code of professional ethics. By means of its detailed regulations of conduct, the code also protects a service provider (because of the fact that details of the conduct regulations of a general ethical frame do not exclude a service provider). The main functions of the code of ethics:

– clarifying of arising problems,
– identifying and resolving conflicts,
– providing a sense of equality and fairness.[381]

The code of conduct for doctors has a long, rooted in antiquity history (who has not heard of Hippocrates?). Nonetheless, it has to be constantly developed on account of the conditions of hospital functioning being changed dynamically. The fact that a very significant factor of success of the code is its implementation itself is also worth noticing. While developing the code, it cannot be forgotten that employees should be allowed to participate in this undertaking, because without their participation it can be treated as an organization's peculiar embellishment.[382] The content of the ethical code depends on an enterprise's profile. It is usually divided into several parts, or chapters, which are distinguished on the basis of particular issues. The most common structure of the code consists of the following parts:

– introduction to the code which presents general rules of functioning of a given organization,
– sections, chapters, parts of the Code which can be organized according to two criteria: issues or clients they apply to,
– the content of codes, which contain recommendations and moral rules declared by a given organization.[383]

It also happens that the code includes a register of cases or situations in which employees may find themselves.[384] The Code of Medical Ethics is a modern version of Hippocrates Oath. It consists of six parts which elaborate on the main problems in the field of medical ethics such as a doctor's attitude towards a patient, the quality of medical care, scientific research and biomedical experiments, a doctor and society and others. The code of professional ethics serves a crucial function in the process of establishing desired norms and values in an organization. Therefore, it should be emphasized that according to De George, the code which is well constructed should meet the following requirements:

– First and foremost, it determines norms and does not contain any unnecessary descriptions of values and ideals to which an organization is devoted.
– Public well-being is the highest good and therefore the code should not include only those regulations which will exclusively secure the interest of an organization's members.

---

[381] L. Karczewski (2008), *Etyka biznesu. Kulturowe uwarunkowania*, Wyd. Politechniki Opolskiej, Opole, p. 158.
[382] *Ibidem.*
[383] Portal.wsiz.rzeszów.pl, March 2010.
[384] *Ibidem*, 162.

– The code is fundamental and honest, i.e. issues which are raised in it should regulate problems of a particular profession, not deal with obvious ones rooted in general morality.[385]

Functioning of the code is an initial stage of developing ethical values. The undertaking should be supported by systematic education of employees. The sole realization of this assumption implies an introduction of diverse educational techniques. The prerequisite condition is to lead employees to an open discussion on ethics. It may be done in the newspapers or bulletins published in a company (in extreme cases it can be done by means of informational leaflets). A qualified person, for instance a consultant, can run an article or a series of articles which will encourage employees to discuss ethical problems.[386] It is the first step to draw members of an organization's attention to the essence of professional ethics and its influence on the whole undertaking. What is more, the beginning of a dialogue may convince employees that they can change the current state. The next, necessary step is to provide a proper training. It should be done using a 'cascade training technique,' namely, it should concern all employees starting from employees holding managerial posts and ending with those holding lower ones.[387] Such trainings can be extended to include clients as well (suppliers, cooperators, patients and their families). Basic training programmes should include a variety of problems concerning the ethics of a medical service worker, place emphasis on showing a number of different standpoints and their application. It is important that its content allows participants to extend a range of their qualifications essential for proper resolving of ethical problems. It is significant to support the content by a study of cases employees have come across or which may occur and this will provide them with practical knowledge in a given field.

There are three kinds of ethical trainings:

– basic programmes, which are to draw an employee's attention to certain ethical issues;

– specialist programmes, directed at managerial personnel whose main task is to provide them with an ability to identify ethical problems and present appropriate tools to solve these problems;

– programmes aimed at developing of the ethical personality, concerned with shaping attitudes and traits of character which are to facilitate ethical cooperation;[388]

It is also worth mentioning that such trainings should not be done as a crash course (ethics during a weekend)[389] but treated seriously by management and employees so that the problems are given a proper meaning. A subsequent stage of building an ethical programme for companies is to appoint a position (or section) for ethics. Experts in ethics should be designated to hold these posts whose main task would be to outline programmes on ethics and implement them into organizations. A vital function of such a programme would be to help employees to solve any ethical problem. It

---

[385] Portal.wsiz.rzeszów.pl (R.T. De George [1990], *Business Ethics*, New York–London, p. 387–388).

[386] *Ibidem*, p. 164.

[387] *Ibidem*, p. 164.

[388] Portal.wsiz.rzeszów.pl, March 2010.

[389] *Ibidem*, p. 164.

carries also a meaning for health service workers who 'cannot be left to themselves and bear heavy responsibility of more and more complicated clinical cases (…).'[390] In Polish hospitals sections for ethics are boards or committees (however, there are only few of them in Poland[391]). Hospital ethical boards are groups of people designated to give advice and offer an opinion in the ethical field to other workers in order to improve the quality of their decisions. This role is performed by realization of the following functions:

– educational which means organizing and conducting ethical trainings,
– normative which means creating guidelines in the form of directives, that is,
– instructions which regulate ways of solving typical problems,
– consultative which embraces advisory actions as well as opinion-forming ones.[392]

An equally important element of functioning of such a board is the fact that its members may serve as a mediator between a doctor and a patient. Especially when it comes to a contentious issue, an objective person who is an expert in solving ethical problems may facilitate the dialogue.

While considering the role of a hospital ethical board its advisory character should be emphasized. This is so because an employee who asks for advice or recommendation in any case would have to make the decision himself and bear responsibility for it. Nevertheless, such professional assistance, even in the form of advice, can be highly beneficial for an employee due to the fact that they will not be left alone with their problems. The fact that the majority of doctors who were asked about ethical boards 'saw the need of appointing some sections helpful in a decision-making process (…)'[393] proves their significance. On account of this, the most important advantage of ethical boards is the fact that workers are not left to themselves and while encountering a difficult case they will receive support. Obviously, this minimizes the danger of making a mistake which consequently would lead to bearing moral, professional and even legal responsibility.

However, even the best idea cannot be realized without a proper promotion. In the case of the norms of conduct, which undoubtedly are the subject of ethical programmes, the best recommendation would be a personal example of a management personnel. Nothing is more appealing to a worker than the commitment of a superior. Other ways of encouraging employees to participate in a project should not be omitted. Among others, they may include various distinctions or rewards for people whose work is based on the values cherished by an organization. Apart from rewards, the managing body may also impose punishments for behaviour which goes against binding ethical rules. Punishment can be administered by means of warnings, reprimands, a financial burden or influencing a career path (demotion, preventing promotion).

---

[390] Karta Pracowników Służby Zdrowia. Watykan, papieska Rada ds. Duszpasterstwa Służby Zdrowia, 1995 [in:] S. Kornas (2009), *Czy w polskich szpitalach potrzebne są komitety etyczne?*, "Medycyna Praktyczna", No. 2, p. 147.

[391] W. Galewicz (2009), *W sprawie szpitalnych komisji etycznych*, "Medycyna Praktyczna", No. 11, p. 120.

[392] *Ibidem*, p. 129.

[393] S. Kornas (2009), *op. cit.*, p. 148.

Ethical programmes are not one-time undertakings. Their implementation is a continuous process which demands constant monitoring whether members of a given organization conform to the norms and ethical standards. The key to success is a constant observation which allows proper orientation of members of an organization and at the same time limits the possibility of the deviation of the accepted standards. Moreover, monitoring of actions makes workers aware of the significance of the undertaking which is proved by a management being interested in it.

The success of the whole ethical programme mostly depends on whether all the members of a given organization participate in it. In the process of work based on ethical rules appropriate tools of communication will enable clients to make use of the programme. One of such solutions is creating an ethical hotline in the form of a telephone line or an email box where all the interested parties (medical workers, patients and their families) could obtain necessary information on ensuing problems of ethical nature or report offences. Anonymity preserved in such a way allows a dialogue without embarrassment and fear. Certainly, such advice should be given by an independent expert who will not only advise, but also carefully listen to any comments. Another solution which is to facilitate ethical programmes is 'whistleblowing'. Used for a long time in the US, this tool excites a lot of controversy in Poland. Until now, there is no Polish equivalent to this term. 'Whistleblowing' is directed at uncovering any improprieties, violations or unethical conduct within an enterprise. A company employee takes actions against inappropriate occurrences. He or she may draw attention to violations committed within an organization by informing his or her superiors about them, or (if there is a possibility of a superior committing those violations) other outside authorities. A whistle-blower (an informing person) acts in a good faith and his or her aim is the best interest of an organization. Such behaviour undoubtedly contributes to creating and propagating ethical norms of conduct, but on the other hand, it may pose some dangers, most notably, for the informing person (he or she may be recognized as a traitor). As to prevent such dangers, the United Nations pledge to 'provide protection from any kind of unjustified treatment for any person who reports in good faith and on reasonable grounds to the competent authorities any facts concerning offences.'[394]

An ethical audit is yet another tool which allows proper functioning of an ethical programme in an enterprise. It is a form of internal control which is based on 'the assessment of the implementation of ethical rules within an organization.'[395] The primary purpose of an audit is to support the existence and preserve an ethical atmosphere within an organization. This should be possible after having analyzed the following issues:

– values which direct thinking and actions of all the members of an organization,

– acting according to these values of all the members of an organization (irrespective of a held post),

– achieving of a desired effect in the social and natural environment in which an organization operates.[396]

---

[394] www.batory.org.pl, *Establishing whistleblowing mechanizm*, Konwencja Narodów Zjednoczonych Przeciwko Korupcji, Artykuł 33 – Ochrona osób zgłaszających.

[395] www.wikipedia.pl

[396] www.ce.uw.edu.pl, artykuł: W. Gasparski, *Europejskie standardy etyki biznesu.*

A conducted audit should give clear answers to the following questions: what strong and weak points can be distinguished in the field of ethics in a given organization and in what way a company can strengthen its ethical position?[397] An audit should consist of two stages out of which the first one is called assessing and the second one implements solutions.[398] An assessing stage allows recognition and revealing of all situations which may adversely influence actions of an enterprise in the field of ethics. It can be concluded that it is an assessment of an actual state of affairs connected with determining whether the state is adequate to the desired one. In practice, this can be obtained by precise analysis of:

1. Internal documents of a company, outsider studies and reports dealing with a given organization,

2. Interviews with representatives of workers, suppliers, customers and other clients.[399]

The main field of interest of this analysis is focusing on issues connected with:

– the process of decision-making by members of an organization to check whether they take into consideration the mission of a company, values and beliefs,

– the degree of understanding by all the clients values preserved by an organization,

– the most common ethical problems, techniques and trainings and the assessment of ethics in a company.

The effect of this analysis is the image of an organization which allows to determine needs in the scope of implementation of all forms of improving ethical actions what is the task of the second audit stage. The result of these actions are recommendations which are to assist the development of an organization's ethics.

An ethical audit is to be conducted by internal as well as outside authorities, however, the best solution is to conduct it by an independent organization, or centers of business ethics.[400] Such an attitude of an organization proves a serious treatment of ethics as an inseparable element of running a business and it confirms social responsibility and the clarity of rules of an organization. Moreover, some enterprises publish the results of a conducted audit and by doing so they show the purity of their business which allows to build trust among all clients. Such a solution is particularly beneficial as far as non-profit organizations are concerned whose main aim is public interest. In the case of hospitals the issue becomes even more significant because its scope of action is the highest value of every person, namely, life and health. By entrusting workers of medical institutions with them, people prove their trust towards a given organization which may serve as the highest recommendation.

---

[397] www.logistyka.net.pl, artykuł: D. Gościniak (2005), *Logistyka w produkcji* (9).
[398] www.ce.uw.edu.pl, artykuł: W. Gasparski, *Europejskie standardy etyki biznesu*.
[399] www.logistyka.net.pl, artykuł: D. Gościniak (2005), *Logistyka w produkcji* (9).
[400] www.emedyk.pl, *Programy i kodeksy etyczne*, March 2010.

3.2.5.3. Implementation of ethical programmes

Implementation of an ethical programme into an organization is a continuous process which embraces all members of a given community. One way of implementing this programme into a company is a 'from top' system known also as autocratic one. It assumes planning all the details of the undertaking at the level of management without workers' participation. Then, the resolutions are imposed on the rest of the members of an organization. However, it should be noticed that such a method very rarely gives a desired result.[401] Certainly, a company can boast of having an ethical programme but it is only a peculiar decoration whose resolutions are of no interest to workers. This is so because imposing top-down resolutions on members of an organization destroys the feeling of participation in a project. And it is this feeling which is the key to the success of the whole undertaking. If employees contribute to the vision and mission and on this basis take part in planning and implementing of the whole system, they become a part of it. Furthermore, it is known that by committing all the interested parties to the project, there is a far greater possibility of their approval of the new order. The fact that the success of an ethical programme is due to its logic and wisdom cannot be omitted. Seemingly obvious, however, the integration of the programme into one coherent whole is not an easy task.

It should be noted that if you want to maintain a higher level of quality in a company by ethical conduct of a personnel, the sole implementation of an ethical programme will not be sufficient. It is essential to constantly cultivate it and to monitor the preservation of the rules. In order to do this, effective systems of communication are to be developed. Firstly, clients should feel that management wants to communicate with them and contribute to a new quality of work and secondly, they should have opportunities to utter their opinions. According to Holms, responsible ethical programmes should be based on three key elements:

1) Identification – enables recognition of existing within an organization patterns of bahaviour by means of providing members of an organization with a variety of ways for communication including whistleblowing and other mechanisms which allow anonymous complaints or accusations. Such a system enables the flow of information on unethical behaviour without embarrassment and fear of retaliation;

2) Investigation – understood as providing a coherent, honest and simple system of solving problems reported by clients and a clearly stated plan of guidelines for an audit board;

Remediation – implementation of repair actions (individual for a particular problem and general) in order to prevent recurrence of bad behaviour within an organization.[402]

All things considered, implementation of an ethical programme to a organization is quite a challenge notably for managers of this undertaking. This is so because the programme needs systematic realization of resolutions. However, it is important for organizations which implement these resolutions to base their actions on eight guidelines which constitute a foundation for next stages of an ethical programme:

---

[401] www.odpowiedzialnybiznes.pl, artykuł: W. Gasparski (2008), *Programy etyczne firm*, May.
[402] S.E. Holmes (2009), *Under Pressure: Maintaing an Effective Ethics and Compliance Program*, "Directorship", October/November, p. 72.

1) recognition of an ethical programme as a continuous process which demands constant coordination directed at a reflection and a dialogue,

2) beginning with a list of preferred values (in the form of a code) which would constitute the base for rules, procedures or trainings,

1) consolidation of a rule that the best way to solve ethical dilemmas is to avoid their occurrence, which only confirms the legitimacy of implementation of codes which would regulate norms of conduct,

2) preventing members of an organization from group decision-making, which would lead to better results and influence integration of a personnel with ethical issues,

3) integrating ethics with other management practices by connecting ethical rules to every aspect of activity such as creating organizational culture or strategic planning,

4) engaging all employees with an ethical programme,

5) forgiving mistakes – the rule sounds as a religious commandment, but it draws our attention to the fact that even the best ones make mistakes all the more they can be made by employees so they should be recognized and addressed appropriately,

6) appreciation of efforts by promoting those who try to act according to the programme, because even if it fails, trying is better than passivity.[403]

3.2.5.4. ADVANTAGES AND DISADVANTAGES OF ETHICAL PROGRAMMES

Application of ethical solutions within an organization's functioning articulated by means of integrated programmes can bring two kinds of benefits. Advantages are not only moral but also practical from the perspective of managing of the whole organization. One of the most obvious pluses is a clear-cut nature of binding rules owing to the fact that desired and forbidden conduct is clearly outlined. An ethical programme regulates workers' behaviour by providing detailed instructions of conduct in a variety of situations which an employee is likely to encounter. Because of this, there are ready solutions to ethical problems which facilitates work. What is more, in situations which are not regulated in the written form, a member of an organization can obtain advice from an expert, even from a board for ethics. In this way, not only can an employee make a better decision, but also he or she does not feel left to themselves owing to an organization's interest in his or her problems. The existence of rules in a written form of a code is the foundation to create ethical sensitivity of members of an organization, which in the process of decision-making allows an appropriate interpretation of accepted values. Furthermore, ethical programmes help to develop an ethical awareness of employees[404] and at the same time draw their attention to the crucial meaning of this aspect in the actions of an organization. As a result of these actions we may observe decrease of unethical behaviour such as theft, corruption and

---

[403] www.managementhelp.org, *Complete Guide to Ethics Management: An Ethic Toolkit for Managers.*

[404] www.ckl.pl/kodeks-etyczny-narzędziem-rozwoju-firmy

frauds.[405] It is also the case that ethical programmes developed by an organization help to decrease conflicts of different groups of clients and if it is so they are basis for a conflict's solution. Additional plus of ethical programmes is creating an organizational culture of an enterprise based on cooperation and honesty. It is cooperation which integrates all members of an organization and their 'union around common, positive values and goals, which results in ordinary people having unusual results.'[406] Abiding by ethical rules in business provides an organization with excellent public-relations (however, it should be mentioned that a company's focus on ethics should not stem only from this reason[407]). Basing actions on rules conforming to accepted ethical standards guarantees a company's good reputation and influences its public image. It is believed that a good reputation is one of the most important assets of a company due to the fact that it assures its credibility and public trust which cannot be gained in any other way. The environment perceives a given company not as profit-oriented but honest and honourable which is of a great importance as far as health service is concerned. It is also worth mentioning that ethical programmes positively influence not only an organization's environment, but also its employees. Working in an enterprise directed at promoting ethical conduct influences also the increase of satisfaction with done work[408] and consequently, it shows enhanced effectiveness and better results.

Effort put in creating an ethical enterprise can be also useful in other fields. Clients' observance of outlined values affects such functions as Total Quality Management, strategic planning or multicultural management.[409] Special attention should be paid to Total Quality Management which is a tool increasing the quality of services. TQM, an approach directed at constant improvement of quality, demands from members of a team actions which are based on outlined rules such as constant improvement, direction at a customer or commitment to work. Distinguished rules rely on ethical values of a team of workers without whose existence and preservation the implementation of this method would be impossible. In Total Quality Management great importance is attached to values such as trust between the interested parties, reliability, efficiency, joint actions, whose promotion is possible only by means of ethical programmes.[410] All the factors influence better performance of a company which is reflected in the highest quality of service and consequently, in a customer's satisfaction or as in the case of medical institutions, in a patient's satisfaction.

In spite of all the advantages, ethical programmes have also some limitations. The most important of them is the fact that all ethical problems cannot be foreseen so in practice, some situations can occur which will not be regulated by the programme.

[405] *Ibidem.*

[406] www.emedyk.pl, Programy i kodeksy etyczne, March 2010.

[407] www.managementhelp.org, *Complete Guide to Ethics Management: An Ethic Toolkit for Managers.*

[408] S. Valentine, G. Fleischman (2008), *Ethics programs, Perceived Corporate Social Responsibility and Job Satisfaction*, "Journal of Business Ethics", p. 161.

[409] www.managementhelp.org, *Complete Guide to Ethics Management: An Ethic Toolkit for Managers.*

[410] *Ibidem.*

It results form the fact that a lot of ethical issues comes down to moral dilemmas specific for an individual situation and it is hard to solve them according to ready instructions. The opponents of these solutions claim that enforcement of a certain way of reasoning results in suppressing during the process of decision-making personal beliefs, and as we already know, even the best programme will not replace human conscience.[411] Furthermore, ethical programmes show certain norms of conduct, advise, teach but in the end the decision-maker must choose and take responsibility for the choice. Certain danger of the discussed method is a possibility of limiting the programme to problems which are important from the organizational standpoint, however, they omit moral needs of its members.[412] Undoubtedly, one of the most serious accusations is also a financial contribution. Especially, taking hospital into consideration, such expenses can be too big. It stems from a very bad economic situation of the Polish National Health Service. In a constant financial deficiency, very often management of an institution does not have money to cover the most basic procedures, not to mention investment in such development.

3.2.5.5. SUMMARY

Nowadays, business ethics is a very popular topic but it also fuels considerable controversy. A lot of people who are opponents of the idea claim that it is unnecessary because eventually every employee makes a decision according to their conscience. It is certainly true, however, because of multitude of people's sets of values, standardization seems to be a good solution so that an organization can enjoy a good reputation. Moreover, we should draw our attention to the term 'business ethics' itself. Here is a list presenting ten myths about this issue:

1) business ethics is more a matter of religion than a matter of management;

2) employees of a given organization are ethical so there is no need to raise this matter;

3) business ethics is a field for philosophers, scientists and not for managers;

4) business ethics is unnecessary because it only refreshes an old idea to 'make good';

5) business ethics is for bad workers;

6) implementation of business ethics is another way to introduce yet another guard to a company;

7) ethics cannot be managed;

8) we can equal business ethics with public responsibility of an organization;

9) if an organization does not break the law, it means it is ethical;

10) ethics management is of little value to the meaning of an enterprise.[413]

---

[411] www.cebi.pl/texty/etyka_w%20_biznesie.doc

[412] http://kpf.pl/obrazki/file/Raport_z_wykonania_Programu_%20Etycznego%20z_a_2008.pdf

[413] www.managementhelp.org, *Complete Guide to Ethics Management: An Ethic Toolkit for Managers*.

Misrepresented interpretations of business ethics may lead to its misperception as an unnecessary expense for an enterprise, which does not need any additional mechanisms of ethical stimulation among their workers. However, it is actually ethics which enables an organization to prevent such aspects as bad reputation, loss of public trust and consequently, loss of competitiveness.

Ethical programmes are a tool of improving effectiveness of actions within an organization. With the implementation of a policy supporting ethical conduct a new quality of actions is created. The quality which is visible to all the customers. Ethical programmes are mainly introduced to these enterprises which value long-term profit. By eliminating unethical behaviour (such as corruption, internal thefts and other frauds) and promoting of moral attitudes, it is possible to enhance the quality of services. This is so because apart from being provided with the service the customer has a chance to cooperate with people who act ethically and honestly. It also influences a positive image of an organization within a society. Thanks to this fact, customers have greater trust in such enterprises and as a consequence, they assess the quality of their services higher. It is true that such programmes carry additional expenses but are not the benefits worth it? In my opinion, they are particularly high in enterprises such as health service institutions whose actions are concerned with the highest value, namely, life and health of a human being. Everything points to the fact that the term 'ethical enterprise' can be related to health care institutions. Obviously, a well-known bad financial situation of the Polish Health Service forces its institutions to seek economical solutions and savings in all fields of their activity. However, should a financial factor be decisive? It is unquestionably vital but we should remember that the development of business ethics influences financial improvement. Because of this, every manager before making their decision should consider the following words: 'Profit is a regulator of the life of a business, but it is not the only one; other human and moral factors must also be considered which in the long term, are at least equally important for the life of a business.'[414]

BIBLIOGRAPHY

1.　Aniszewska G. (2007), *Kultura organizacyjna w zarządzaniu*, PWE, Warszawa.
2.　Armstrong M. (2002), *Zarządzanie zasobami ludzkimi*, Oficyna Ekonomiczna, Kraków.
3.　Austen A., Frączkiewicz-Wronka A., Majowska M. (2008), *Odpływ profesjonalistów medycznych – postulowane narzędzia jego ograniczenia*, "Zarządzanie Zasobami Ludzkimi", No. 2.
4.　Bartkowiak G. (2008), *Dobór personelu medycznego* [in:] Dobska M., Rogoziński K. (ed.), *Podstawy zarządzania zakładem opieki zdrowotnej*, Wyd. PWN, Warszawa.
5.　Bartkowiak G. (2009), *Psychologiczne aspekty zarządzania zasobami ludzkimi w zakładach opieki zdrowotnej*, Wolters Kluwer Business, Warszawa 2009.

---

[414] Jan Paweł II, Centesimus Annus, 1991.

6.   Berliński L. (2009), *Modelowanie strategii biznesu*, Wyd. Dom Organizatora, Toruń.
7.   Blachlińska E. (2008), *Doskonalenie jakości usług świadczonych przez szpital przy wykorzystaniu metod QFD i FMEA na podstawie PZZOZ Szpital w Czeladzi*, praca magisterska obroniona na wydziale Organizacji i Zarządzania Politechniki Śląskiej, pod kierunkiem naukowym dr. inż. Radosława Wolniaka, Katowice 2008.
8.   Brilman J. (2002), *Nowoczesne koncepcje i metody zarządzania*, PWE, Warszawa.
9.   Brown P.R. (2009), *The phenomenology of trust: A Schutzian analysis of the social construction ofknowledge by gynae-oncology patients*, "Health, Risk & Society", Vol. 11, Issue 5.
10.   Buchelt B. (2008), *Metodyczne aspekty projektowania strategii personalnej w jednostkach sektora usług medycznych*, "Zarządzanie zasobami ludzkimi", No. 2.
11.   Buchelt-Nawara B. (2006), *ZZL w jednostkach sektora usług medycznych* [in:] Król H., Ludwiczyński A. (ed.), *Zarządzanie Zasobami Ludzkimi*, Wyd. PWN, Warszawa.
12.   Buchelt-Nawara B., *Podmioty zarządzające zasobami ludzkimi w zakładach opieki zdrowotnej*, [dostęp online: 11.04.2010 r.] http://gollum.uek.krakow.pl/bibl_ae_zasoby/zeszyty/pdf/122879827.pdf.
13.   Bukowska-Piestrzyńska A., Fijałkowska A. (2007), *Znaczenie jakości w budowaniu pozytywnego wizerunku placówki zdrowotnej*, "Problemy Jakości", No. 6.
14.   Chappell T. (1998), *Dusza biznesu*, Wydawnictwo Studio Emka, Warszawa.
15.   Choongsup L.E.M. (1999), *Optimal medical treatment under asymmetric information*, "Journal of Heath Economics", Vol. 14 (4).
16.   Clausing J.R., Clausing D. (1988), *The House of Quality*, "Harvard Business Review", No. 5–6.
17.   De George R.T. (1990), *Business Ethics*, New York–London.
18.   Dobska M., Dobski P. (2004), *TQM zarządzanie przez jakość w zakładach opieki zdrowotnej*, Wyd. Mars Graf, Poznań.
19.   Durlik M. (2008), *Zarządzanie w służbie zdrowia. Organizacja procesowa i zarządzanie wiedzą*, Wyd. Placet, Warszawa.
20.   Dz. U. Nr 115, poz. 749 z dn. 19 sierpnia 1998 r. Rozp. MZiOS: W sprawie szczegółowych zasad przeprowadzania konkursu na niektóre stanowiska kierownicze w publicznych zakładach opieki zdrowotnej, składu komisji konkursowej oraz ramowego regulaminu przeprowadzania konkursu.
21.   Dz. U. Nr 30, poz. 30 z dn. 29 marca 1999 r. Rozp. MZiOS: W sprawie kwalifikacji wymaganych od pracowników na poszczególnych rodzajach stanowisk pracy w publicznych zakładach opieki zdrowotnej.
22.   Dz. U. Nr 44, poz. 520 z dn. 17 maja 2000 r. Rozp. MZ: W sprawie wymagań, jakim powinny odpowiadać osoby na stanowiskach kierowniczych w zakładach opieki zdrowotnej określonego rodzaju.
23.   Dz. U. Nr 91, poz. 408 z dn. 30 sierpnia 1991 r. Ustawa o Zakładach Opieki Zdrowotnej.

24. Filipowicz W., *Białe konkursy w szarych odcieniach*, [dostęp online: 11.04. 2010 r.], http://www.tvnwarszawa.pl/33026,51818663,Bia%B3e_konkursy_w_ szarych_odcieniach_cz_II,artykul.html.
25. Forgas J.P., Bower G.H. (1986), *Mood effects on person-perception judgments*, "Journal of Personality and Cocial Psychology", No. 53.
26. Frąckiewicz-Wronka A. (2009), *Zarządzanie publiczne w teorii i praktyce ochrony zdrowia*, Wolters Kluwer Business, Warszawa.
27. Gaertner S.L., Mann J., Dovidio J.F., Murrell A., Pomare M. (1989), *How does cooperation reduce intergroup bias?*, "Journal of Personality and Cocial Psychology", No. 59.
28. Galewicz W. (2009), *W sprawie szpitalnych komisji etycznych*, "Medycyna Praktyczna" (11).
29. Gałuszka M. (2007), *Korupcja i działania antykorupcyjne w systemie ochrony zdrowia*, "Lekarz Rodzinny", September.
30. Gilbert D.T., Nixon G. (1991), *The trouble of thinking: Activation and applica-tion of stereotypic beliefs*, "Journal of Personality and Social Psychology", No. 60.
31. Gruca-Wójtowicz P. (2009), *Jakość usług medycznych w kontekście zróżni-cowanych oczekiwań stron zainteresowanych*, "Problemy Jakości", No. 3.
32. Hamrol A. (2005), *Zarządzanie jakością z przykładami*, PWN, Warszawa.
33. Harris P.B., Ross Ch., McBride G., Curtis L. (2002), *A Place to Heal: Environ-mental Sources of Satisfaction Among Hospital Patients*, "Journal of Applied Social Psychology", Vol. 32, Issue 6.
34. Herrera-Espiñeira C., Rodríguez del Aguila M., Rodríguez del Castillo M., Val-divia A.F., Sánchez I.R. (2009), *Relationship between anxiety level of patients and their satisfaction with different aspects of healthcare*, "Health Policy", Vol. 89, Issue 1.
35. Holmes S.E. (2009), *Under Pressure: Maintaing an Effective Ethics and Com-pliance Program*, "Directorship", October/November.
36. http://kpf.pl/obrazki/file/Raport_z_wykonania_Programu_%20Etycznego%20 z_a_2008.pdf
37. http://www.cbos.pl/SPISKOM.POL/1999/K_032_99.PDF, 09.03.2010.
38. Jan Paweł II, Centesimus Annus, 1991.
39. Jończyk J. (2008), *Diagnoza i ocena wybranych elementów zarządzania za-sobami ludzkimi w jednostkach sektora usług medycznych*, "Zarządzanie Za-sobami Ludzkimi", No. 2.
40. Jończyk J. (2008), *Zarządzanie zasobami ludzkimi w zakładach opieki zdrowot-nej*, Difin, Warszawa.
41. Juchnowicz M. (ed.) (2000), *Strategia personalna firmy*, Difin, Warszawa.
42. Kapała W. (2006), *Pielęgniarstwo a jakość*, "Problemy Jakości", No. 3.
43. Kapliński A.K., Łysiak M.R., Pięcińska T.S. (ed.) (2001), *Zakład opieki zdro-wotnej w praktyce*, Wydawnictwo Verlag Dashofer Sp. z o.o., Warszawa, cz. 10, rozdz. 5, podrozdz. 5.1, p. 10–11.
44. Karaszewski R. (2003), *Systemy zarządzania jakością największych korporacji świata i ich dyfuzja*, Wyd. Uniwersytetu im. M. Kopernika, Toruń.

45. Karczewski L. (2008), *Etyka biznesu – kulturowe uwarunkowania*, Wyd. Politechniki Opolskiej, Opole.
46. Karski J.B. (2003), *Praktyka i teoria – promocja zdrowia. Wybrane zagadnienia*, Wyd. CeDeWu, Warszawa.
47. Karta Pracowników Służby Zdrowia. Watykan, papieska Rada ds. Duszpasterstwa Służby Zdrowia, 1995.
48. Kautsch M. (2010), *Specyfika zarządzania zakładem opieki zdrowotnej* [in:] Kautsch M. (ed.), *Zarządzanie w opiece zdrowotnej. Nowe wyzwania*, Wolters Kluwer Business, Warszawa.
49. Kautsch M., Whitfield M., Klich J. (ed.) (2001), *Zarządzanie w opiece zdrowotnej*, Wyd. Uniwersytetu Jagiellońskiego, Kraków.
50. Kijowska V. (2010), *Zarządzanie zasobami ludzkimi* [in:] Kautsch M. (ed.), *Zarządzanie w opiece zdrowotnej. Nowe wyzwania*, Wolters Kluwer Business, Warszawa.
51. Kolman R., Tkaczyk T. (1996), *Jakość usług. Poradnik*, Wyd. Ośrodek Postępu Organizacyjnego, Bydgoszcz.
52. Kornas S. (2009), *Czy w polskich szpitalach potrzebne są komitety etyczne*, "Medycyna Praktyczna", No. 2.
53. Kotler P. (1994), *Marketing. Analiza, planowanie, wdrożenie i kontrola*, Gebethner i S-ka, Warszawa.
54. Kozłowski W. (2010), *Zarządzanie motywacją pracowników*, Wyd. CeDeWu, Warszawa.
55. Kraśniak I., Kraśniak J. (2009), *Kompetencje zarządcze pielęgniarki oddziałowej w świetle wyników badań* [in:] Lewandowski R., Walkowiak R., Kautsch M. (ed.), *Współczesne wyzwania menadżerskie w ochronie zdrowia*, Wyd. OWSIiZ, Olsztyn.
56. Kreier E., Łuczak J. (2006), *ISO 9000. Łatwy i skuteczny sposób uzyskania certyfikatu jakości*, t. 1–3, FORUM, Poznań.
57. Krot K. (2009), *Jakość i marketing usług medycznych*, Wolters Kluwer Business, Warszawa.
58. Król H. (1999), *Strategie personalne organizacji*, Humanizacja Pracy. Zarządzanie Zasobami Ludzkimi, No. 1–2.
59. Krukowska-Miler A. (2010), *Marketing wartości w zarządzaniu niepublicznymi zakładami opieki zdrowotnej w województwie śląskim*, Politechnika Częstochowska, rozprawa doktorska, Wydział Zarządzania.
60. Kunecka D., Karakiewicz B. (2010), *Procedury konkursowe na stanowiska kierownicze w ZOZ-ach. Co dalej?* [in:] Rudawska I., Urbańczyk E. (ed.), *Studia i materiały Polskiego Stowarzyszenia Zarządzania Wiedzą* (25), Wyd. Bel Studio, Bydgoszcz.
61. Kuperberg K., Caruso A., Dello S., Mager D. (2008), *How will a room service delivery system affect dietary intake, food costs, food waste and patient satisfaction in a paediatric hospital? A pilot study*, "Journal of Foodservice", Vol. 19, Issue 5.
62. Kwaśniak W., Horzelska-Matyja A. (1998), *100 lat szpitala w Czeladzi*, Czeladź.
63. Langreth R. (2009), *Miracle story*, "Forbes", Vol. 183 (4).

64. LeVine R.A., Campbell D.T. (1972), *Ethnocentrism: Theories of conflict, ethnic attitudes, and group behavior*, Wiley, New York.
65. Lipka A. (2000), *Strategie personalne firmy*, Wydawnictwo PSB, Kraków.
66. Listwan T. (1999), *Strategie personalne* [in:] Krupski R. (ed.), *Zarządzanie strategiczne. Koncepcje, metody*, Wydawnictwo AE Wrocław, Wrocław.
67. Luboiński G. (2008), *Standardy etyczne*, "Standardy Medyczne" (5).
68. Lundy O., Cowling A. (2000), *Strategiczne zarządzanie zasobami ludzkimi*, Oficyna Ekonomiczna, Kraków.
69. Łuczak J., Matuszak-Flejszman A. (2007), *Metody i techniki zarządzania jakością. Kompendium wiedzy*, Quality Progress, Poznań.
70. Maciąg A., Kuszewski K., Topczewska-Tylińska K., Michalak J. (2007), *Rola procesów, standardów i procedur w kształtowaniu jakości świadczeń zdrowotnych*, Wyd. Alfamedica, Bielsko-Biała.
71. Maister D.M. (2006), *Zarządzanie firmą usług profesjonalnych*, Helion, Gliwice.
72. Mazur J. (2001), *Service Marketing Management*, Difin, Warszawa.
73. McLaughlin B.K. (2009), *Identifying methods to communicate with patients and enhance patient satisfaction to improve return on investment*, "Journal of Management & Marketing in Healthcare", Vol. 2, Issue 4.
74. Mruk H. (2010), *Przywództwo w zakładach opieki zdrowotnej*, Wolters Kluwer Business, Warszawa.
75. Musielak M. (2004), *Wybrane etyczne aspekty zarządzania służbą zdrowia w Polsce*, "Nowiny Lekarskie", No. 4.
76. Mykowska A. (2002), *Satysfakcja pacjenta a jakość obsługi medycznej*, "Zdrowie i Zarządzanie", Tom IV, No. 6.
77. Niezależne Forum Pielęgniarek i Położnych: *Konkursy Tak czy Nie.* [dostęp online: 11.04.2010 r.] http://www.forum-pielegniarek.pl/viewtopic.php?f=22&p=1034.
78. Nogalski B.I., Rybicki J. (ed.) (2002), *Nowoczesne zarządzanie zakładem opieki zdrowotnej*, Wydawnictwo Dom Organizatora, Toruń.
79. Nogalski B., Śniadecki J. (2001), *Etyka zarządzania przedsiębiorstwem*, Wyd. Oficyna Wydawnicza Ośrodka Postępu Organizacyjnego, Bydgoszcz.
80. Olzak S. (1992), *The dynamics of ethnic competition and conflict*, Stanford University Press, Stanford.
81. Opolski K., Dykowska G., Możdżonek M. (2005), *Zarządzanie przez jakość w usługach zdrowotnych. Teoria i praktyka*, Wyd. CeDeWu Sp. z o.o., Warszawa.
82. Opolski K., Dykowska G., Możdżonek M. (2009), *Zarządzanie przez jakość w usługach zdrowotnych. Teoria i praktyka*, Wyd. CeDeWu, Warszawa.
83. Ostrowska S. (2009), *Koncentracja na wewnętrznym otoczeniu jednostki* [in:] Frączkiewicz-Wronka A., Austin-Tynda A. (ed.), *Przywództwo w ochronie zdro-wia. Idee i instrumenty*, Wolters Kluwer Business, Warszawa.
84. Pabian A. (2008), *Promocja – nowoczesne środki i formy*, Difin Sp. z o.o., Warszawa.
85. Palczewska A. (2008), *Jakość usług medycznych w opiece paliatywnej*, "Problemy Pielęgniarstwa", No. 16.
86. PN-EN ISO 9000:2001, *Systemy zarządzania jakością. Terminologia*, PKN 2001.

87. Pocztowski A. (1999), *Zarządzanie zasobami ludzkimi w teorii i praktyce*, Humanizacja Pracy. Zarządzanie Zasobami Ludzkimi, No. 1–2 (3–4).
88. Pocztowski A. (2004), *Zarządzanie zasobami ludzkimi. Strategie, procesy, metody*, PWE, Warszawa.
89. Pocztowski A. (2007), *Zarządzanie zasobami ludzkimi. Strategie – procesy – – metody*, PWE, Warszawa.
90. Pocztowski A. (ed.) (2008), *Zarządzanie talentami w organizacji*, Wolters Kluwers Business, Kraków.
91. Popis M. (2009), *Systemy zapewnienia jakości w opiece medycznej w Polsce*, "Problemy Jakości", No. 10.
92. Portal.wsiz.rzeszów.pl, March 2010.
93. Priporas C.V., Laspa Ch., Kamenidou I. (2008), *Patient satisfaction measurement for in-hospital services: A pilot study in Greece*, "Journal of Medical Marketing", Vol. 8, Issue 4.
94. Rodzewicz A. (2008), *Jakość usług medycznych (prywatne czy publiczne)*, "Problemy Jakości", No. 3.
95. Rudawska I. (2005), *Jakość relacji pacjent–profesjonalista w sektorze usług medycznych*, "Problemy Jakości", No. 3.
96. Rumerlhart D.E., Hinton G.E., McClelland J.L. (1986), *A general framework for parallel distributed processing* [in:] Rumerlhart D.E. et al. (ed.), *Parallel distributed processing*, MIT Press, Cambridge.
97. Skotnicka-Zasadzień B., Glenc D. (2006), *Rola pacjenta w ocenie jakości usług medycznych*, "Problemy Jakości", No. 6.
98. Skrzypek E. (2000), *Jakość i efektywność*, Wyd. UMCS, Lublin.
99. Sobaski T., Abraham M., Fillmore R., McFall D.E., Davidhizar R. (2008), *The Effect of Routine Rounding by Nursing Staff on Patient Satisfaction on a Cardiac Telemetry Unit*, "Health Care Manager", Vol. 27 Issue 4.
100. Spake D.F., Bishop Jr. J.S. (2009), *The Impact of Perceived Closeness on the Differing Roles of Satisfaction, Trust, Commitment, and Comfort on Intention to Remain with a Physician*, "Health Marketing Quarterly", Vol. 26, Issue 1.
101. Stangor C., Lynch L., Duan L., Glass B. (1992), *Categorization of individuals on the basis of multiple cocial features*, "Journal of Personality and Social Psychology", No. 62.
102. Stankiewicz J. (1999), *Komunikowanie się w organizacji (Communication in an Organization)*, Wyd. Astrum, Wrocław.
103. Stanowisko NRPiP z dn. 12 marca 2008 r. w sprawie nieuzasadnionej likwidacji kierowniczych stanowisk pielęgniarskich/położniczych w zakładach opieki zdrowotne, [dostęp online: 11.04.2010 r.] http://www.izbapiel.org.pl/uploadf/uchwalystanowiska/marzec2008/stanowisko2.doc.
104. Stephan W.G., Stephan C.W. (2007), *Wywieranie wpływu przez grupy. Psychologia relacji*, Gdańskie Wydawnictwo Pedagogiczne Sp. z o.o., Gdańsk.
105. Stępniewski J. (2005), *Jak opanować sztukę negocjacji. Przewodnik praktyczny*, Wyd. Wyższej Szkoły Zarządzania i Marketingu w Sosnowcu, Sosnowiec.
106. Styś A. (2003), *Marketing usług*, PWE, Warszawa.

107. Sullivan M., Adcock D. (2003), *Marketing w handlu detalicznym*, Oficyna Ekonomiczna, Kraków.
108. Thistelthwaite J. (2005), *Those Little white lies*, "Update", Vol. 70 (1).
109. Torres E., Vasques-Parraga A.Z., Barra C. (2009), *The Path of Patient Loyalty and the Role of Doctor Reputation*, "Health Marketing Quarterly", Vol. 26, Issue 3.
110. uchwalystanowiska/marzec2008/Stanowisko2.doc.
111. Ustawa z dnia 6 listopada 2008 r. o Prawach Pacjenta i Rzeczniku Praw Pacjenta (Dz. U. z dnia 31 marca 2009 r.).
112. Valentine S., Fleischman G. (2008), *Ethics programs, Perceived Corporate Social Responsibility and Job Satisfaction*, "Journal of Business Ethics".
113. Wikipedia. Wolna encyklopedia. *Hasło: konkurs*, [dostęp online: 11.04.2010 r.] http://pl.wikipedia.org/wiki/Konkurs.
114. Wiśniewska M., Nowoszyńska J. (2009), *Akredytacja i systemy zarządzania jakością w placówkach opieki zdrowotnej*, "Problemy Jakości", No. 7.
115. Wolniak R. (2003), *Koncepcja trzydziestomacierzowego rozwinięcia metody QFD*, "Problemy Jakości", No. 9.
116. Wolniak R. (2006), *Wybrane metody zarządzania jakością w sektorze usług finansowych – teoria i praktyka*, Wyższa Szkoła Bankowości i Finansów, Bielsko-Biała.
117. Wolniak R., Skotnicka B. (2008), *Metody i narzędzia zarządzania jakością*, Wydawnictwo Politechniki Śląskiej, Gliwice.
118. Woźniakowski A. (2005), *Globalizacja – różnorodność – zarządzanie talentami* [in:] Borkowska S. (ed.), *Zarządzanie talentami*, Wyd. IPiSS, Warszawa.
119. www.batory.org.pl, *Establishing whistleblowing mechanizm*, Konwencja Narodów Zjednoczonych Przeciwko korupcji, Artykuł 33 – Ochrona osób zgłaszających.
120. www.ce.uw.edu.pl, artykuł: Gasparski W., *Europejskie standardy etyki biznesu*.
121. www.cebi.pl/texty/etyka_w%20_biznesie.doc.
122. www.ckl.pl/kodeks-etyczny-narzędziem-rozwoju-firmy.
123. www.emedyk.pl, Programy i kodeksy etyczne, March 2010.
124. www.logistyka.net.pl, artykuł: Gościniak D. (2005), *Logistyka w produkcji* (9).
125. www.managementhelp.org, *Complete Guide to Ethics Management: An Ethic Toolkit for Managers*.
126. www.odpowiedzialnybiznes.pl, artykuł: Gasparski W. (2008), *Programy etyczne firm*, May. 126. www.opoka.org.pl/biblioteka.
127. www.wikipedia.pl.
128. www.wyborcza.pl, artykuł: Domaszkiewicz Z., Miączyński P., *Obywatel kapuś, czyli samotność demaskatora*, "Duży Format", 20.

CONCLUSIONS

The proposals included in the present book point out clearly the direction which should be taken in the process of innovating hospitals in Poland. So far the attempts of reforming the health care system in our country concentrated rather on changes in financing, ownership or responsibility regulations while it is important to implement innovating solutions in the hospital organizations concurrently.

To achieve success, understood as realizing patients' expectations, health care units must place a particular emphasis on modern methods of management, taking into account cost accounting, their structure, controlling and taking care of income by using all possibilities of its earning. At the same time they should take advantage of new organizational and technological solutions, staying financially in balance. The health care systemic reform still in process cannot be regarded as an excuse for management ineptitude, not applying its basic instruments or even ignoring the environment areas essential for the organization.

Health care has always been a discipline which requires innovations in particular way both by providers of medical services and their patients. The development of medicine with a change in the recognition of the importance of so called 'evidence based medicine,' openness of medical profession towards other countries' checked solutions, aiming at most effective treatment of a patient, taking advantage of the latest technical and technological achievements to support medical activities make health care units willing to implement innovations. Unfortunately, the inventiveness is very often limited to medical aspects of hospital's activity, neglecting the aspect of its organization and management.

It is puzzling why in such conditions favoring inventiveness, it is so difficult to implement organizational or management innovations. Are they not modern enough? Do the managers not know how to use them? Or is there a reluctance to implement the innovations, which has not allowed for solutions in Polish hospitals but present in other financial institutions and enterprises?

In fact the medical world is divided into a 'white' part devoted to treating patients, saving health and life and a 'grey' one, focused on administration, organization and management. Both parts stand in opposition, which is wrong. The solutions provided by their representatives are mutually defied, as every single medical professional is also a part of health care unit organization in organic way. While they expect clear rules on financing and good working conditions, they are expected to be open and contribute to the management of the organization. These two aspects constitute the hospital's managers domain and should be common for all hospital environment activity to innovate the organization.

Transposing organizational solutions from other economy areas to medical units is the task to be undertaken by both scientists and health care managers, who are responsible for hospital' s existence and creating the ground for collaboration with medical professionals. However, the latter should contribute to the system of management as all its parts are equally important. If any part that seems unimportant, happens to be neglected all system stops functioning.

SUMMARY

Management of hospital consists in the analysis of costs and introducing innovative organizational solutions which influence the effective use of human and material resources. Legal regulations concerning the sector are defied by managers and they are shown to be inappropriate for real requirements in hospital management. The authors present the possibilities of making cost accounting modern, with French experience set as an example, which might be introduced with success in Polish hospitals.

Organizational innovations should become a priority for the managers of hospitals. The solutions introduced by the French and also chosen ventures in Polish hospitals are presented in the book. In that aspect, the functioning of endoscopic and one-day surgery wards have been described as constantly developing fields of medicine, highly required in the market. As a result of systemic transformation, privatization of hospitals takes place in Poland therefore this problem is presented in the book as well. The ideas of process management and integrated system of medical information, supporting hospitals functioning have been shown against a background of French hospitals solutions.

Medical professionals are important in the process of health care but often underestimated in publications. Doctors, nurses, midwives, diagnosticians and technicians are directly responsible for the treatment effectiveness, felt by patients thus proper innovative solutions introduced in HR sector should influence the shortening of treatment and improve its effectiveness.

The problems of quality in health care have been also discussed in the publication. The authors describe the methods of quality tests, not common nowadays, which may influence the system of quality management positively. There are many examples of practical solutions, also taken from German hospitals in the book.